Yours truly
Thos Whittaker

LIFE'S BATTLES

IN

TEMPERANCE ARMOUR.

BY

THOMAS WHITTAKER.

WITH PORTRAIT.

London:
HODDER AND STOUGHTON,
27, PATERNOSTER ROW.
MDCCCLXXXIV.

To
JOSEPH LIVESEY,

THE FOUNDER AND LIFELONG UPHOLDER

OF THE PRINCIPLES OF THE SOCIETY

TO WHICH THE LABOURS OF MY LIFE HAVE BEEN DEVOTED,

I DEDICATE,

IN HIGH ESTEEM AND DEEP AFFECTION,

THIS BOOK.

TO THOSE WHO HAVE BECOME DISCIPLES OF THE FAITH, AND

ON WHOM THE SUCCESS OF THE FUTURE DEPENDS,

I WOULD ALSO COMMIT THESE RECORDS,

AND IN DOING SO,

URGE THAT THE ANCIENT LANDMARKS BE NOT REMOVED,

AND THAT THEY BUILD ON THE FOUNDATION

LAID BY THE EARLY APOSTLES,

AND BE NOT CARRIED AWAY BY EVERY WIND OF DOCTRINE.

SCARBOROUGH, *August 22nd*, 1884.

CONTENTS.

CHAPTER I.
CHILDHOOD: SCARS.

How we Learn.—Scars.—My Mother's Kitchen.—Looking not Seeing.—My Mother.—The Parson and the Doctor .   PAGE 1

CHAPTER II.
CHILDHOOD: THEOLOGY.

Early Impressions.—Memories.—Theology.—Bright Spots.—Buttons 13

CHAPTER III.
CHILDHOOD: THE FACTORY BOY.

Home Influence.—My Father.—Might against Right.—How I came to be a Factory Boy.—My Father in Prison . 19

CHAPTER IV.
CHILDHOOD: LEAVING HOME.

Removal to Blackburn.—Removal to Preston.—A Fright.—Strange Providence.—My Mother 25

CHAPTER V.
YOUTH: MACHINERY AND MOBS.

The late Lord Derby.—William Cobbett.—Henry Hunt.—Mobs and Machinery.—Joseph Livesey and the Galvanic

Shock.—Success and Danger.—Cheap Rum.—Removal to Bolton and to Glossop.—Mutual Forbearance.—Early Marriages.—How I Came to Marry.—The Way it was Done.—Excitement in the District.—A Sad Mistake.—My Dead Child.—Timely Help 33

CHAPTER VI.
THE DAWN OF TEMPERANCE MANHOOD.

Joseph Livesey, and how the Preston men did it.—Life Stories and the Quaker Chairman.—My Brother William, and how I was Caught.—The Influence Felt.—The Gallery.—Gospel Temperance 47

CHAPTER VII.
SELF-HELP AND SELF-RESPECT.

Aimless Lives.—Temperance not Everything.—My Education.—Disadvantages of Working Men.—Modern Oracles.—The Sabbath-school.—The Bible and the Life of Franklin.—My Learning to Write, and my Poetry.—My First Letter 55

CHAPTER VIII.
TAKING THE TIDE AT THE FLOOD.

The Law of Life.—The Manly Resolve.—The Dwellings of the Poor.—The Lever that Lifts.—Prejudice and Persecution.—Payment of Wages in Public-houses.—Another Trouble.—The Letter.—My Dedication.—The Open Door.—A Severe Temptation 65

CHAPTER IX.
MY COMMISSION.

In Full Commission.—"Bacchus" and Dr. Grindrod.—Beardsall, Burns, and Barker.—The Mighty Fallen.—The Lost Found.—Thomas Swindlehurst.—John Cassell . . 77

CHAPTER X.

LANCASHIRE AND WESTMORELAND.

Lancaster Ale.—Only Once.—Never Again.—Mr. Livesey in Lancaster.—My Commission Opened.—The Quakers and Methodists.—The Rulers did not Believe.—A Contrast . 85

CHAPTER XI.

WESTMORELAND AND CUMBERLAND.

Marching On.—The Teetotal Rattle.—The Market Cross.—The Second Visit.—Two that were not One.—A new Acquaintance.—Where will you sleep?—The Town Crier.—" I'll Sign."—My First Procession.—The Drunkard's Home.—John Mawson 93

CHAPTER XII.

CUMBERLAND.

Out of the Fire.—A Light Heart.—Rather Depressing.—Unexpected Help.—Bread upon the Waters.—A Remarkable Circumstance.—How the Doctor was Saved.—Still Pursuing.—The late Sir Wilfrid Lawson.—The Poor Widow.—The Rev. Owen Clark.—Extremes Meet . . 105

CHAPTER XIII.

CUMBERLAND.

John Cluer.—Carlisle.—The Young Preacher.—Brampton.—The Shoulder of Mutton.—Naworth Castle.—The Hon. Mrs. Howard.—My Curiosity Gratified.—John Slack . 119

CHAPTER XIV.

NORTHUMBERLAND.

Good Wishes.—Much out of Little.—The Sight of Newcastle.—My Arrival and Reception.—James Rewcastle.—The Two Open-air Meetings.—A Quart of Ale better than a Quart of Water.—A Trick of the Devil.—The Big Chapel and the Goodman.—The Town Crier and his Companion 127

CHAPTER XV.
WIFE AND HOME.

John Bright.—My Wife Signs.—The Slattern Wife . . 141

CHAPTER XVI.
FRAGMENTS.

Brave Men.—Importance of Little Things.—The Quaker Lady and her Mug.—The Countess of Zetland . . 151

CHAPTER XVII.
MEMORIES OF MEN AND THINGS.

My First Dinner.—Harry Wilkinson.—Blanchland and the Lead Miners.—The Scene on the Moors.—My First Mount.—Stanhope.—The Mountebanks.—John Candlish.—The Man in the Gig 159

CHAPTER XVIII.
MEMORIES OF MEN AND THINGS.

Bavington Hall.—The Inventor of the Sweeps' Machine.—W. E. Forster.—The Two Processions 175

CHAPTER XIX.
MIDLANDS.

James Teare.—Rotherham and Nottingham.—John Cassell.—Not all Fish that Comes to the Net.—The Brewing Utensils.—The Boots.—Newark 185

CHAPTER XX.
NORTHAMPTON.

Thomas Cook.—The Sermons at Kettering.—The Meeting.—The Wine Seller and Maltster Join.—Kettering To-day.—Wellingborough.—How the Rattle Turned up Again.—Why I made an exhibition of it when elected Mayor . 195

CHAPTER XXI.

MY ARRIVAL IN LONDON.

My First Sunday There.—Strangers in London.—John Meredith.—J. S. Buckingham, M.P.—My First Speech.—Earl Stanhope.—Exeter Hall.—My Speech there and what Followed.—The Letter from Campbeltown, N.B.—The First Meeting in Smithfield.—My Colleague Taken to Prison.—The Meeting on Tottenham Green.—London Suburbs 205

CHAPTER XXII.

LONDON.

The Work Done.—James McCurry.—The London Letter.—Thomas Hudson.—Ratcliff Highway.—The Quakers' Clothes.—John Meredith.—C. H. Spurgeon . . . 217

CHAPTER XXIII.

THREE "GEORGES."

London Slums.—Emigration.—Father Mathew . . . 229

CHAPTER XXIV.

MARRIAGE.

The Chamber of Death.—From Manchester to London by Road.—Loneliness.—The Rev. R. Aitkin.—Public Men.—Marriage.—Death 241

CHAPTER XXV.

THE EASTERN COUNTIES.

Francis Marriage.—Harlow.—The Riot.—The Race.—The Besieged House.—Plaistow not Glasgow.—James Larner.—Sir H. Thompson.—The Race between Light and Darkness.—Luton.—The Brewer 253

CHAPTER XXVI.
THE WEST OF ENGLAND.

The Rev. B. Parsons.—The Men who were to the Front.—James Teare.—Stogumber Ale.—A Word for Hitchin . 265

CHAPTER XXVII.
THE WEST OF ENGLAND.

Kingsbridge.—Richard Peek.—Good *Sort* of Men.—Valued Friends 273

CHAPTER XXVIII.
HISTORY.

The Rev. G. Carr.—John Dunlop.—Mr. Forbes.—The Beer Bill.—The Elder Brethren.—Experiments . . . 283

CHAPTER XXIX.
OUR MEANS AND MEN.

The Original Article.—Divisions in the Camp.—The Breach Healed.—The National League.—The British League.—The Alliance 297

CHAPTER XXX.
MANY, BUT ONE.

Ireland and Scotland.—The Rechabites.—The Sons of Temperance and the Templars.—The Band of Hope.—Life Insurance.—Temperance Hospital.—Sunday Closing . 309

CHAPTER XXXI.
GOSPEL TEMPERANCE.

Physic in Jam.—Nothing New.—People who have been Sleeping.—Making No Charge.—Samples of the Past.—Truth the Same.—Early Medical Men 321

CHAPTER XXXII.

BANDS, HALLS, AND PROCESSIONS.

The Gospel and Teetotalism on all Fours.—There is no Full Gospel where True Temperance is not Taught.—Temperance Halls and Temperance Bands and Processions. . 333

CHAPTER XXXIII.

EXTREMES MEET.

More Light.—"All that Glitters is not Gold."—The Carriage.—The Stage Coach.—The Donkey Cart 345

CHAPTER XXXIV.

FAITH AND PHYSIC.

Motives.—The Exceptions.—The Sacrament.—A Sad Mistake.—The Fire of Hell.—The Terrible Passion for Drink.—Learned Nonsense.—The Rev. F. Beardsall's Pledge.—Doctor Higginbottom's Teaching.—Is Medical Practice a Science?—The Invalid Banker and his Wife.—Family Faith. — Personal Illness. — Family Affliction. — The Doctors.—The Risk.—The Victory.—The Temperance Hospital 355

CHAPTER XXXV.

REFLECTION AND PROSPECTS.

Benefit of Temperance Advocacy to the Advocate.—Memories.—Effect of Liquor Traffic on National Conscience . . 373

CHAPTER I.

CHILDHOOD: SCARS.

WE know nothing but what we learn, and we learn from those by whom we are surrounded. We naturally, and in some cases irresistibly, imitate what we see and hear. The power to imitate, and the facility with which it is done, sometimes, in very young life, is not only astonishing but very amusing. Take the dialect of Somerset and compare it with those of Lancashire and Yorkshire; they are almost as different as is Welsh from German. Why should there be this difference? We are all sons of the soil, and belong to one common stock. The circumstances differ, and we imitate the sounds and phrases of the locality in which we live, excepting in cases where special efforts are made to avoid and correct this. People must and will learn something; and it is a great mistake to suppose that, because persons have not been to school, they know nothing. The fact is, many who have not been to school know too much, while those who have been, in some cases, know sadly too little.

It is the *kind* of knowledge people get, on which so much of the future depends; and the more precocious and capable the child, the more important is it that the school life be right, and the home training and example be safe. A knowledge of letters, other things being equal, is in all cases undoubtedly a great gain; but a knowledge of letters in itself is but a poor provision for life. An educated man is said to possess a third hand, but that is only true when the other two are there; and everybody will see how helpless, even to ridiculousness, a man is who has no power in his two natural hands, however much he may possess in the artificial or educated one.

He lacks the ability to apply his sense, and becomes as useless as is a cork leg without the body to carry it.

A knowledge of letters is not enough to make a full man. There must be a knowledge of life, and an observation of men and things. There must be a discipline of the will, and an influencing of the heart, if the existence is to be decent and creditable, and the life-work a power and a blessing. This is admitted; and what can better discipline the will, and influence the heart, than the home of childhood? Who amongst us does not know that a scar in the flesh made when young in life is with us to-day, and we can put our finger upon it; and though the component parts of our body in every particular have been completely and entirely changed again and again, yet the scar is there, and will be our companion to the grave; and if we were to be lost, and found dead in some lonely land, or cast on some foreign shore, in the absence of every other means of identification, that scar would spot us, and that blemish be our recognition. What is true in our physical nature applies with much force to our moral and mental character; and if in our making and education there be blemishes and scars, those blemishes and scars can never be erased: they may not always be within our moral and mental perception, any more than the physical scar can be seen by the passer-by, but they are there nevertheless. Every man has his life-story, and every man has his scars, not for parade, but for instruction,—not for glory, but for warning.

The time is coming, and in the nature of things cannot be long, when the opportunities I now possess will be gone; and as it is believed there are lessons in my life and experience worth putting on record, I will now, in this jubilee year of my public life, so far seek to gratify my friends as to perform this task.

The miserable folly and egregious delusion of sowing what are called " wild oats," and while doing it presuming upon the ability and the opportunity of withholding one's hand and correcting one's life at will, is only equalled by the vain and empty excuse so frequently offered for such delinquencies by older persons who ought to blush in the presence of those who have been guilty of such deeds as are implied by the phrase in question. There is no such thing as exemption from moral or mental scars when once made, any more than there is to be obtained an obliteration of a physical scar when once stamped on the body. We may divorce ourselves from one another, and we can shut our eyes and stop our ears to sights offensive and sounds distressing, but from ourselves we can never get away. In that court there is no divorce, in that law—the law of life—there is no repeal; and I venture the opinion that though we may survive the scars of the mind and the morals, as we do the scars of the flesh, still their very remembrance proves their existence,—and as existence is life, the effect never dies. If the breath of the nostrils affects the atmosphere, and a stone dropped in the centre of a pond tells upon the entire mass of water the pond contains, there is no act or deed of life performed in the midst of animated nature that does not give motion to good or evil. It may not be seen,—nay, it may not even be felt; but it is there, and often in spite of ourselves, and frequently unknown to ourselves, it is mixing with and making part of life. What, then, can be of greater importance than character? and where do we get our character if not from our homes and our surroundings? The grandest thing that can happen to this country is to improve the home life, and fill our surroundings with physical advntages, mental pleasure, and moral life.

In a little cottage on a small farmstead near Grindleton, across the Ribble from Chatburn, and on the borders of Yorkshire, on the 22nd of August in the year 1813, I made my first public appearance. I fear I did it then, as I have occasionally done since, at an inconvenient time, and before I was wanted. My parents had taken a small farm at Clitheroe, to which they meant to go, and on which spot, so far as they had the power to manage things, it was determined I should be born. But my propensity to come to the front, as well as my determination to have a will of my own, was manifested very early in life, and, because of that, my parents felt it best to stay where they were till the little trouble in question was got over. That was how I came to be a son of York instead of Lancaster, and that is one reason why I have often said that "I could have been born in Lancashire if I had had a mind."

It is true in more senses than one, though the statement has often puzzled some of my friends.

When I was born, as I have heard my mother say, I was the tiniest bit of a thing that ever was, to live, and she wondered how I did live, and at times *why* I lived; but somehow or other these things that we can very well spare, often stop, while some that we know not how to do without are frequently taken away. I belonged to the sort that stop. The only article about me which could be called big, when I was born, was my head. It would seem that nature early in life made an effort to give me a head, so much so that it has grown comparatively little since. For a child, I had a remarkably large head; for a man, I have a rather small one. This head of mine has been like a good deal of railway property—such a large outlay in the beginning that there has been no dividend since. In consequence of this peculiar appearance in me as a child, I was constantly subject to annoyance and insult, and that annoyance and insult had a wonderful influence in the formation of my character. I seldom went out in the neighbourhood in which I lived when a child without boys calling out after me, "thick-head," "round-head," "numskull"! This begot in me the spirit of retaliation and revenge, and I became a fighter. The consequence was, that at ten years of age there were few boys in the neighbourhood of the same age that I had not thrashed, and few boys of fifteen years of age who had not thrashed me for thrashing their little brothers. It will be seen how I became a fighter, and as "practice makes perfect," at twenty years of age there were few men whose noses I could not have hit.

These circumstances have influenced my life, and will do so to my dying day, and in consequence I have had temptations and besetments to which I should have been a stranger had it not been for those circumstances. The *scar* is there. True, good can be brought out of evil; and had I not been good for fight, how I should have been qualified for a temperance advocate, it is difficult to say. But everybody knows we may "buy gold too dear." Whether that has been true or not in my case, others must judge. There are more ways of fighting than one; and when the qualification and propensity exist, it will not be long in finding some one or something to attack.

There is a legitimate exercise for every power and faculty, however dangerous and disgraceful its misapplication may be. The late Hon. F. H. F. Berkeley, member for Bristol, who for so many years championed the Ballot Question in the House of Commons, was an astonishing and most determined upholder of the Game Laws.

John Bright, as everybody knows, was a bitter and persevering opponent of them. On one occasion when their repeal was before the House, Mr. Berkeley twitted Mr. Bright with his fighting propensity, and said, "If the honourable member for Durham (Mr. Bright then represented that city) had not been a Quaker, he would have been a prize-fighter."

Mr. Bright retorted, "Had not the honourable member for Bristol been the son of a peer, he would have been a gamekeeper," and there is no doubt that circumstances do alter cases, and hence it is that I lay so much stress on the importance of circumstances.

I can go back in my memory to the scenes and circumstances of childhood. They are fully and vividly before me now: I can see the kitchen in which I spent my young life, and in many particulars and details distinctly note down its furniture and fittings, and certainly I have never forgotten the lessons there learned. I can see the fire, the hooks, crooks, pots and pans, and all the paraphernalia of cooking.

I can see my mother moving about the kitchen trying to make home happy. I can see the dresser against one side of the kitchen, and the shelves over it, decorated with earthenware, pewter plates and wooden trenchers for naughty boys who were apt to let their plates fall. I can see on the top of the kitchen a vessel kept beautifully bright—a thing almost idolised, and only used on special occasions and for particular people.

In this land we have lords many and gods many. I can see on one side of the fire a large arm-chair for special people; and on the other side I can see a little stool, which until I got to a certain age was called "Tommy's stool," and on that stool I used frequently to sit. Some people can see without looking, while others cannot see if they look. There is a wonderful difference between looking and seeing. I saw what was done in that kitchen, and I saw it without looking; and if parents and adults fancy that children cannot see and do not know, they make a great mistake.

I was not more than four years of age at the time I now speak of, yet I saw, and I know now what I saw. The *scar* is there. "A wise man's eyes are in his head, but a fool's eye is in the ends of the earth." Much, therefore, depends on where our eyes are. Who of us does not know hundreds of people who are like the rest in all the main features, but very dissimilar in some most important particulars? They have got the "fool's eye," they look everywhere, and all over, but see nothing. It is a vacant, unmeaning, unintelligent stare. They look, but cannot see. The hills, the valleys, the dancing stream, the bubbling spring, with the singing bird and charming landscape, and all earth's joys and heaven's blessings, are but one vast space and unmeaning medley in the "fool's eye." Such as these go to church, attend chapel, visit the lecture hall. They look like being there, but they are *not* there. They bring their clothes, and put them down in a pew or on a form, and then they themselves go out; they know nothing practically of the service; there is not a single fact in the lecture they retain, nor an argument they understand. They went because they had got their clothes on, and could see other people who had got theirs on. In that is the beginning and the end, the rest is all stubble and rubbish, mere fillings-in. They have got the "fool's eye." They can tell you lots about people who were there, where they sat, and to whom they spoke, but they know nothing of the service or the speech; they are not there, and if you make a collection, it will be found they are out, and have been gone for some time. Looking is therefore not seeing. How many have, as they call it, "looked" at the Temperance question, and could not for the life of them see any obligation on their part in connection with it, and these, too, well informed and in some cases most respectable Christian people! They have "looked," no doubt, but how? Why as I used to look for my clogs, when I was a factory lad.

Before I was seven years of age, I had to be up by five o'clock on a cold winter's morning and go a mile to the cotton mill. When I got there, I had to run after a spinning "mule" piecing up threads and cleaning about, covering a distance of twenty miles a day, and getting home at eight o'clock at night. Of course I was very tired; and I wore clogs. I had half a crown a week for my work, but if I happened to be a few minutes late in a morning the factory gates were shut, and I was admitted on a fine of twopence. Well there were not many twopences in a half-crown, so my mother made it her business to see that I was up in time in the morning, for she wanted, poor soul, the whole half-crown badly enough. She seemed never to sleep in the night, if she did it was only with one eye at a time, and that was not always shut, for she would often call out in the night, "Thomas, are you asleep?" and I would say, "Yes, mother."

I remember one morning being called up in a great hurry and fright. "Eh!" said mother, "it is daylight, thou wilt be fined." But it transpired it was only half-past two o'clock; it was a very bright moonlight night. When she discovered her mistake she was very sorry for her poor boy. "Go to bed again, my child," said she; "there's two hours for you yet; I will see that you are up in time; I do believe I had been to sleep a bit, and I awoke and the room was all light, and I thought it was daylight."

After a night like that, I was not always very vigorous at getting up. Being promised a treat if I was a good boy and went to the mill, I would be stimulated to get up and dress myself; but sometimes when I got downstairs in the dark and cold, my heart would fail me. The rain would be beating against the window, and the wind howling round the house, and I wanted an excuse for not going to the mill, and I would call up the staircase, "Mother, I can't find my clogs." She would reply,—

"They are in the corner," where they were left the night before, and I would then look round the house as if they had been hung up like pictures, and I would say,

"I can't *see* them." Just so, I did not want to see them.

I am afraid that is the way in which a great many good sort of people have looked at the Temperance question. They did not want to see it.

Nothing is easier than believing what we *wish* to believe. There is not only the fool's eye, but there is the prejudiced eye, and "None are so blind as those who will not see."

I remember there was a door leading out from the kitchen into a place called the pantry; in that pantry were three large stone bottles, small beer, strong beer, strongest of all.

My mother was a good housewife, she could not only bake, but she could brew, and it was as common, and believed as desirable, to brew as to bake. We were living near the highway, on the outskirts of the town, and the minister or ministers of the church of which my mother was a member would often make a call: "They were going into the country," or "coming from the country"; "they had passed through a storm," or "storm threatened"; "they had been visiting the people," or "were going to visit them"; "they were tired," or "expected to be tired." Under any of these circumstances they felt free to call at our house, and they were very welcome. I can now see one of those good men enter the kitchen, and take his seat in the arm-chair on the opposite side of the fire to that on which I was sitting.

My mother would take down from the top of the kitchen the vessel kept beautifully bright, and retire into the pantry and pay her respects to the *strongest*. Taking out the cork and turning up the bottle, it would say, "good, good, good," as its contents went into the vessel, as I sat and heard it, and I can hear it yet. The *scar* is there. The vessel would then be put on the fire, and the liquor warmed and spiced and made very nice, then presented to the minister. Now I saw that; my education was going on, even when my presence was not recognised, and my consciousness and observation were ignored. The minister said "the ale was good." I heard it: I believed it. I had been taught to respect and believe the minister. Those who taught me that, had no reference to his praising ale, they had reference to him as a man. I heard him smack his lips: I smacked mine and thought, "Oh! it is good!" but I got none, but I got the *desire;* and there was evidence enough in the preacher's act and talk to make me believe in beer, and I determined then, that when a man I would have it.

The doctor would frequently call. I was one of eight brothers, and we had every one a sister, and there were but nine of us after all. The doctor, like the minister, was ever welcome. The home was, though humble, a very hospitable one, and my mother had a big heart, and could do a deal with a little. I remember I could take greater liberties with the doctor than with the minister. He would often be treated in the same way as the minister, and father would occasionally take a glass with him, but never with the minister; it was too awful and too solemn. It was different with the doctor; he was really one of us; and if doctors wish to get on with the people they must notice the children, take them on their knees, and occasionally kiss them. Never mind if the way is not always clear, it will have a wonderful effect! The mother is almost sure to say, "What a nice man that doctor is!" and whatever blunders he may make in the administration of physic, they will never be seen, for the art of medicine is the art of pleasing, and wise men study the constitution of the mind.

I could not only see the doctor without looking, but I was not afraid of him seeing that I was looking; not so with the minister, but I saw him nevertheless. The doctor knew what the look meant. We can speak with our eyes as well as with our tongues, and he took me on his knee, patted me on the back, and said, "what a fine boy I was getting." I liked that. He then let me sip a little out of the bottom of his glass, thick with sugar; then setting me down on the floor, telling me to hold up my head and stretch myself; then, "You will soon be as big as father." That was nice; it was the height of my ambition to be like my father. I thought no man under heaven like my father. But to be "like father" seemed to say, do as father does, and he would be taking a glass with the doctor.

Now all this was very becoming and very agreeable; everybody did it, and no one suspected any mischief, or doubted the wisdom and propriety of the act. It was done in ignorance, ignorance at which no doubt God would wink, but it has left a *scar*. That conduct strengthened my desire for, and belief in the liquor. Long before I was a man, I got it, but neither the minister, nor the doctor, nor my parents could give me their knowledge and experience and grace, and in the absence of it I was sadly wronged, and two out of the eight brothers were slain.

CHAPTER II.

CHILDHOOD: THEOLOGY.

THE events of childhood make impressions which are indelible, and the character of future manhood is invariably cast in the mould of early life. There can be nothing therefore of greater moment than the condition of things by which the morning of our days is surrounded· and the spring-time of our being placed, for they not only give form to our manhood's deeds, but colour to our thinkings in the autumn of our life. This being so, the schoolroom and the homestead will ever be the great factors of national life, as well as givers of individual character; it is here where individualities are formed, and the foundations are laid on which the future structure will be built. From this basis will go forth the life and likenesses which shall characterize the country's coming age, and stamp with injury or with honour our mother's sons and our national progeny.

In the most favoured circumstances of young life there is necessarily much learned which has to be unlearned before anything like substantial progress can be made; but in a vast number of cases there is scarcely a bright spot to be seen, and nothing but one continued accumulation of disaster, ignorance and guilt besets the path. The selfishness which results in a life of isolation, or at most in simply just getting as much out of men and things as will contribute to our mere personal ambition or morbid tastes, and individual pleasure, is little more than existence, it is not life, and scarcely deserves the name; and yet what multitudes so exist, and pass from our midst not leaving a single blessing in their trail, nor doing a single deed deserving a record. How much of time and opportunity is gone with many of us, and what vacant places in the homes and solitude in the hearts with others! Yet there comes round to us all the ever welcome season of social festivities and family gatherings. How much the life before us will be influenced by these intercourses remains to be seen.

The results of the past we know, and we are but dull scholars if that past has taught us no lessons. There is much in life worth the living for, notwithstanding the many drawbacks which beset our path, and it is astonishing how much of joy and of blessing will come to our lot, if we will but put a sunny countenance on, and give what little portion of good falls to our share a fair and legitimate chance of fructification amongst others.

Nothing is so refreshing to the soul as a generous outlet. It begets warm impulses in others, and these react upon ourselves, and in that way not only families but entire neighbourhoods may be made glad.

I know not if the thoughts which now occupy my mind can be put before those who may read them in such a way as to become useful as well as interesting; but my past experience in such matters has not been unsatisfactory, and I therefore ask the indulgence of those who may think differently.

My book knowledge is, I regret to say, limited; but my knowledge of actual and practical life is considerable. It is from that source my inspiration comes. If there be "sermons in stones, music in running brooks, and good in everything," why not draw lessons from every-day life, and give the facts and incidents which have done so much to make us what we are? If in the making we have been spoiled, then by all means discard the material; but if otherwise, then cherish what is worth using. "Let there be light" was spoken with an authority which is infinite, and every effort made to bring to pass that fulness of joy and completeness of blessing which the consummation of the command implies, is a working together with God, to which is given the promise of success, and for which is provided rich consolations and satisfactory rewards.

Those of us who can go back to the days of dip candles and oil lamps, dim fires and bare floors, can more readily count up our acquaintances and recollect the events and incidents of childhood, than those who live in railway times, penny newspapers, and telegraphic messages. The hills which surrounded the localities in which some of us dwelt, were to our minds the boundaries of the earth, and the few prominent men of the little town in which our lot was cast, were the most awful and authoritative. This was especially so with the borough bailiff and the town crier. The rector lived in another atmosphere, and walked in silk stockings and buckled shoes; and if it was a narrow way in which he walked, it was made so by the fact that nobody else dared to tread in it. The occupiers of the chapel pulpit often made one's hair stand on end by the fearful looking for of fiery indignation which was said to await most of us poor little wretched sinners, sitting with legs dangling on high forms without backs; and lest any of this lively and loving exhortation should be lost upon us, the teacher's long staff would come down upon our little heads with such a whack as not only to stir us up, but considerably agitate the entire congregation. Under this gentle and reviving treatment, our vacant and half-shut eyes would be directed towards the preacher. He in the meantime was filled with what was called holy zeal, and by way of showing what condition most of us were likely ultimately to be found in, he drew the curtain aside and gave us a peep at the unseen world. The picture then drawn is with me still, and has been my companion by night and by day from my youth up until now. There stood his satanic majesty, a most forbidding figure, horns on head, a malicious grin on his face, and a wild chuckle in his mouth; a tail composed of serpents' heads, from the mouths of which came issuing sparks of fire and streams of poison, and resting on the foot that was not cloven, and holding in his hand a long pronged fork with which he was kept busy turning over the bodies of those doomed to live for ever in that fire which was never to go out! As he turned them over the flames licked round the mouth of the pit, and ten thousand sparks flew from the conscious bodies of those who by creative wisdom had been made in the image of the Infinite. This was the horrible teaching to which I was subject, and these were the manifestations of the government of a God of love and wisdom as given to me before I knew my right hand from my left, and they have left their mark upon me to this day.

There were, however, some bright spots on this cloudy sky, and gleams of sunshine in the midst of the terrible tempests with which my child-life was sadly too familiar. One of the occasional occupiers of this chapel pulpit was a man of gaunt form and robust intellect, and very marked individuality. He dressed in plain drab with smalls and gaiters; buttons he abhorred where there were no button-holes. When, however, he had a button, it was a button—something to be seen and used and handled. The coat was always of the frock or surtout cut, single-breasted, reaching down to the knees, and buttoning right up to the throat. The buttons were as large as a good-sized medal, and of white bone or ivory. He never curled his "topping," or parted his hair—that to his mind would have been unscriptural. He was careful withal in his dress, and respectable in circumstances, and good in character. The hair on his head lay in silken serenity, and was as orderly and undisturbed as the thatch on a well-rigged farmstead. The face clean shaven, and his linen as spotless as his heart was pure. When he occupied the pulpit his presence was welcome, and there was a cheerfulness and brightness in the whole congregation which filled the little temple with sunshine. In his presence there was no sleeping; in what he said there was good sense and sound logic; but in what he did there was much interest and great curiosity. We, the boys on the benches, kept our eye upon him, especially when it was seen that he had begun to feel for the bottom button on the front of his long surtout. That it was known was a prelude to what often proved to be an exciting performance with a somewhat ridiculous climax. As he warmed to his subject these buttons would, one after another, be attached to and secured in the corresponding button-hole until the throat was reached. At that point all eyes were fixed; the boys especially were usually in a state of intense excitement, for the preacher would then lay hold of his coat, which he had unconsciously buttoned up so carefully, and with great force tear it open, in the doing of which some of these big buttons would not unfrequently fly off over the pulpit down into the singing pew below, and occasionally roll in the direction of the forms where the boys sat. This became a temptation too strong for the youthful mind, and there was consequently a spontaneous and general rush for the prize laid at their feet. Several heads upon this display were brought into disagreeable contact with the long staff, and then with faces awry and rebellious hearts, we were called upon to join in singing,—

"Praise God, from whom all blessings flow."

Now if the Sabbath is to be made the most irksome and doleful day of the week, and in connection with that we are told that the heaven to which we are incited, and for which such a price has been paid and such sacrifices have to be made, is to be one "eternal sabbath," it cannot be said, so far as the mass of the people are concerned, to be a very attractive way of putting the case.

CHAPTER III.

CHILDHOOD: THE FACTORY BOY.

IF "the child is father to the man," the impressions of early days cannot but form a prominent feature in the influences guiding our after-life. The extent and force of the development will of course, in some measure, depend upon our natural constitution and the construction put upon things by those amongst whom we live. There is nothing, as it seems to me, to compare with home influence, and that that should be true and loving is of the utmost importance. Oneness at home and unity of families, even in the midst of poverty and sore trials, has in it a strength which will beget respect, and a majesty that dazzles even when covered with rags.

Nature's nobility depend not on coronets, princely character and manly bearing can be found where there are no belted knights or proud courtiers. Among the sons of toil and the daughters of sorrow there have ever been found those whose history would give glory to any land, and whose lives have "left footprints on the sands of time" which, when seen, gave heart to many a despairing brother. That there are despairing brothers, and that life's journey is one which has in it many circumstances trying to our minds, and events crushing to the hearts, needs no proof. Yet when early winter has walled up our doors, and the north wind is bringing to us blinding snow and biting sleet, do we ever think of the homeless poor, the fireless grate, the bare cupboard, and the cold hearthstone? "When thou makest a feast, call not thy rich neighbours nor thy friends, lest they invite thee again." If that be the teaching of infinite wisdom, what fearful folly, if not monstrous wickedness it is, to spend money like water in feasting and fuddling those who could not see us if they met us in the street under other circumstances, and who laugh at our imbecility, and ridicule our apeing the aristocrat in what after all is only practised by the snobs of society. The tinsels of life have a wonderful attraction to certain minds, and an opportunity to don official robes becomes irresistible to men whom tailors make. But how empty and hollow is all this! and when the time for disrobing comes, and come it will, and there is nothing left but what the man is himself intrinsically worth, who would buy the article? "Handsome is that handsome does" is a wholesome adage, and the glories of life have no value excepting so far as they may have been fairly earned and are honestly used.

The following is a literal account of an event in my childhood which I have never forgotten, and from which I have drawn lessons. My father was an unlettered man, honest and industrious, with a firm will, and an undying love for his family and his home. He was one of eight brothers, all very powerful men physically, and he himself had eight sons. My mother, mentally, was much his superior, and almost equal to him physically; she had a large heart, a warm temperament, and an intensely religious nature. When I was but an infant they left the borders of Yorkshire for an ancient and somewhat famous borough in the north of Lancashire.

The hand-spinning wheel and hand loom which were

then the feature of the district, and by which, in connection with a little land and a cow or two a decent living was got, and a comfortable home maintained, were threatened by the building of factories and the introduction of machinery. People of forethought who had young families growing up around them, migrated to the neighbourhoods of these factories, where a prospect of employment for young children as well as adults was held out.

That condition of things resulted in my parents renting a small farm in the neighbourhood of this town, and within reach of a flourishing print works and a rising cotton manufactory. The owner of the farm was a leading gentleman in the town, officially connected with the borough, and an employer of labour. My father entered into his service as well as being a tenant on his land; the master prospered, the servant's family increased, and the responsibilities and difficulties increased also. There was a strike at the print works, and as my parents had opened a small grocery in addition to occupying the land, several of the families employed at the print works became their customers, and were allowed credit through the strike, but when they returned to their employment many of them forgot to pay their debts. That made my poor parents poorer still.

About this time, a gentleman living opposite to us, who had a saw-pit and timber yard taken from one of our small fields, desired further accommodation, and he was told by my father's landlord to stake out as much more land as he needed for his business. This being done without even consulting my father's wishes, or considering his feelings, was more than could be borne, and my father, with a giant's strength, tore the stakes up as fast as they were put down, and snapped them in twain like so many chips. That resulted I believe in an assault, and certainly in a long and expensive lawsuit, in which my father was worsted and cast into prison. Our beds were taken from under us, and we were left desolate. A more unrighteous and wicked thing I never knew, but it was only one of the many instances in which might overpowered right in the past, in ways which could not be practised, and I think would not be attempted, now.

It was under these penniless and helpless circumstances that, when I was but a few months over six years of age, by five o'clock on a cold winter's morning I walked a mile to a cotton mill, getting home again at eight o'clock at night, and for which at the end of every two weeks my wages came to five shillings, that is supposing no deductions had taken place for being a few minutes late in going to my work in a morning. I know something, then, of cold, and want, and hunger. I also know something of the oppression of power and the iniquity of law. In my early life these had come home to me in all their force and bitterness, and from that day to this I have cultivated a strength which should enable me to do battle with them, and I have grown in my desire to beat back that which wronged the poor, as well as to check undue assumption and vain presumption on the part of the rich.

On the 25th of December, 1820, with the rest of the family I spent my Christmas-day and night with my father, who was then in the Moat Hall of the borough, which at the time was the local prison of that town, and from which my father would not, and did not, come until he had had restored to him his rights in respect to the tenancy of his land, which was ultimately done by the landlord himself; but not before my father had been kept in confinement over six months, and had been stripped of what little earthly good he possessed.

I know not the exact process by which this deliverance came, but I fancy there was some particular law special to this particular borough, which gave the claimant power to cast into prison, but which at the same time held him responsible for much of the cost, and in that way I think my father wearied his prosecutor out. I have, however, no recollection of any similar case in the same borough, either before or since. I believe my father settled that business. It was not an ordinary prison, it was simply a large room in what was called the "Moat Hall," with several large windows looking into the main street, and through which any one could readily see. So the place was neither dull nor cheerless, and my impression is that it was never intended or expected that my father would remain there. It was done as I believe to frighten him, and was more a case of personal authority than of law or justice; for the gentleman with whom the contention lay, was at that time a little king, and could with certain limitations say,

> "I am monarch of all I survey,
> My right there is none to dispute,
> From the centre all round to the sea,
> I am lord of the fowl and the brute."

Yet there was one who did dispute him, and though the battle was most unequal, conquered him, conquered him by firmness of purpose, and stubbornness of will, sustained by a sense of right.

For a few weeks my father was kept there twirling

his thumbs. The family and friends, however, fitted him up a bed, and found food and fuel, but all that was a severe tax. Subsequently, a loom was introduced, and the heart of the oppressor began to thaw, and members of the family had pretty free access to the place and could stay nearly as long as they liked. My father was a good weaver, and some of us used to go and wind the bobbins, so that so far as comfort went the place had the advantage of our then family home. Money was earned, and as there was no rent to pay, circumstances improved. Tyranny was crushed, and oppression was put to shame. The door of the prison-house was opened, but my father was in no hurry to avail himself of it; he took his own time and came out in his own way, not having suffered in character or reputation by the incarceration. But the iron had entered his soul notwithstanding, and he could not bear the sight of the place afterwards. That fact determined him at the first opportunity to remove from the scenes which brought to his remembrance much of oppression, if not of shame, and we were from that time plunged into the thick of the manufacturing towns of Lancashire. That circumstance changed the entire course of our family life.

CHAPTER IV.

CHILDHOOD: LEAVING HOME.

I WAS then ten years of age, and though there had been many, very many dark days in my short history, the companions of my child-life were all there. The river on the banks of which I had often sported had about it many charms; its streams were of the purest and most limpid character. The town well, from which I had often drunk, to my mind was a fountain of life; and its ladle secured by an iron chain, and the stepping-stone by which we entered the well, were memories pleasing to recall. The brow down which I had trundled my hoop, and the old castle towering up high above our little farmstead, had all linked themselves to my wondering mind, and to wander away from them into the great hive of industries, and live in the midst of unknown voices, and amongst the rattle and burr of noisy machinery, and the strifes and ambitions of life, was to me simply to go into a whirl of workshops and a maze of mobs. The house to which we went was in a crowded, cramped neighbourhood, filled with unearthly sounds and foul with unwholesome odours.

We crouched down on the evening of that eventful day round the embers of a fire which had never been very brilliant, huddled up in a small house, in the corner of a narrow and confined street. The family consisted of seven children, the eldest sixteen, the youngest two years old. My parents sat in the midst of this solemn responsibility, and waited for and wondered what the coming morn would bring. I had then become, though so young, a companion of their inner thoughts, and when my father broke down, which was a most unusual thing with him, but which he did on this occasion, I remember being so touched that I wept as a child only could weep who had been spoiled of its treasured joy, and whose highest pride had been smitten and laid in the dust.

Much of the suffering of this life is no doubt self-inflicted, and the imprudence and dissipation of vast numbers of the working population is patent to all observers; but there are apart from these an innumerable company of patient, helpless sufferers, who by a combination of circumstances over which they have no control, and which no forethought could prevent, have been brought into the most abject penury and inextricable difficulties. The following day brought employment in one of the cotton mills of the town to my father and two of the children. I had also been presented as one likely to be of some service, having already had more than three years' experience in contributing my quota to the daily wants of the family; but the managing partner shook his head, and thought I was too small.

It was not long, however, before an opening was made for me, so that four of us managed in combination to keep a roof over our heads and the wolf from the door.

This condition of things continued for about a year, and my father succeeded then in obtaining a somewhat responsible though humble position in the famous Horrocks' cotton mill in the town of Preston. The Messrs.

Horrocks were the largest and most prosperous manufacturers in the district, and in addition to appointing my father as the night watch over their extensive premises, they took my brother and myself into the weaving department, with the view of our being thoroughly trained in all the arts of the trade, and the intention as soon as we were qualified of our taking responsible and what were at that time much to be desired positions in the business. That prospect justified the removal of the family from Blackburn to Preston, in which town we lived for several years. Every year added to the strength and value of the family, and as the children had ability they were put to profitable employment. This brought both comfort and plenty to our home, and we became what was looked upon as a better-class working family.

One night, after two or three years' residence in Preston, my father had gone to his duties as night watch, and the family were in social comfort seated round the cheerful hearth, while my mother, as was her wont, would be rehearsing to us some of her early histories, and relating those thrilling stories of Lancashire witches in which she was a strong believer, a knock was heard at the door. The tale of witches, boggarts, hobgoblins, and haunted houses with which our ears had been regaled had already made our hair stand on end; faces could be seen in the fire, and figures flitted through the flame. We hitched closer to each other, and held our breath in awe, but gave no answer to the knock. The house was a new one, and at the extremity of that part of the town, a churchyard filled with graves was our nearest neighbour. To breathe audibly, let alone to speak, was to die! Keeping our seats with wondering and consternation, we jointly cried, "Who's there?" At that the door opened, and a figure stepped in. From behind wrappers and from under cloaks a voice was heard to inquire if that was the home of my father. The voice when heard was known to be that of my father's former landlord and master. He asked for shelter and protection. He was not only a waylaid traveller, but a pursued fugitive, flying from creditors and in desperate circumstances. He was lodged for the night, and had given to him the best bed the house could afford. Mother could only look upon him still as the "squire," and notwithstanding the memories his presence brought back, she could but treat him as such. He had come to grief, and, after the shades of evening had set in, he had walked twenty miles to escape his creditors. The only door open to him was the door of the man he had so unrighteously wronged and oppressed, and under his roof he was secreted, nursed, and fed, for six weeks, till the storm passed by. For those six weeks, long before the squire rose from his bed in the morning, my father had returned from the duties of his night watch, and had cleaned the old yellow-topped boots, that he who had once been his lord might feel there was even yet one hand left which did not refuse to do him service.

In calling to mind the circumstances, I have often wondered at the strange fatality which clung to the history of the little squire. When he ruled with a high hand over the interests in which my father was involved, there seemed to be no bands in his death. That Providence should be charged with bringing about family ruin by such instrumentality as this story records, and that the same Providence should be charged with subsequently punishing the same instrumentality for bringing it about, is amongst the things which I confess my inability to understand, and therefore cannot explain. The whole thing is not only opposed to common sense, but can never be made to harmonize with the character of Him who delighteth in mercy. When in the darkness of that winter's night those weary twenty miles were trod by the pursued squire, there would undoubtedly be communings and reflections, and many have been the experiences in which "man's extremity" has been "God's opportunity." How far that was so then I know not, but that he bitterly regretted the deed done, when it was too late to remedy it, there was no doubt, and that the acknowledgment of his error was one of the impulses of his nature which led him to seek our home when trouble had overtaken himself, was again and again made manifest. During that sojourn at our Preston home, explanations and acknowledgments were made on the one hand, while kind and forgiving deeds were performed on the other, which led to mutual friendship and lasting esteem continuing to the end of the natural lives of those immediately concerned.

I should hesitate to charge Providence with the responsibility of redressing every wrong, and correcting every abuse, and punishing every transgression common to life; but it seems to me there are certain fixed laws which govern our being, and the rule is, that in conforming to laws we secure results in character with them, and these results harmonize with justice and reason. When, therefore, Scripture speaks of men "reaping what they sow," and "man measuring to man that which shall be measured to him again," it simply announces a truism which experience teaches and every day proves.

There are, of course, exceptions to this rule, many

exceptions; but the exceptions themselves prove the rule, and if men would but notice the frequency with which high-handed oppression and undue advantage taken come sooner or later home to themselves, there would be less cruelty and dishonesty than there is.

The very selfishness of our nature, if nothing else, would hold back our hand in the hour of temptation and though it may be the lowest of motives, it is a motive which is in universal operation, and often exists when there is no other influence at work. "What ye would that men should do unto you, do ye even so unto them," is only another side of the same thing; consequently all laws and all resolutions which lack these just and natural elements, can never commend themselves to a civilized people, and will be repelled until they are repealed.

This "coming home to roost" is not confined to mischievous and evil things—it would be a miserable and unsatisfactory arrangement if it were so—it has another side. Just as "an evil tree bringeth forth evil fruit, so likewise a good tree bringeth forth good fruit;" and of all the blessings which belong to life, that of good doing is perhaps the greatest. "More blessed to give than to receive," may be a strange doctrine, but it is no more strange than true, and many, very many, revel in it as a luxury, and will not part with it but with life. My mother had a big heart, even in her penury she gave much; and when I remember the hospitality of her home, the abounding plenty of her table, and the religious devotion of her nature, it looks to me like having much of the presence and blessing of Him who fed the multitude with so little, and when they had done, gathering up more than was possessed when the feast began.

When David cut off the skirt of Saul's garment, it was pretty clear what might have been done had the spirit of retaliation and revenge been dominant.

The world's life has in it many grand and glorious records. There is something left, after all, about this human nature of ours, notwithstanding its many disfigurements, which tells us that the image of God, though marred, has not been destroyed, and that we are yet capable of, and do frequently perform, deeds proving that we are not bastards, but children—children born of heaven. Saul was not more completely put into David's power than was the poor squire in that of my mother, and those who read these recollections must forgive me if they think it undue presumption of me when I say that I think one record has a value and a lesson in it as well as the other.

CHAPTER V.

YOUTH: MACHINERY AND MOBS.

DURING our residence in Preston two or three events happened of a public nature which deserve a record.

The late Lord Derby was returned to the House of Commons for the first time as one of the members for one of the two or three boroughs in the country which enjoyed manhood suffrage. Every man of twenty-one years of age and of so many weeks' residence, not being a pauper, and untainted with crime, was in Preston entitled to vote. By that constituency the late Lord Derby was first sent to the House of Commons as the Whig candidate. He was a very handsome young man of brilliant talents, and these, combined with the family influence in the town, which at that time was great, secured his return.

The celebrated William Cobbett was also an unsuccessful candidate at the same election, but he secured such a hearing and gave forth such teaching as paved the way for the success of the famous Radical candidate, Henry Hunt, at a subsequent election, while Cobbett himself was returned in triumph as one of the first members for the newly-enfranchised borough of Oldham. Lancashire during those years was afflicted, like many other manufacturing districts, with the mania for machine breaking. Mobs collected and marched *en masse*, armed with bludgeons and other offensive and destructive weapons, making dreadful depredations in many directions. Blackburn had suffered much from these wild intimidations and foolish illegalities. Soldiers were called out, hundreds of special constables sworn in, and the peaceable and law-abiding portion of the community put on self-defence.

The crisis of this period was in the year 1826. The people madly thought that machinery would be their ruin, and in pursuing the destruction of this competing foe, they sacrificed in many cases both liberty and life. We in Preston were threatened, and reports came thick and fast that thousands of men were marching on the town; and as Horrocks's was one of the largest mills, and in advance of many others in the use of the latest improvements in machinery, they were specially named for the vengeance of the mob. Brown Besses and blunderbusses were furbished up and put into requisition, and all official men armed. My father, I remember, was one of them. Having never handled fire-arms in his life before, what would have been the consequence, had he been called upon in all seriousness to do so, I don't know. This I am sure of, his aim would have been more sure with his fists, and the truncheon to which he had become accustomed would have done surer if not more deadly work. In one of the upper rooms of the new mills in which I was then employed, there were stored several tons of paving stones. The lower rooms had already been filled with the latest improvements in looms, and in them my brother and I, who were the only males in that department, were employed; the rest were young girls and women, to the number of two or three hundred. When the mob came, and supposing they forced their way through the entrance gates and overcame the men of fire-arms and official authority, then we, the women and children, were to fly to the upper rooms of the building it was expected the mob would especially attack, and shower down through the open windows upon these thick heads the delicate and tender appliances of paving stones. We were, however, saved the soft impeachment, for the mob never came, better counsels having prevailed, and the women and children were saved a warfare in which, after all, I think there was more fear than danger.

Joseph Livesey, a name which for fifty years has been a household word with all temperance reformers, was at this time made known to me. He was a tradesman living near to our home, and then took a deep interest in everything which concerned the poor, as he has never failed to do, even down to the present day. A heart which always welled over with kindly sympathy to the helpless and neglected, having himself been one of them, induced him to open a night-school for youths and children of neglected education. To it I was myself attracted, partly by some companion boys who had begun to attend, and partly by the entertainments he mixed up with the education. One of them, I remember, included some experiments in electricity. That was a most popular affair, and when the entire school was joined into a circle to receive the shock, the room in which we were assembled being but small was not considered large enough for the full demonstration of the power of the galvanic battery, so we all turned out into the street. The neighbouring mothers and grandmothers were also invited to join hands with us, which many of them did; for there was no limit then, as there has frequently been no limit since, to Mr. Livesey's desire to confer pleasure and blessing. The wonderment with which we waited for the result was depicted on every countenance, and when the shock came, the dancing and prancing and grimaces which characterized that mixed and astonished circle were worthy of the pencil of a Hogarth or a Cruikshank. I don't know that I made much, if any, progress in my irregular and somewhat spasmodic attendance at Mr. Livesey's night-school. One thing, however, I did learn, and it has continued with me to the present day—I learned to love and esteem Joseph Livesey; it is a name never to be forgotten. The owner of it still lives; and though ninety years of age the heart is still young, the countenance sunny, and the hand holds the pen of a ready writer, and thousands have risen up to call him blessed.

My success in my work while at Horrocks's in Preston led me into sorrow and became a temptation. It was a practice to give bounties to such of us as could turn out a special quantity of work in a given time from a given loom, and I was not unfrequently successful in doing so. This made me an attraction, and no doubt flattered my vanity. My success was talked about, and the girls and women who worked with me in the same business made a pet of me. They took me with them to their dances, which were invariably held in public-houses, and as there were occasional prizes given for the best hornpipe, and as I had the good fortune or the *misfortune* to win sometimes, that was fuel to the flame.

There was always a considerable amount of drinking in connection with these performances; indeed, I know of no other means the publicans had of covering the cost, and getting paid for the trouble, than by the promotion of drinking. It will be seen how readily and naturally one would run with the stream. Then the bounty money, as it was a speciality, could fairly be considered a private perquisite, and my parents had no claim upon me for that. They had already received my ordinary wages for what was ordinary work.

A public house at the bottom of Friargate announced rum at "fivepence a noggin,"—the usual price was sixpence. I was then living in New Preston, the other extreme end of the town. The advantages here offered were irresistible. I was fourteen years of age. My elder brother and I started off on the Saturday night we had received our first bounty, I think it would be a shilling each, and invested the entire amount in this rum. How we got home I know not to this day, but on the Sunday morning I was so sore I knew not what to do, and my face was so cut and bruised I was not fit to be seen, and on the Monday morning, when in the mill, my appearance was such as to beget unkind and doubtful feelings on the part of the foreman in the room in which I worked, and I was never able to live it down while working there. That spoiled my prospect of promotion and success at the famous Horrocks's, and it seemed to touch and taint the whole family, and once more turned the current of our family life.

We were all boys with one exception, and as we bid fair to become big and powerful men, and the authorities in Preston seemed slow as my parents thought in putting us into advanced positions, they removed to Bolton, and we secured better positions at "Ormerods and Hardcastles'," a firm scarcely less famous in that town than was Horrocks's in Preston. From Bolton we went to Glossop in Derbyshire, and in doing so secured further advantages for the family. It will be seen how we clung together as a family; when one was touched the rest sympathised. This no doubt is a pleasing feature, and has in it many advantages; but when the family is large, as was the case with us, and there is also a considerable amount of self-will and individuality, it sometimes results in inconvenience and suffering. That was our condition more than once. Had it not been for this we needed not to have left Preston, or Bolton, or Glossop.

"A rolling stone gathers no moss" was never more clearly exemplified than in our own case, and we had more than once, when seated in the family circle, to say it would have been better if we had "let well alone." It was well in Preston, and in Bolton, and in Derbyshire, but we would do better; we did better for the time being, but when the cost incurred in doing better was taken into account, the better doing left no margin. If "three removals are as bad as one fire," what a lot of fires we have had! and as they were fires to cover which no insurance had been effected, it will be seen the loss and suffering must have been very considerable.

Factory workers of to-day know nothing of bad materials, defective machinery, and oppressive employers as compared with fifty and sixty years ago. It is not now the favour to give work in a mill that it was then, and the hours for work are much fewer, and the machinery with which the work is done much more effective and less destructive to the material worked; this being so, there are not the occasions for disputes, fines and abatements which existed in the past, and which unprincipled men were far too ready to put into force.

The factory child of sixty and seventy years ago had no protection, and the operative in the mill would frequently submit to an injustice, rather than sacrifice his bread.

There is now much more consideration on both sides, and far greater equality between employer and employed than then existed. Then they were emphatically two parties, living and working as if there were no community of interest; now a better and more rational spirit prevails, and this should be cultivated more and more. We cannot afford to live as if we were not one, and it is a serious mistake, and a manifest injustice, when either master or man (because of his power, or fortuitous circumstances) seeks an undue advantage.

"Honesty is the best policy," and never more so than when exercised in a community of interests; and I have faith enough in human nature to believe that in all ranks of society, when the common weal is fairly understood and honestly sought, there will not be those sad outbreaks of disaffection and irreconcilable differences which have too often paralysed our trade and ruined both masters and men.

My success in Glossop was premature. When but a youth I was a better man than my father. I could earn more money, I was young and active, and could fly about the machinery in a way he could not. This no doubt has much to do with those early marriages that are too common amongst mill-workers. Two young people look at each other, they are sixteen or eighteen years of age, they can each earn a pound or twenty-five shillings a week. Two twenty-fives are fifty, and that is a lump of money and a temptation to people who can live on ten or twelve shillings a week. They put themselves together, and their wages too, and for a time there is abundance, but usually this is not long lived. The practice, too, of taking the young wife or the young husband to the home of the parents of one of them is most objectionable; but as it dispenses with the necessity of house furnishing, and leaves both at liberty to go to the mill, it is in many cases an inducement rather than a hindrance to early marriage.

This in my judgment is a great mischief, and it will be well for all concerned when no two people will consent to become one until they are able to furnish their own house and find their own home. In factory districts a large and well ordered family is in the main a help and a blessing, and where there is industry and sobriety with combined family life, that is, one table and one purse, there will not only be every necessary supplied in abundance, but many luxuries as well.

It is from this class that many of our prosperous manufacturers and merchants, both of the past and present, have sprung, and as these multiply poverty will disappear, and home wrecks be a thing of the past.

I had seven brothers, and all with one exception married before they were twenty-one years of age. Some of them at eighteen, and one little more than sixteen years of age. This is an evil in more ways than one. It impoverishes the family homestead, and not unfrequently results in physical weakness and premature old age; and when there is added to this, young and helpless family life, it will be seen how resources are dried up, and self-respect destroyed. The practice too of young people *boarding* with their parents at such prices as are often fixed upon is most unfair and unbecoming. Why seek at the earliest opportunity to deprive parents of any little benefit which may result from skilled labour in young life? Surely nobody can be more entitled to the first-fruits than those who have watched our infant steps and nursed and trained our growing life. "Honour thy father and thy mother, that thy days may be long in the land which the Lord thy God giveth thee," is the first command with promise. We are too apt to forget the command, and no wonder so many pass through life without inheriting the promise.

I boarded with my parents, and though I could not at all times meet even the modest and (as I think now) shameful consideration of seven shillings a week for that board, I thought myself rich enough to get married. That I was in love there is no doubt, but that the bonny little creature who became my wife should have been so was the marvel to everybody. We were much together, working next to each other; there were many opportunities of showing kindness and rendering mutual help, and in that way our oneness grew into warm affection, but we were very young. My habits and character were very objectionable to the father of this choice of mine. How she herself could be so reliant and hopeful in my case was a mystery to all. The men with whom I associated were continually tantalising me by saying "she would never have me," that her "father would not allow it," and all that sort of thing.

At length I was provoked into betting a wager of so much drink that I would marry her within a month. I could earn money, but I had none, neither had I a decent suit of clothes, and as to a home that was out of the question. The banns were forthwith published, but the father in hot haste forbade them; we were both under age, and my companions got drunk in anticipation of the further revel that was coming to them by my losing the wager; but they reckoned without their host, for instead of waiting the month I was married within two weeks of the wagering business.

It was managed in this way. My sister, who was the oldest member of our family, and a second mother to the rest, was in high esteem by all who knew her. She was very fond and very proud of my choice. I made her my confidante; she hoped the connection would improve and bless me, and no doubt it did for a time. She went to the provision shop where the family traded, and gave her guarantee for the loan of three pounds; that being secured, some eight or ten of us, men and women, agreed to leave by four o'clock, on Sunday morning, and walk to Stockport, twelve miles, where I bought a licence of the vicar, and was married by him before one-half of Stockport had got breakfast. Having arranged to help my intended away from her home with such clothing as she required during the early Sunday morning, she was taken to my best man's house, and there prepared for the journey, my friend and his wife accompanying us, with others, who were also in the secret. I slipped down home, having put on my brother William's suit of Sunday clothes, and off the cavalcade started, in high spirits and in great feather; some of the feathers, it will be seen, were borrowed for the hymeneal altar. Brother William, when he awoke and found his clothes gone, was in sad plight, and the father of my wife on missing his daughter was in great desperation, and messages flew in all directions but the right one, to prevent the consummation I was bent upon.

The whole neighbourhood was up in arms, for the news had spread like wild-fire, and as the evening of the day approached, the road leading to the town from where we had been, and which became known as the day advanced, was lined with crowds of excited people. We all walked back from Stockport to Glossop, with our hats and bonnets decorated with ribbons, creating great excitement, and having much fun all along the line. On our arrival, we had quite an ovation. The people formed an avenue along which we passed. My best man had been in the army, and was more than six feet high; he led the procession in great form, like a drum-major. My parents (influenced by my sister) had made quite a nice provision for us, and gave us a welcome more than was expected or deserved, and the victory such as it was, was complete. I had got a gem of a wife, and that was my stock-in-trade.

On the Monday morning we both went to our work in the mill, and we applied ourselves to our duties, and it was not long before I had a nice little home of my own, and I was promoted to better and more profitable employment; but I did not break with my companions nor change my habits, and the result was I got into trouble with my employers, and left once more with the rest of the family for Lancashire.

This was a terrible mistake, and a great disappointment to our employer Mr. Wood. The family was large and capable, and we were at the time an acquisition to any employer of labour in the cotton trade; but a little temper on the part of the master, with too much defiance on the part of the servant, brought about the crisis, which both parties, I have reason to believe, subsequently repented.

Belmont, near Bolton, was our next destination. It was a wilderness of a place, and we could not settle in it. Some little interference with our work was quite enough to beget a quarrel with our employer, and one day at noon we all refused to return to our duties.

Then it was I knew what it was to be hungry, without what was needful to supply my wants; that was the case with the entire family.

We still stuck together, and two of the sons had added wives to the stock. The next day father, one of my brothers, and myself, started out in search of employment, calling at several mills on our way to Blackburn. We were unsuccessful; we had no love for Blackburn, and it was not our intention to apply for work there, but to go on to Clitheroe, the town of early days and of mixed memories.

After partaking of a very meagre tea at a public-house in Penny Street, weary, faint, and some of us lame, we started on the eleven miles' walk for Clitheroe.

We had not got more than a mile and a half out of the town when father broke down. He had never turned his face towards Clitheroe since leaving it some ten years before, under circumstances already described.

The recollection of the way in which our home had been broken up in that town, choked him, and literally falling by the wayside he said, "Thomas, I cannot go." My father was a strong, powerful man, and not easily broken down or unmanned; but on this occasion he trembled like a leaf, and wept like a child.

It was more than brother and I could bear, so we urged him to return to Blackburn and spend the night.

The next day he called on the firm of Eccles and Company, by whom the family had been employed on the occasion of our residence there ten years before, and they at once promised employment to some of the family, holding out prospects to the rest.

That determined our removal to Blackburn, which was done within the week.

There was but one small house at our service, and my furniture had to be distributed with such neighbours as were kind enough to take the trouble to oblige me. My wife and babe and I were in the same dependent condition, and to make matters worse the baby died within three days of our arrival. This was a climax. There was not a soul in the town I knew outside my own family, I was out of work, and had not a penny in the world. Here was I, a stranger among strangers, penniless, homeless, childless, not twenty-one years of age, with a good trade in my fingers, but before I was twenty spoiled for life, and now, for the time being at least, incapacitated for work at my own trade. My shoulder was so weak that it could not be applied to anything requiring physical strength, and that entirely the result of abuse and neglect.

The father of my wife had never been reconciled to her choice, and now to feel I had brought her away from the scenes of her childhood, and the beautiful surroundings which the Dale of Glossop presents, to herd with the crowds of a strange and unattractive town, and to be dependent on such service as they could render, filled me with a wounded spirit. I could not live among the dead, while the charity of the living was worse than death to me.

I wandered in loneliness and remorse for many hours,

reaching Preston nine miles away, in the vague hope that an elder brother who had got work there would be able to do something, but it was not possible.

The crushed heart and troubled conscience drove me to desperation. All moral power seemed dead in me, and my physical infirmity made me mad; and had it not been for a remarkable coincidence which occurred while I was away, I have reason to believe I should never have survived the burial of that child.

My mother in walking down King Street on some domestic errand met with a gentleman whom she had not seen for I think twenty years. He had been her class-leader in Clitheroe. She was not aware of his residence in Blackburn. She made known to him the straits of the family, speaking specially of the difficulty concerning my dead child. He came to our relief, and brought with him sunshine and hope. This kindly and unexpected deed made me feel that all was not lost, and that there was some good in the world after all. That nerved my arm and strengthened my will, so that in my poverty I determined never to say die; and though I could not work at my own trade, which was a terrible humiliation to me, I determined to do what I could in other ways, and so recover if possible my lost position. Lancaster, a town in which I was not known, supplied the opportunity for a few months, after which I again returned to Blackburn, taking up my usual position and doing my usual work.

During this period my eye caught the bill announcing the temperance meeting at which I signed the pledge, and it is of what followed I am so anxious to speak.

CHAPTER VI.

THE DAWN OF TEMPERANCE MANHOOD.

LANCASHIRE and Yorkshire during the years 1833, 1834, 1835, was the ground mainly worked on the new plan, and the Preston men electrified, delighted and astonished the people wherever they went. Mr. W. Pollard, a respected local preacher in the Wesleyan Connexion at Manchester, and a very good platform man, put in good seed as the agent of the "Moderation Society" in other parts of the country; and Mr. Finch, a merchant from Liverpool, who, at the time was in partnership with Mr. Swindlehurst of Preston, also, when on his journeys, did brave and efficient service on behalf of the new crusade, and in that way the fire spread. Many others no doubt, in different parts of the country, caught the flame and relighted other torches, but it is not my purpose to write a history, and I cannot therefore particularize. Somebody else with more time than I possess must do that; one with greater patience for detail, and more correct chronological knowledge than I can command, will, I trust, be found in our ranks to do justice to our cause in all departments, and to all its workers.

I can only see what is near, and throw off a few remarks belonging to my own immediate circle.

As I have outlived my compeers, it is thought that many facts and incidents considered interesting, which nobody but myself can tell, should be attempted. That is really the reason why my surviving friends, who have so often been afflicted by my tongue, are now exposed to the same ordeal from my pen.

Joseph Livesey, who by common consent is recognised as our founder and guide, was a man ever commanding the respect and confidence of all who knew him, a man of strong common sense, of the strictest commercial integrity, combined with the kindest of natures, and the most unbounded sympathy for the poor and the helpless, grasped this question in all its fulness and power. Constitutionally a combination of Franklin and Cobbett, philosophic in thought, and forcible in expression, he had the heart of a father, and the pen of a ready writer. He opened the first temperance hotel in the world to give the teetotallers a home, and he published the first temperance periodical that ever saw the light, in which he for some years kept our hearts cheered and our hopes bright. It was during the time I refer to largely circulated and much appreciated, and will be found at this day, by those who can lay their hands on it, most interesting reading.

How the Preston men missioned the district in their temperance car has been told more than once: taking the responsibility of hiring rooms, and where that was not practicable, taking the street or the market-place, and from the car on which they had travelled, exhorting every man and teaching every man, then returning home, sometimes after a day's and sometimes after a week's excursion and resuming their ordinary duties. It was in carrying out this programme that they came to Blackburn, the town in which I then lived, in the early part of 1835.

The Theatre Royal was engaged for the entire week. The town being freely and attractively placarded, the movement begot great excitement and much interest and curiosity. I was then in my twenty-second year, and considered to possess quite the average amount of skill. In my department, as an operative in a cotton mill, I could hold my own with my fellows. I was thoroughly down, both in circumstances and in prospects, and was glad to be employed on the worst machine in the worst mill in the town. Man's extremity is said to be God's opportunity, and no doubt it is often so. I could a story tell, but I would rather not. I know the value of a sensational story, and it is quite a fashion to tell one, and not uncommon or unprofitable to publish it. Possibly I got spoiled on the threshold of my temperance career for performances of this sort by the following incident. Quakers, it is well known, are proverbial for their quaintness and sagacity. One of this class presided over a meeting, to be addressed by reformed drunkards, and by them only. Tale after tale was told by speaker after speaker, each one it would seem trying to outdo his predecessor in the catalogue of brutalities perpetrated and the neglect of obligations. At length one got up and topped the rest by saying,—"Mr. Chairman, ladies and gentlemen, if I were to tell you all that *I* have done, I should be *hanged.*" The chairman, rising from his seat and quietly putting his hand upon the shoulder of the speaker, said, "That will *do*, my friend; thou hadst better *sit down.*" It is not that I fear being hanged, but that I have no pleasure in the things whereof I am now ashamed, that I now abstain from a rehearsal of the follies of my youth.

On the Sunday prior to the meetings in Blackburn,

I had been strolling and floundering about in a meaningless and objectless way, with some more of my companions, in the fields in the neighbourhood of the town, and returning home we mutually agreed to call at a certain public-house and get something to drink. On entering the door I saw a large bill posted announcing those temperance meetings. It attracted my attention, and I read it. On the bill were printed the names of the speakers. I *knew* some of them, and that excited my curiosity, and begat my interest. They had themselves been heavy drinkers. I told my companions so, and we determined to go to the meeting. If, as I was going, any one had said to me, "Whittaker, you will become a teetotaller," I should have felt inclined to have knocked him down, if I could have done so. I sat in the gallery, the part of the building that was free. There was a great crowd. My brother William hearing that I had gone to the meeting, followed, unknown to myself. He was a strictly sober and God-fearing young man. He knew my habits, he was like a twin brother, and we were bedfellows for years. The meeting was most impressive, and I was dumb-founded by the recitals and appeals of the speakers. There was an earnest purpose and a religious power in that meeting which lives with me to this day.

At the close my brother came to me and challenged me to sign, and though I hesitated, I was at length overcome. Knowing the influence my brother had on myself, can it be wondered at that I should, in the freshness of my youth, and the vigour of my new life, call upon the Church individually and collectively, to stand, like Aaron of old, between the living and the dead, that the plague might be stayed? Yet when that was done, they called us "uncharitable," and told us not to put teetotalism in the place of religion. The fact is, (and it will be well for the modern teachers of temperance to make a note of it,) we had then sadly *too much* religion in our teetotalism for the Church, while the Church had not enough religion in it to make its members teetotallers.

In those meetings, in that theatre, during that week there was a manifestation of the power of God that I, and many others had never seen or felt before; it was a pentecostal week, our hearts were touched, and the Holy Ghost fell upon us. Yet there was no singing, no reading of Scriptures, no prayer, public or audible; but there was something more than all that—there was the quickening Spirit, there was life from the dead, and influenced by that Power, and renewed by that life, the teaching ran like fire among dry stubble, and God only knows how dry some of it was. Teetotallers in those days were born in the fire, and were not readily choked (as many subsequent ones have been) by the smoke. There was a price to pay, and a cost to be incurred, of which the people of to-day know nothing, and when our junior friends know at what *price* their *own* freedom in these days was bought by the men of the past, they will be more disposed to make acknowledgment of, and be thankful for, the righteous though rough work then done. It is a mistake to suppose that though the Church bodily was not with us, that therefore we were destitute of the Spirit of Christ, and had no fellowship with religion. Comparing the past with the present, some of us know we never had so much of either of these things as when all men spoke evil of us.

Can any one be so ignorant as to suppose that the vast numbers of rollicking, rolling, rough stones, tumbled together as they were, could have formed themselves into buildings which have in many cases become palaces, had not the Master Builder been about, and the cement of Christian fellowship adhered to them? These wild asses' colts might be caught by the skilful throwing of the lasso, but who could have tamed them and put bits in their mouths, had not some unseen hand been at work, and some power like that which spoke "peace" to the troubled sea been near, though possibly unseen and unacknowledged?

Going back to the gallery of that theatre, and the circumstances under which I signed the pledge, was not that brother's example in my case a carrying out in a minor degree of the example of Him who for our sakes became poor? Suffice it to say that up to that point my passion for drink was a power, and my belief in it most sincere; but I signed the pledge then and there, and made a clean sweep of the whole business, and I would not to-day lend anybody a pot to put the liquor in. This is the great deliverance achieved by God through temperance. I have simply closed the account and done with the shop. In that I insult no man, I wrong no man, and I think there have been periods in my history as a temperance worker, when I could earnestly and sincerely say with Paul, "I could wish myself accursed for my brethren and kinsmen according to the flesh."

There is a piece of personal and private experience which I think will be an omission of duty if I do not relate here, as it may help to correct mistakes not unfrequent in these days, and put a trifle into the scale of *old*-fashioned teetotalism, which more than once in my presence has been made to kick the beam, by the bouncing bundles thrown into the *new*. Readers will perhaps bear with me.

I am the son of a mother in Methodism. My only sister and my twin brother (as I call him) were creditable and worthy members of the same growing and useful body of Christians. I had myself been a scholar when a young child in one of their Sunday-schools, so it may fairly be supposed I was neither destitute of religious knowledge, nor ignorant of a sense of religious duty. I had, at the time I signed, a young wife and child. She was also the offspring of Christian creditable people; yet not for three years at least, so far as I remember, had I ever privately and of my own accord bowed my knees in prayer. When I reached home, I told my wife what I had done; it took her breath, and she answered not a word. The remainder of the evening was spent in quiet thought. On retiring for the night my mind was exercised as to whether I should submit to ask my wife to join me in prayer, asking God to help me to be true to my pledge and firm in my resolution. At length turning to her I said, "Shall we pray about the matter?" She burst into tears, and we fell on our knees together, and oh! the memory of that night! It is with me still! That was the grandest prayer-meeting I was ever at, and I have been to many. There were more tears than words, and a grand rainbow followed the storm, giving promise of brighter and better days, and I have not been disappointed.

Now whatever good may have come to the world through the simple act of my signing the pledge (and there are those who think that not a little blessing followed that deed), though I had been much impressed at the meeting, had not my brother William, to whom drink was no snare or temptation, set me the example and urged me to the deed, I should, in all probability, have left that meeting (as my companions left it, who went with me) as I *was*, and never had another desire, and never had another opportunity, as I believe was the case with every one of them. They, to a man, passed away years ago, and passed away as they had lived.

Is there nothing then due to my brother? and has there been no guilt in the past, and may there not be guilt in the future, on the part of those who may have been and who will be like him in character and habits, who have been and who will yet be selfish and indifferent in this business?

To argue, as many good men do, in favour of the use of strong drink, and present excuses for their continuance in its use, is in my judgment to libel the profession they make. Driving a bargain with Deity for the retainance of an indulgence may be a clever but it is not a creditable performance, and cannot but be classed with those acts which give offence, and against which woe is pronounced.

CHAPTER VII.

SELF-HELP AND SELF-RESPECT.

SELF-RESPECT, if not a necessity to a creditable existence, is certainly an important factor in it. A blank mind may survive a blighted life, but no life gets far beyond the dullest and most monotonous existence, that has not in it some ambition. To rise in a morning and know not what to do nor where to go, unless some one else has made provision for our thought and occupation, and to retire at night without feeling that the world in our absence would have suffered at least *some* loss, can scarcely be called, and surely it is not, a patriotic, philanthropic, or a Christian life.

Occupation oils the wheels on which life runs, and we all know how much better it runs and how much longer it lasts, when its energies are applied to useful and practical purposes. An objectless and listless life is a dangerous and deadly one. That "Satan finds some mischief still for idle hands to do," is not only poetry but practical experience, and nobody is more to be pitied than the people whose forefathers spent their lives in making such provision, that their offspring should be what are called ladies and gentlemen. They live on their means, and that is about *all* they *do*. Provision is good, provided that in connection with it there be an understanding that when dependence upon others is not an obligation in us, others who depend upon *us* shall not lack that service. The lives many men live remind one of the application made to King James by a man who wished the king to "make him a gentleman." The king replied, "I cannot make you a gentleman, but I can make you a nobleman." No doubt he did so, and as nobility is inheritable, that may explain why noblemen in some quarters are so numerous, while gentlemen are so scarce. It will be found that neither refinement nor gentility are dependent on, or regulated by, either wealth or title; and while there may be, and no doubt is, something in the breed, circumstances and conditions mould and fashion life.

Temperance, as we have often been told, is not everything. Now nobody knows this better than its disciples; neither is bread cheese, but the man who gets bread and no cheese, or cheese and no bread, is better off than he would be if he got neither. There is one thing temperance does for everybody who adopts it, though it may do nothing more, it alters *conditions*. Why is a shop worth a hundred pounds a year in one street, and not worth a hundred pence in another? The circumstances and conditions make the difference. If a man drinks, and keeps drinking company, the chances are against him; if he abstains, and keeps virtuous company, the chances are in his favour.

There is much truth in the teaching, that we are the creatures of circumstances, but it is not the less true that circumstances are not unfrequently begotten by ourselves. When the necessity for my frequenting the public-house ceased, which it did when I ceased to need and use the liquors there sold, it became necessary that I should have other objects, and do something else.

The bright fire and welcome hearth, with the additional presence of a beautiful and cheerful wife, was not all that I wanted. The songs of Zion in which we joined, gave me some outlet; but I could not "sit and sing my soul away to everlasting bliss," though I kept saying that I could in the songs we occasionally sung; so I began to take stock of my acquirements and qualifications for life's work. They were limited and small, and the more I saw, and the more I knew, the weaker and more incompetent I seemed to be. Schooling I had had none, excepting a somewhat limited attendance at a sabbath-school could be called such.

That sixty and seventy years ago was not what it is now. Week-day schooling I had none at all, neither had any of my seven brothers. My father was also an unlettered man, so that there was not much help in that direction at home. The food of the family had to come through the fingers of the family, and as appetite is not dependent on education, we must have food whether we knew letters or not. The consequence was, that as soon as a shilling or two a week could be earned by any of us, we had to do it. My term of toil began when but a few months over six years of age, and from that moment continued, either in print shops or cotton mills, to the time of my becoming a teetotaller. The hours were fearfully long, and the work oppressively hard, so that I often, when in the midst of my work, fell fast asleep, standing bolt upright, and was not infrequently awoke by the man whose helper I was knocking me down like a dead fish on the floor.

I had to rise very early in the morning, not later than five o'clock; then walk a mile to the mill, and when there I was kept going with very little intermission for meals. There were no laws then regulating the labour of young children. The mill was also turned by water power, so that it cost but little to keep the machinery going, and men were at liberty to keep on from morning to night, and many of them did so keep on, and of course those who worked with, and had to help them, had to keep on also. That was *my* condition, so that when I did get home at eight o'clock, and sat down, I would often drop asleep at once, from weariness and fatigue. It will be seen, then, that the opportunity and ability to improve my time and educate my mind, so far as the knowledge of letters was concerned, was simply *nil*. Education will not cure intemperance, excepting so far as it tends to show the folly of drinking, just as it demonstrates the disadvantages of ignorance; but it will give the person possessing it resources and occupation that will both limit the temptation to drink, and greatly modify the passion for self-indulgence. That thousands of unlettered, but otherwise well skilled, decent working men, when off work, from whatever cause, are, from sheer inability to know what to do with their leisure time, swept away into the corner dram-shop and nearest public-house by passing influences, just as the wind drives the unswept dust along our streets, or the floods wash down our gratings the loose and ill-assorted material carelessly left, an offence to passers-by, there is every reason to believe, and it is a mistake to suppose that temperance reformers are not conscious of that fact; but, on the other hand, it is not the less palpable that refined natures, nervous temperaments, acute intellects and cultivated minds, one and all, are not infrequently seized upon by the devil "Drink," and debased and destroyed.

The revelations by G. R. Sims and others, in response to and in connection with "The Bitter Cry of Outcast London," prove that; but in doing so, they tell us nothing we have not known before, in connection with our fifty years' experience as temperance workers. But society will listen to them, they have got its ear, and it is well, just as society listens to Sir William Gull, Sir Henry Thompson, Dr. Richardson and others; yet these men tell us nothing that we had not before learned from such medical men as John Hegginbottom, Thomas Beaumont, John Fothergill, Henry Mudge, and others, fifty years ago. Canon Farrar, Canon Wilberforce, and such as they, are doing Herculean work, and their words are worth the record and commendation they get. They have got the public ear; but people who quote and parade these utterances as something wonderful or unheard of, only show how limited is their own knowledge, and how very late in the day it was before they themselves awoke to what was going on in the world. Dr. F. R. Lees, long before any of these worthy and deservedly esteemed men had a name amongst us, waded deep and dug down low in ancient literature and classic lore, stripping science of its hidden meaning, and the practice and teaching of it of such theories and actions as were irreconcilable with common sense, and misled the simple and destroyed the ignorant.

He, the child of our youth and of our first love, and the growing giant of advancing years, has never lost a single mental combat; while with a courage and intrepidity marvellous to behold in so frail a physical tenement, he again and again scattered to the winds our theological and scientific foes. The light now but just touching the fringe and tapestry of the Church of God, and resulting in the eloquent and overwhelming denunciations and efforts of a few of its best sons, concerning its unholy alliance with the liquor traffic, and its sanction of the cup of cursing on the Table of the Lord, has been a fire in our own bones for nearly fifty years. If the world, and the Church in the world, knew how much we have kept in, during those years, they would more than forgive us for all we have let out. It is enough that the day has dawned in which men who will be listened to, have spoken plain and wholesome words on this condition of things; and it forebodes the coming noon, when the meridian of the land's deliverance shall blaze upon us, and the long winter of our inconsistencies and discontent shall pass away. I fear by my theories and imaginings I have been carried away from the plain practical details of the beginning of my teetotal days and home life, which were meant to be the feature of this chapter.

Company was my besetment. I was fond of company, and company was fond of me. Indeed I was a big man amongst little ones. I could tell a story, I could sing a song, I could dance a hornpipe. That, with my belief in and love of "drink," was a world holding me tight and strong. My mother gave me a small Bible, and said, "Thomas, read it." I did so, for I could read; I had learned to do that in the sabbath-school, and I say, "God bless the sabbath-school! and the men and women who so nobly work in it." I bought, I remember, an abridged "Life of Dr. Franklin" from an old book-stall; I think I gave tenpence for it. How I came to do that, I think, was because Joseph Livesey, in his "Malt Liquor Lecture," had referred to Franklin when he was a pressman in London doing without beer while all the other men took it, and how much better he got on than they did, and what a grand and wonderful man he became. So I bought his book. The Bible and Franklin's book were almost my sole library for the first few years of my temperance life; I read them thoroughly and well, and became intensely interested, and the striking passages—I mean passages which seemed to suit my case, and help me in my views and work—I copied out in writing. This gave me work and interest at home, and entirely broke my public-house connection, and in that way the appetite and desire for drink left me—so much so that in three months' time I could, if needs be, have worked up to the chin in it, without putting out my tongue to lick it.

In two years there was not a passage in the Bible speaking of wine or strong drink in any shape or form that I had not written out in full. I did the same with any passage referring to water in any shape or form, also with every passage referring to Christ or salvation. This strengthened my memory, it gave me information, and improved my writing; and those who have any practical knowledge of my teaching, will remember how much of those two books got into my brain, blood and bones, and were they taken away how little I should have left. I have said I was fond of company. In reading Franklin I found the teaching, "Better be alone than in bad company." I put that down. Again, "Buy what you do not want to-day, and you will want what you cannot buy to-morrow." I put that down. I had been made to see and feel that I did not want the beer, so I did not buy it, and the to-morrow has not yet come in the which I could not buy what I did want. Again, "If you have only sixpence a day, and live on fivepence, you will save money." I put that down.

Turning to my wife as I read that, I said, "Look here!" and she looked and read. After doing so she exclaimed, "Of course we shall." Then I said, "We will do it," and I have saved the penny ever since.

My writing, or rather my learning to write, was a formidable undertaking. I bought pens, ink, and paper, and commenced operations by my own fireside, in the presence of my wife and child. My first copy was a straight stroke, and it was very crooked. I then tried to make an O. What a job I had with the O's! I had a copy-book full of O's. My idea was, that a perfect O should be a circle, and that nobody should be able to tell where I began or where I left off, and I could not manage it. They were more like men's heads and faces than O's. I tried a word; the first word I attempted was THEN, and I could not get it into shipshape; it took nearly one page of the copy-book, and *then* the other, and *then* over leaf. From that I got to passages out of the Bible and Franklin's life as already described. Getting tired of copying, I said one night to my wife, "I do believe I am a poet." She replied, "I am *sure* thou art." Well that settled it, and I began on the spot. I will not here give a sample of my powers in that department, for I have no ambition to be made a *peer*, and were I to do so it might place Her Majesty in a difficulty at the present moment with the Laureate. I can only say that in the early days of my public advocacy of temperance, when I at any time, as the saying is, "dried up," whatever that may mean, I quoted a few verses of one of my poetical effusions; it invariably "brought down the house," and I was always asked if it was in print, and I as invariably replied, "No; printers always spoil my poetry as they do my speeches." By perseverance I got so to write that I could at least read it myself, if I were not too long after its composition in referring to it. I occasionally now come across some original copies of the days I am now reviewing, and I know no more about their meaning than does the proverbial Man in the Moon. This is very much to be regretted, at least to myself, for the thoughts of my youth were fresh and vigorous, and were not destitute of originality, and in these hackneyed days of a twice-told story, it would be refreshing to know what originality and young life meant.

May I be excused saying here that I have been a profuse letter-writer to almost all sorts of people, and on a great variety of subjects. The first I ever wrote in my life, if my memory does not mislead me, and I think it does not, was written to Joseph Livesey. It was a very short one, and penned at Kendal in Westmoreland, giving an account as well as I could to the gentleman named of my proceedings up to that point as a temperance missionary. It appears in the *Preston Advocate* for the month of June, 1836, which was at that time published and edited by Mr. Livesey.

I have been writing letters ever since. Scores of them are in print in various temperance and ordinary newspapers. What with printers' blunders, and more especially my own unreadable writing, terrible mistakes have been made in names, dates and places in the morning of the Temperance Reformation, and one reason amongst many for my attempting the task I am now engaged in, is that these mistakes may be corrected. Perhaps the following letter, received from a friend and frequent host then living in Nottingham, to whom I had written intimating my intention to pass that way shortly, will best explain the condition of things then. "Dear sir, the postman brought me a letter the other day from some one living somewhere, but from whom and from whence I know not. As you are the only correspondent I have whose writing I cannot read, I judge it is from you. Should you be coming this way soon, and will call and explain what you mean, I shall be very much obliged!"

It would seem as if my progress in the mechanical part of letter-writing was but slow, for many years after the Nottingham correspondence occurred, I received a letter from a very worthy clergyman then living in Yeovil, with whom at the time I was in almost constant correspondence, to the following effect: "My dear brother, may I be permitted to suggest how very much it would add to the pleasure of my dear wife and myself if your letters, which are so very interesting and welcome, could be written a little more legibly and plain." The amusing part of this correspondence, for one does sometimes get amusement out of difficulty and annoyance, was in the fact that this letter, coming in correction of mine from this scholar of the university, was itself so indistinct and incomprehensible, that it took me nearly a week to get anything like an intelligible appreciation of what was intended, and that was only done by calling to my aid neighbours on my right and left, one of whom fortunately happened to be an adept in orthography. Perhaps never since the day of Burns could two men looking in the face of each other more appropriately say, "Oh, wad some power the giftie gie us ta see ourselves as others see us." It is, I hold, wise to take comfort and encouragement where and when we can, and there must have been a little advance in my case or this book would never have seen the light.

CHAPTER VIII.

TAKING THE TIDE AT THE FLOOD.

THE teaching which says, "There is a tide in the affairs of man which, if taken at the flood, leads on to fortune," is a forcible and pleasing way of showing how advantageous it is to "strike while the iron is hot."

Indecision and vacillation may be but a physical or mental weakness, but it is often a crime; a crime which is often repented of, but seldom forgiven. The chance is gone, and gone for ever, and repentance and forgiveness can have no value where such repentance and such forgiveness do not secure to us the blessing gone! Presence of mind and firmness of purpose are worth more than gold, and to be true to one's self is not only to be in harmony with the laws of life but with the works of God. He that is true to himself "cannot then be false to any man;" and my experience and observation go far to prove the value of the teaching: "When thou doest well to thyself, thy friends will praise thee." The miseries of life spring up from, and are very much made out of, the wrongs we do to ourselves; and we never wrong ourselves more than when we wrong others.

The law of supply and demand is ever in operation, and will sooner or later make its own terms, and those terms will in the end balance the account. There may be a little margin here and there, but in the main the law holds good. There are fixed laws which govern nature animate and inanimate, and any departure from those laws cannot but work to the disadvantage of all concerned. If we watched and worked out this thought, how much more of harmony there would be in our existence than there is, and what fulness of joy would be found in quarters where it is now unknown!

The morning after I signed the pledge brought with it new hopes and new aspirations. I felt all was not lost, and, God helping me, the future should more than redeem the follies and waste of the past. The home that had satisfied my wants as a drinker was not in harmony with my self-respect as a teetotaller, and I soon put myself in possession of a house rented at twelve pounds a year. Then I was living in one the rental of which was a shilling a week. In that hole, for it was literally a hole, I sang, "Rule Britannia, Britons never shall be slaves." My politics centred in the thought: "When will Government do something for the working classes?" and yet I had no voice or power in choosing a representative. When I took my money from the public-house and put it on to the rent, the rent enfranchised me. No candidate for parliamentary honours after that would pass my door; before it they never knew where I lived, nor cared for what I wanted.

The dwellings of the poor and "The Bitter Cry" have, from time to time, begotten considerable discussion and eliminated much thought; but when Prof. Huxley says, "the people must be improved from the inside, and not from without," he only announces a truism which has been taught from the temperance platform for half a century. Put a pig into a palace and the palace becomes a pig-stye, while a prince in thought and heart will make a stye a palace.

Did it never strike those who are everlastingly talking about improving the dwellings of the poor, and about the poor being driven to the public-house because of the wretchedness of the homes in which they are compelled to live, that if these poor would only take a few shillings a week, now constantly left at the public-house, and put it on to the rent of a home, how much better a home many of them might have? There are exceptions, I know, but they *are* exceptions: the rule is, that this would be the case. The cleansing of the outside of the platter never was and never will be an inside cure, but no internally clean person will ever eat off a dirty plate. Who does not see that if my family had been born to me under the circumstances and in the condition in which the friends of temperance found me, how different their influence and position in the world would have been to what it is now, having been born in a home that blessed and brightened them?

Had the teetotallers lifted me physically out of a hole into a palace and left me there, the probability is that the next time they came around they would have found me in the old place again. That would have been a new patch on an old garment with a vengeance, with the proverbial consequences. No, no; they did not do that. They pointed out the folly of spending my money on "that which was not bread," and my time and strength on that which profited not. They appealed to my knowledge of life, and my personal consciousness of right and wrong. They showed how much of my present happiness and present success, as well as my future joy, depended upon myself. They made me feel that a man's position and success did not, after all, depend so much on his birth and parentage as on his own efforts and perseverance. They turned before my eyes the wheel of fortune, exhorting me to stand upon my feet and hold up my head, and lay hold of it; that I was to act well my part—'twas there the honour lay. It was then I felt an inspiration of manhood which up to that time had almost gone dead within me, and I was drifting down and down that miserable descent along which vast masses of my countrymen had gone, and were then going, shutting their eyes to the light, and throwing up their hands in the presence of "thieves within and a troop of robbers who spoileth without." That was the platform on which rested the lever that lifted me, and this is the platform from which has been proclaimed liberty to many a captive, and the opening of the prison door to many that were bound, and without it all the binding of the strong men in our midst will be but as the green withes in the case of Samson.

It is not meant that nothing else shall be done, but without this we put our money into bags with holes and draw from wells that have in them no water.

It was not to me at first a smooth path, nor is it so now at all times. There have been moments in my experience when the way was so dark that I knew not where to turn, nor to whom to look, and could but sit still and weep. But deliverance always did come, not in the way wanted, nor at the time looked for, perhaps, but it came, and again and again I have realized that that which was my greatest care and trouble subsequently proved my greatest good. "There is a Providence which shapes our ends;" and that feeling, even if a delusion, has certainly had its value in my case. The general

feeling at the time to which I now refer was very bitter against the Temperance Movement, especially that phase of it which excluded and denounced the use of wine and beer.

The working men had been taught to believe that it was a system got up by masters to ascertain how little working men could live upon; and when they had done that they would drop wages! When I signed the pledge I was a working man among working men. They looked upon me as their enemy, and they taunted me as such. They secretly spoiled my work, and damaged my machinery. They refused me the help common to each other and frequently necessary, and misrepresented me to my employers. In fact they did all they could to make my practice of teetotalism an impossibility.

Nobody but one who has experienced it can conceive the trials and irritation to which I was subjected. I had got a comfortable and happy home, with prayer meetings, preaching, and class meetings, to which my neighbours came with constancy and in great numbers. I had identified myself with an active and useful church, and when my day's work was done I took an active part in conducting public temperance meetings both in the town in which I lived and also in the towns and villages in the neighbourhood. Bands of us would not infrequently go out in the evening four or five miles to neighbouring places and hold meetings, then return home the same night, walking both ways, and do that several nights in the week, and at the end of the week go ten or twelve miles. The work was a joy to us, and our success was our reward. Those were happy and useful days—days before lecturing became a profession, and days consequently when adventurers were not so numerous as they subsequently became. A practice then common at the mill at which I worked was a constant source of trouble and annoyance to me. The men of my branch of business in the cotton trade were paid in a body by a cheque. It was a custom on receiving it to go to a public-house near the works and there get the cheque cashed, and then pay one another. A room was apportioned to us; the money was not always prompt in coming. We could not occupy room and consume coal without some return, so we became customers for liquor, and many a time a considerable score was run up before it was convenient or possible to get the cheque changed into cash. That not infrequently resulted in a night's drinking and a Sunday's dissipation, and an utter disqualification or disinclination to work on the following Monday.

The bill passed forbidding the payment of wages in public-houses, in 1883, was not a moment too soon, but fifty years too late. Hundreds of men have in the interim been robbed and ruined by the practice. What business has any employer of labour, when a man's wages are due, to shuffle out of the trouble and direct responsibility of payment by anything so unfair as leaving men responsible to one another and subjecting them to a positive reduction on the principal to which they are fully entitled? It was no uncommon thing in the past to have secret arrangements between middle men in public works and publicans, by which a mutual advantage was secured at the cost of the workmen. It was so in the case now in question, and I knew it, and took exception to the arrangement, and was determined not only not to drink, but not to go to the place where the liquor was sold. I spoke to one of the principals, asking that my wages might be paid to me at the counting-house. He at once said, "Of course, if you wish it," and from that time it was done. I may say here, that the foreman and general manager concerned in this business subsequently both became publicans, and were killed by drink. Thus separating myself from the men in the payment of wages embittered their spirit, and made my position in the mill more trying than ever. Things became so disagreeable that it was reported to one of the principals by the foreman, who had been my foe all the way along, that there would be no peace among the men in the large room in which I worked unless I left. There were many of them, and they were good workmen and could not well be spared; so I was sent for down into the counting-house, and told that it would perhaps be best if, as soon as I could suit myself, I would leave. They regretted the necessity, for they wished all the men were like me, but they must have peace. That was a terrible blow: I liked my employers, I liked my work, and I liked my home. My Church fellowship and surroundings were a little heaven to me. I had, though a very young man, changed my home more than once since my marriage, but such changes gave me no concern, for I neither understood nor appreciated what was implied by the word "home;" and it is that "happy go lucky" or "devil may care" kind of life, that has in it so much of the wreck of home and the ruin of family life. Now I had a home, and knew something of the joy of domestic life, and the threatened disturbance of that home and unsettling of that life was a deep and heavy sorrow. I don't know that I can describe what followed better than it was done in a letter to the never to be forgotten Joseph Livesey, in the year

1867, in response to an application from him to supply him with some particulars of my origin as a temperance advocate. The letter was embodied in his "Reminiscences of Early Teetotalism."

"DEAR MR. LIVESEY,—

"The circumstances under which I was moved to devote my life to the Temperance Cause were as follows:—

"I was a cotton dresser in Blackburn, and spoke freely in that and the neighbouring towns and villages in behalf of teetotalism. This made me somewhat obnoxious to the men of my own trade, so that my situation became anything but comfortable, and I determined to leave. Preston was then (this was in 1835) to my mind the model town, and its band of brave teetotallers were the men after my own heart, and I felt I could live and die among them. Early one morning, with a heavy heart (for I had become attached to Blackburn, and especially to the Church with which I had become united), I walked to Preston. On my arrival there I called at the temperance hotel to get a little breakfast, before applying at any of the factories of that town for work. You came into the room where I was seated, expressing your surprise at my early visit, and then your sorrow at the occasion for it. You knew some little of me then, for at your request I had said a few words in the theatre at Blackburn, two weeks after I had signed the pledge on the occasion of you giving your malt liquor lecture in the same place. I had also spoken in the theatre at Preston on the occasion of your Whit-Monday demonstration, but the thought of becoming a public teacher had never crossed my mind. During the conversation you asked me if I would like to go out as a temperance missionary. The moment you mentioned it the finger of Providence pointed out to my mind most clearly and distinctly, 'This is the way, walk in it.' I had not then a doubt of it, I have not now a doubt; it is the glory of my life, and my only regret is that I cannot more fully magnify my calling. The result of that conversation was that I never asked for another situation, and I walked back the nine miles to Blackburn with a heart as light as a feather. I felt that the Lord had delivered me out of the hands of man, and made my brow brass, and that by His help I would war a good warfare.

"When I got home there was sorrow at the thought of parting from my little family, but it was only a passing cloud. If the world could have heard my little wife pour out her soul in gratitude to God for the blessings temperance had brought to her home, and seen the earnestness with which she cried that her husband might carry light and life and joy to many a poor drunkard's heart, and blessings and songs of joy where cursing and tears prevailed, it would better understand the power and triumph of our early days.

"By your advice I went to the conference of the 'British League,' held in Manchester in September, the year 1835; I spoke freely at several meetings in connection with that conference. I laboured mainly under your own direction from that time to the following May, chiefly in Lancashire. I was then sent out by your recommendation as the agent of the League, and visited Westmoreland, Cumberland, Northumberland, and Durham, and you know what followed. I have always looked upon you as my teetotal father; I signed the pledge with you. The first letter I ever wrote in my life I wrote to you, and it is printed in the *Temperance Advocate* for June, 1836, that is thirty-one years ago this month.

"When my path in life seemed blocked up, you unlocked the door which led me into the good land, while the Providence of God said, 'Go and possess it.' I have done so, and when I went out into the world a poor raw Lancashire lad, knowing not whither I went, and without purse or scrip, you guaranteed a provision to my family. This is how, and when, and *why* I became a temperance advocate. I am one still, and hope to remain such to my dying day. I have just returned from the thirty-third conference of the League held in Bradford. There were few, if any, besides myself who were present at the first. It was a satisfactory meeting upon the whole. There is not the simplicity and godly sincerity about the movement which we witnessed in our first years, but there is a growing feeling to put aside or forget the bickerings which at one time nearly destroyed us, and an evident desire to work for the consummation we all devoutly wish—a sober world. If neither you nor I should live to see it, the next best thing is to die working for it.

"Yours faithfully,
"THOMAS WHITTAKER.

"SCARBORO', *July 1st*, 1867."

I look back upon these days, now, with wonder and amazement. How I came to do it, and how I lived through it, puzzles me yet; but I am so glad, now the winter has set in upon me, that the spring and summer of my life was not entirely lost, that some good seed was put in and took root, and that there was a glorious summer and an abundant harvest.

It will be interesting to some, perhaps, if I give one phase of my life not yet mentioned. I have always been a fighter, and could do, if put to it, a destructive work in that department. The conduct of the men in the mill tried me terribly; more than once I was sorely tempted to break the pledge, if for no other purpose than to put me in character and position to smash one of the men who had been specially tantalizing and provoking. My salvation I have always felt was partly due to the fact that in the Church, and on the temperance platform, I had committed myself as a disciple of peace, and I have ever since believed it most wise and most safe to commit ourselves to a course of life which will strengthen our obligation to do right. To be one of many, makes us feel that others have to be considered as well as ourselves, and whatever we might feel disposed to do as individuals, yet if the doing of that touches the status and character of others, then comes in the claim, if not for ourselves yet because of others, to pass that offence, to abstain from that attack. The other circumstance that helped, was, that in the mill there was one Christian man who had joined me in my teetotalism. He was a simple-minded, passive man, and had never been a drinker, so was let alone. He feared God and worked righteousness. We were neighbours. I loved him much and respect him still; he, if living, is a long way on towards ninety years of age. Last time I was in Preston I saw him. He has been true all along the line. At noon, during the dinner hour, we used almost daily to go into an empty house near the works. He knew my exercise, I felt my own need. In that house many a load was taken from my heart, and many a blessing came into my soul. I have had some hesitancy in stating this fact, because it looks like a parade of one's goodness and devotion, and I would not here have done it, only there are those now who think we were a godless and a prayerless lot in early days.

They do this ignorantly and in unbelief. If they knew, as I do, how frequently the early men were driven, if not into dens and caves and thickets of the forest, yet into quiet corners to pour out their souls in prayer to God, and that too, under a deep sense of the vastness and difficulty of the work they had engaged to do, and of their own helplessness in it, we should not have our hearts wounded, and our spirits grieved, as we frequently have by the vain and foolish assumption, not uncommon on our platforms now, on the part of men who in effect say, "The people of the Lord, The people of the Lord are we, and all the rest are heathen."

CHAPTER IX.

MY COMMISSION.

MY first official journey on behalf of "The British Association for the Suppression of Intemperance" (now "The British League") was taken on the 9th of May, 1836. I then left Preston for Lancaster, a raw Lancashire lad 24 years of age, well supplied with "Livesey's Malt Liquor Lecture," *The Temperance Advocate*, and a good assortment of temperance tracts. I had, prior to that, laboured almost exclusively in Lancashire amongst a people with whom my life up to that time had been mainly spent, and every few days returning to my home. In those labours I had mainly been directed by Mr. Livesey and the Preston Committee.

Now my position became more important, and my labours more extended. The centre of the Association I then represented was Manchester. In that city the executive mainly resided. The Revs. Joseph Barker and Francis Beardsall were the joint secretaries, and Mr. Grindrod was the treasurer. The late Dr. Grindrod was then a young medical practitioner in Manchester, and did undoubtedly a brave and heroic work as a medical man in the early days of teetotalism. He was most gentlemanly in his demeanour, and thoroughly Christian in character, and was both intelligent and courageous in the advocacy of the cause and defence of its principles.

The organ of the Society was then *The Temperance Star*, conducted by Mr. Beardsall and Dr. Grindrod. It was a short-lived periodical like many other temperance papers, but for the time it did a good work, and contains some very able papers on the question. The subsequent life of the doctor is pretty well known, how for a few years he travelled the country and lectured chiefly on the medical and physiological phase of the question, and then settled down in a large and well-known hydropathic establishment at Malvern.

As author of "Bacchus," he supplied all future temperance teachers with a very valuable text-book, and rendered in the publication of that work an invaluable service to the Temperance Cause.

I had not seen the doctor for forty years, but paying my first visit to Malvern so recently as last November, 1883, I lost no time in trying to get an interview with him. On calling at his house I found he was too unwell to see any one, and a few days after a record of his death was made known.

I regret exceedingly that I did not see him, and can only hope that he was well enough to be made acquainted with my intent. The Temperance Cause is very much the poorer by the loss of Dr. Grindrod, and the country at large has suffered a great deprivation by his death.

The Rev. Francis Beardsall was the minister of Oak Street Chapel, Manchester, in our early days; and in that chapel, in the heart of that busy and enterprising city, we held frequent meetings in the years 1835 and 1836.

My visits were frequent, and it was during those

years especially that I was brought into near communion and intimate relations with these two men. They were godly men. The power of the Most High was upon them, and the Spirit of the Infinite no doubt influenced them. They not only counted the cost, but they paid the fine, as all men in those days had to do, who had anything to lose. The adventurer and professional had not in them the metal essential to the work, and consequently they were thin on the ground. The rulers had not then believed, and it was as much as a man's respectability was worth to be known to have identified himself with such a low-bred and ill-mannered set as teetotallers were thought to be.

Mr. Beardsall was, I think, the first minister who took exception to the intoxicating cup at the table of the Lord. Of course that was heresy, if not blasphemy, of the most dangerous and horrible kind, an insult to God, and a reflection on Christ. He wrote and spoke freely on the wine question, and was the compiler of one of our first, as well as one of our best, temperance hymn-books. He was a delicate man, and left the country for Canada more than forty years ago, and I believe died on the passage out.

He was a minister in connection with the Baptist Church, and he and Dr. Jabez Burns, of London, a minister in the same Church, were the two men who, as ministers, were among the first, if not the very first, to raise our banner and hold it firm and high in the Church on the sacramental wine question. All honour to them! The Church is not yet free of that offensive incongruity, and many difficulties present themselves even *now*, but what must it not have been fifty years ago!

The Rev. Joseph Barker, "the joint secretary with

Dr. Beardsall," was a minister in the Methodist New Connexion, and was stationed at Chester; he was consequently not so frequently in direct communication with me as the others.

I saw him for the first time one Sunday morning, in the little chapel at Hawarden, the locality now famous as the residence of our Prime Minister. It was early in January, in the year 1837. He was the preacher on the occasion. At that time, and for a few years subsequently, he had the esteem of the Christian world, so far as his name was known. He obtained a wonderful influence over the minds of young men, and was exceedingly popular, both in the pulpit and on the platform.

On his appointment to the Gateshead and Newcastle-on-Tyne District, he was almost idolized by the people. The pitmen and ironworkers drank in his words, and sat at his feet with joy and gladness.

Whether from the pride of intellect, or mortified ambition, or moral blindness, I know not, but for years succeeding his residence in the North he became one of the most dangerous men to religious truth, and was more destructive to its influence than any man I ever knew. Those who had followed and idolized him as a teacher of Christian truth seemed in thousands to turn from it as by common consent with him, and as amongst these there were many of our active teetotallers, religion and temperance suffered equally alike. Those two interests were put back for years in the North by this sad circumstance; and it was the same in many other districts in the country, for Mr. Barker was well known and much esteemed.

I met with Mr. Barker for the last time in the city of

Brooklyn, U.S.A., in the spring of 1875. We dined together at the house of the Primitive Methodist minister of that city. He was then doomed for this life; I could see it, and *he* was conscious of it. He was an altered man; he had returned to the faith of his youth, and had on the previous Sabbath been preaching in connection with the Primitive Methodists.

Poor man! my heart bled for him. He was in great peace and full of hope, but oh! how he regretted the great mistake of his life, leaving the Church of his fathers and of his youth! He was as simple as a child, and tender as a woman. He seemed very pleased to meet with me. Our course had been very diverse for thirty-five years, and we had had no intercourse. Joseph had been true, in all his changes, to teetotalism. He had never wavered on that point; and indeed no charge could, I think, at any time be brought against his commercial honour or moral character.

When we parted he gave me his hand; I felt it was the hand of death, and that we should never meet again in this life. "Thomas," he said (referring to the work to which my life had been devoted), "I congratulate you on your fidelity and perseverance. 'This one thing I do' has been your motto, and you have done it. God bless you! I have tried too much and done too little, and now the time of my departure is at hand, and it is too late to redeem much of the past." And so it was, and he died! I never could feel unkindly towards Joseph Barker, and I think the Churches of the land were not so cordial to him when he did return as they ought to have been. I thought while he lived, and I think now, that his mistakes were mental more than moral, and there was a good deal of jealousy and envy

G

amongst his brethren before he left the Church, and that soured his temper and embittered his spirit, and helped on the calamity which followed.

It will be seen that the society whose first agent I was, had for its two secretaries and treasurer three men of mark—Dr. Grindrod, the Rev. Francis Beardsall, and the Rev. Joseph Barker. John Cassell, the "Manchester Carpenter," as he was called in early days, has left a name that will never perish. He was amongst our early friends in Manchester, and he was constant in his attendance at the meetings superintended and conducted by Dr. Grindrod and others. The Preston men went frequently by invitation to address those meetings, and I was in 1835 and 1836 much amongst them. At one of these meetings Mr. Swindlehurst, of Preston, was the main speaker; Mr. Cassell signed, and Mr. Swindlehurst is credited with the honour of Mr. Cassell's conversion.

It is only due to say here, that at that time Mr. Swindlehurst was a power on the temperance platform. His story was a thrilling one. I heard it in the town of Lancaster in the year 1834, and I shall never forget the effect produced. He was a generous, open-handed, and open-hearted man, always ready, always willing for the work. Had he been less generous and less ready, maybe, as a business man, he would have been richer. He had a ruddy complexion and a stentorian voice, and at times a most pathetic style. He was a great favourite and in great demand; and as teetotalism, in those early days, gave to everybody and took from nobody, no wonder that many of its noble sons died poor; still, to be credited with a result like John Cassell is in itself a crown of rejoicing.

John Cassell, in himself, would make a most interesting and readable book. He was a marvellous man, young, bony, big, and exceedingly rough and uncultivated. He was working as a carpenter in Manchester when picked up by us. He followed me to almost all my meetings in Manchester, and got his mind pretty well stocked with what I had to talk about. I was his model man as an orator; and as he subsequently told me, for we were good friends to the time of his death, which was somewhat premature,—he died at the age of forty-eight,—it was his desire to be like me that determined him to take the road and the platform.

He committed to memory several of Anderton's characteristic poems, and repeated them in the Lancashire dialect, amusing the people very much. He never let go the desire to be somebody and to do something from that moment; and when it is remembered how unlikely he was, and with what difficulties he had to contend, and that he lived to leave such a name as he has done, as the founder of the famous publishing house known as Cassell, Petter, & Galpin, and that he was at one time within an ace of being chosen candidate to represent the borough of Marylebone in Parliament, it will be seen that John Cassell, the Manchester Carpenter, had got some stuff in him.

The country is full of men who have made their mark, but from no source have they come so freely as from the temperance ranks. It must be so. Other things being equal, the teetotallers must win, and it is a fallacy to suppose that drinking in any case helps to success, or that the cultivation of such social customs as necessitate the decanter and the spirit bottle give respectability.

While it is true that the land is full of men who do credit to their position, and to the cause through which they have attained to what they now are, it is not the less true that the land has in it hundreds who, although they owe all that they possess to the fact that they had the good sense to become teetotallers, now cheat themselves with the thought that it will help them and their children in the social scale, if they kick away the ladder by which they have reached to what they are, and follow the fashion of customs more honoured in the breach than in the observance. Such people make a fatal mistake, and run a fearful risk, in addition to bringing upon themselves the pity and contempt of all men who have a true sense of honour and put a proper estimate on consistency and common gratitude. John Cassell, Joseph Barker, Francis Beardsall, and Dr. Grindrod were true as steel to the Temperance Cause in every phase of their varied lives. All honour to them!

CHAPTER X.

LANCASHIRE AND WESTMORELAND.

THERE was a special interest in my beginning my commission to the north of England at Lancaster. In the year 1834 I was employed in a cotton mill there, and I lived in the town six or eight months. I had in wrestling, and in other less creditable ways, crippled myself, and my left shoulder had been so weakened by frequent dislocation, that I was for the time being incapable of following my ordinary employment as a cotton dresser, so I got right away from the neighbourhood in which I was known, and came down to machine weaving, and not caring to be known as a weaver, I went and worked amongst strangers. I had a brother then engaged at the same mill, and through him I got the employment in question.

Lancaster ale was of a much more potent character than that to which I had been accustomed, and it made sad havoc of me, and the six months I spent in that town were in every sense the worst six months of my life. I never took a house all the while, for from the first it was my intention to return, as soon as I was able, to the neighbourhood of my old quarters.

My brother unfortunately was not a good example, nor a safe companion for me, and if the memory of my life in Lancaster could be blotted out, I should be thankful.

The only man I ever saw hanged was in Lancaster, and I never wished to see another; I had heard his trial in part, and it seemed to me that his life was sworn away by an unfaithful wife. He had been, prior to this case for which he suffered death, imprisoned for some months in Preston house of correction. During his incarceration his wife had formed an intimacy with another man, and on his return home she refused to receive him; she, her niece, and the man who had supplanted her husband, were the witnesses who swore that he had been guilty of an offence which was at that time punishable by death. The evidence to my mind was very weak, but he had no friends, and no help, and was condemned to death, and was hanged. I believed then, and I believe now, that the man was innocent of the charge, and I have ever since been opposed to the taking away of life under any circumstances whatever. It drove me mad, and I went to the execution under a sort of vague idea that if the crowd would join me, we would rescue the man. Of course that was out of the question, but I was nearly getting into trouble through it; to make the matter worse, I found that the man who had hanged him was lodged during his visit in the very same house in which I was lodging myself, and he had to make short tracks on my arrival.

During my residence in Lancaster, Mr. Joseph Livesey came over to give his malt liquor lecture in the Theatre Royal. I had a great respect for Mr. Livesey, and went to hear him; the uproar and disturbance was very great, and the place was very crowded. Much as I esteemed Mr. Livesey as a man, I did not like his teetotalism, and I was too willing to join the disturbers and enjoy the fun. The chairman on the occasion was Squire Dawson, a proper man and a Christian gentleman living near Lancaster.

The meeting had scarcely commenced when a man's *legs* came through the ceiling over the pit, and down tumbled the plaister: he had missed his footing in the dark. Presently an old paint-pot was suspended through the hole made, and paint dropped from it on to the people below, and they could not get from under it because of the crowded state of the pit. The squire with his gold spectacles on his nose, and with much suavity and persuasion, exhorted the people for the credit of the town to listen to Mr. Livesey. A dusty stuffed imitation *fish* was hurled at the squire's head; he was hit across the nose, his sight dimmed by dust, and his spectacles disordered; then at this point some one got to the main gas tap and left us in darkness; then we had imitation thunder and lightning. Yet, Mr. Livesey managed to give his lecture, and put in seed that took root, and they have had teetotalism in Lancaster from that day to this.

I have before me now a letter from the present squire of Lune Cliff, the son of the chairman of the meeting I have just described, asking me to go to the reopening of the Palatine Temperance Hall, on the 28th of January, 1884, and I hope to go. It will be seen then that it was most fitting that I should commence my work in Lancaster. It will also be seen what strange memories would fill my brain, and how I should wonder what would happen to me. I was not unknown in the town, and there would be some curiosity to hear what I would say by those who did know, and what I was like by those who did *not* know me.

I travelled by what was known as the *Flying Packet*,

on the canal between Preston and Lancaster, a very pleasant mode of conveyance indeed, but there was a licence to sell drink on board, and on this occasion the drinking was rather free. I untied my tracts and began to distribute them, and there was soon a hot discussion.

The captain did not like it at all, for it interfered with the sale of drink. I have not just now a very clear recollection of the kind of meeting I got in Lancaster, but I remember that the town crier was made drunk by the publicans while he was on his round to call the meeting, and I saw him reeling in the street, a laughing-stock for the boys and girls.

That was very annoying, and it was only the beginning of annoyances from that source. The same thing happened to me in several places, during my first month's work, and it was in consequence of that that I became possessed of what is now known as the "Teetotal Rattle," which I freely used in connection with that journey.

Kendal, at the time I now speak of, was in advance of most towns on the Temperance Question; they had a good working committee, of which the late member for the borough, Mr. John Whitwell, was the secretary.

His youngest brother, Edward, who has been so true a friend and constant a worker in the cause, and who is now so diligent in the Sunday-closing effort, was then a stripling youth. His parents, who were then living, showed me great kindness, and manifested much sympathy; and indeed several members of the Society of Friends living there, (and they were a somewhat large and influential body at that time,) gave me much encouragement. I will say here, that had it not been for the people commonly called "Quakers," in my early days,

I don't know what would have become of me, and indeed of the cause generally.

They were at one time almost the only people who had got a decent home, who gave us habitation, as the Primitive Methodists were the only people who, with anything like freedom and willingness, opened their chapel doors and preaching rooms to us.

The Methodist Free Churches, and "Warrenites," as they were then called, came next, but they had not at the time many places to offer.

The Established Church treated us with silent contempt. The nonconforming Churches, in the drinking business were anything but nonconformists; and the Wesleyans, in very many cases, stepped out of the way to hit us, and as is well-known treated our petitions and memorials to Conference with scant courtesy indeed; and so far as Conference power went, the doors of their chapels, and even schoolrooms, were closed against us. In nonconforming and Wesleyan Churches, as well as in the Establishment, the drink power was in the ascendant, and it was not an uncommon thing then (and we knew it), for leading members in these various Churches to be largely interested in the liquor trade, and in some cases to own and supply with drink some of the worst houses in their several localities.

This we exposed and denounced, and that too before Canon Wilberforce was out of his swaddling-clothes. If he, after fifty years of light and labour, found it no easy thing to "kick against the pricks," notwithstanding he is the son, and the brother of a bishop, and the grandson of a Christian statesman and gentleman, whose name is still verdant in our midst, while personally he ranks high in the Church of state patronage, and amongst a body of ministers who are usually understood at least to be gentlemen, what must have been the condition of things, with a handful of comparatively poor obscure men, with the Church and the world in combination seeking to crush them? That was the time to cry out "Oh! ye mitred heads, preserve the Church, and lay not careless hands on skulls that cannot teach and will not learn."

That we had great numbers of individual Christians in all sections of the Church with us, there is no doubt, and especially so amongst the Methodists, but the ruling powers were against us. In certain localities, because of special circumstances and a few determined men, we possessed ourselves of the schools and chapels, but it often gave great offence, and it resulted in the Wesleyans enacting laws excluding us from all their places.

As a sample of the spirit and prejudice then prevalent, I may say that at Bingham in Nottingham, in the spring of 1837, where my labours had been abundantly blessed, and where most of the leaders in connection with the Wesleyan Church had heartily espoused the cause, I was asked to spend the Sunday with them, and preach in the Wesleyan Chapel, and did so to crowded congregations. Upon which an ex-president of the Conference, who had been accustomed to preach for them annually, in the interest of their trust funds, and whose visit was relied upon to help them in their difficulty, in this instance declined the usual favour and service, because they had allowed *me*, a teetotaller, to occupy their pulpit. A more popular, or a more genial man than he, the Church had not got in it, and yet on this question his spirit was embittered.

What wonder then, that in Conference we were

snubbed, for he was president more than once! What a contrast between those days and the days when the Rev. Charles Garrett has been the universally beloved president!

In December, 1881, I was asked by the resident minister in a leading circuit in the West Riding, whose appointment it was, to preach the temperance sermon, as arranged by Conference. I did so. Yet thirty-five years previous to that, the most popular and promising local preacher in the district was expelled from the Society by the superintendent of that very circuit, because he had, contrary to the wish of this representative of Conference, preached a temperance sermon.

We were amazed at the conduct of the Southern Churches in America on the slave question, but in what sense have we been better than they? The Church in America was blood-stained by slavery; the Church in this land is blood-stained by drink. America hounded down such men as Lloyd Garrison, in the name of religion, and in this land the temperance advocate has been hounded down for the same reason, and by the same influence.

He of America told the Church an unpleasant truth; we have done the same in this land: and in both cases the cry came, "Away with him." It is the old story. But Lloyd Garrison lived to see his country freed from the blot of slavery, and to be honoured and fêted by the civilized world: that has not yet been our good fortune, but we look, and long for the coming day, when the last drunkard shall be reclaimed, the last public-house shut, and the flag of sobriety shall wave over a sober and regenerated land.

CHAPTER XI.

WESTMORELAND AND CUMBERLAND.

THE Temperance Society in Kendal kept me going for about two weeks, and the meetings were remarkably successful, and my labours were concluded at a large public tea on Whit-Monday, 1836. The Saturday before I shall never forget; it was one of the hottest days I was ever out in, and I had to walk across Cortmel Fells to Ulverstone. I think it is twenty miles. After that long and fatiguing walk, I had a meeting in the evening, and returned by the same route and in the same way on the following Monday for the Kendal tea and meeting.

It was during this fortnight I went to Holme, a small manufacturing village, half-way between Lancaster and Kendal, and about a mile and a half from Burton. This Burton was a famous posting town on the high North road, having several hotels and hostelries, the residences of many good families, and about it an air of respectability, as it has even yet, in its somewhat decayed condition, but withal, a host of loafers and hangers-on, no uncommon feature in such towns in the old coaching days.

Steeped in drink from the clergyman down to the common cadger. At the flax-mills near Holme, then in the occupation of Waithman Bros. (Quakers), we had a strong temperance element. This was encouraged by the master, and the foreman and manager. I had a very happy time with them, and before leaving it was determined that we should go down in pretty strong force on Burton. Saturday afternoon was the time fixed for attack, and the Market Cross for the centre of action.

The square in which it stands was pretty well covered with public-houses and hotels. The principal one, nearest to the Cross, had a good sized window looking right upon the meeting from one of its best sitting-rooms. In that room, with the sash of the window lifted up, sat the parson of the parish, the leading lawyer of the place, and one or two others. Just outside, and under the window, were several loafers and loungers and hangers-on, more or less under the influence of drink.

At that time, and in that place, it was a common saying that "if you want the parson or the lawyer, you will find them at the hotel."

There was a town crier there, but he would not disgrace himself by crying a teetotal meeting, so what was to be done to make known our intent? A joiner working at Holme mills, who had been blessed by my visit, and knowing how I had then been put about by drunken and obstinate bellmen, made a "rattle" and went with me to Burton, and said, "Now if you will tell the people what you are going to do, I will spring the rattle." That was agreed on, and was done.

The rattle was a new thing, and brought the people out. The whole town (so to speak) came to see.

"Now then," said my friend, "you see what can be done. You take that rattle, and if ever you are fast for a bellman again, use it," and he gave it to me. I accepted it, although at the time I never thought I should use it, but it became part of myself, and has cut no small figure in my history. I have it yet, and I treasure it very much.

While I was speaking on the Cross, the lawyer and the clergyman sent a man who was standing outside the hotel, and near the open window, with a large mug of ale to ask me to drink. This man was a descendant of an old and decayed family in the town, and was related to the lawyer, but was willing to do any mean job for a drink of beer. He came close to me and offered me the mug, the parson and the lawyer enjoying it very much, for they were no more sober than he was. Of course I declined the offer, upon which the contents were thrown in my face. Then the entire spirit of the meeting was changed; the women present had their sympathies touched, and cried out vengeance on the brute. How I managed to restrain myself I know not, but I could have made havoc of that scoundrel, had I chosen to put forth my strength; but I was calm and self-possessed, and finished my address as if nothing had happened. The fellow soon made himself scarce, and the hotel windows were shut, and I walked back to Holme and slept in peace, and with a thankful heart.

The following Sunday in the little preaching room at Holme was a happy day to me, and one full of blessing to the band of men whose hearts God had touched.

I never saw Burton again from that day till last summer (1883). In view of writing this account, I thought I would take the opportunity of seeing the locality, and verifying certain facts which had come to my knowledge within three years of my first visit.

I saw the old Cross and the old window, and set my foot as near as I could remember on the spot on which

I stood in 1836. The Rev. Mr. Robinson, the clergyman at Holme, who got me up a little meeting in his school-room, and who is a most earnest and well-informed teetotaller, went with me to Burton to see the site of ancient battles. I am much indebted to him for his kindness and hospitality during my visit.

The clergyman now at Burton is also a sound and good teetotaller, but unfortunately I had not the opportunity of seeing him. Both Burton and Holme have changed in the interim, in some cases for the better, in others for the worse.

Well then, what has become of those persons who came so conspicuously to the front in connection with my first visit to Burton? Within three years of that visit they were all dead!

The parson fell through a window, after drinking, and died in consequence.

The man who brought the beer to me, fell down some steps when he was drunk, and died in consequence.

The lawyer went mad, and had to be taken care of, and died a lunatic! The two former were dead within two, and the latter within three years of my visit. Truly the "wicked is driven away in his wickedness, but the righteous hath hope in his death."

During my stay in Kendal I had an invitation to go on to Penrith. That invitation came through a friend, not by post. Those were not penny post days, and people were glad to avail themselves of friendly acts in that way. I was told to travel by a certain coach, and some one would meet me on my arrival and tell me where to go and what to do. I went.

On my arrival I saw a gentleman bustling about amongst the passengers, accosting everybody but myself.

Presently I was left alone, and in his extremity he appealed to me.

"Pray," said he, "may I ask if you saw a gentleman on the coach of the name of Whittaker?"

"My name is Whittaker," was the reply. Upon this he fell back several paces, evidently troubled and disappointed. I was dressed in a check shirt, a brown coat, with more pockets in it than I had use for, fustian trousers, and ankle jacks, and my wardrobe, I think, was tied up in a large blue cotton handkerchief. I was a poor raw Lancashire lad. I had not then been much from my mother's fireside; I was a stranger to every foot of the road I took, and to every face I saw, and my speech was contemptible. This gentleman was donned in yellow top-boots and smalls, a large flapped beautifully embroidered waistcoat, a blue coat with bright buttons and large silk velvet collar, a massive gold chain hanging from his fob, at the end of which there was a bunch of gold seals nearly as big as my fist. He had a silver-knobbed cane, and a professional hat. We didn't match.

"Pray," said he, assuming a tone and manner of self-conscious superiority, "how long have *you* been a member of our society?"

I have no doubt I looked very *raw*, and that to his mind would be a sufficient reason for putting me through my facings. Though my education had been very much neglected, and my knowledge of men and things limited, I did know my own name and how old I was. So I replied, "I have been a teetotaller eighteen months." This announcement almost knocked the breath out of him; and when he had recovered himself he said he was sorry to hear it, they had no teetotallers there and did not want any. Theirs was a Temperance Society; they abstained from ardent spirits as poisons, but they took beer, wine, and porter, the good things sent for their use. They had heard of the teetotallers of Preston, from whence I had come, but they didn't like it, it would split up the society and spoil the movement, and if I spoke at the meeting I was not to say a word about it.

"Well," I replied, "it is the only thing I can talk about, and what am I to do?"

"Why," said he, "you must not speak at all. Our treasurer is a *brewer*, and he takes the chair to-night, so you see it will never do." And he left me. In the street at five o'clock at night, eighty miles from home, not railway days, nor ten shillings in my pocket! On the opposite side of the street from where the coach stopped, and during the time of this interview, there stood a poor man, a nailmaker, a reformed drunkard. A capital second edition of the Pharisee and publican. He stood a great way off while the big man came near. Seeing me left, he crossed over to me, and asked, "Are you the speaker?"

"Yes," was the reply, "I can talk."

"Why then," with astonishment he exclaimed, "did you not go with the doctor, our president?" referring to the man in boots.

"He won't have me."

"Why not?"

"Because I'm a teetotaller."

Opening his eyes like saucers, after this interchange, and putting his hand in such a way as meant business, a hand with a heart in it, he said, "So am I. Rare and glad I am to see you; I never saw one before."

In those days a teetotaller was a curiosity—a curiosity

which in small towns and large villages every one came out to see; and when two met, as we met then, it was a sensation.

"Well," said my new acquaintance, "what will you do? Where will you sleep? I can't give you a bed, but I can give you a cup of tea, but if you had come five months ago, I could not have done that. I heard of your teetotallers at Preston, and I have abstained four months. I have not signed the pledge, they won't have one here, but if you will give me one I will do it," and he did it.

After much trouble a gentleman was found who was rich enough to keep a spare bed, and who ventured, being a tradesman and fearing the loss of his business, to run the risk of lodging me, and it was a risk in many towns in those days.

The next morning, after breakfast, my nailmaking friend was in my presence, asking, "What shall *we* do?" *We* were a society, and had got a responsibility. I said, "I am here to hold a meeting; and now I am here, I will have one, by hook or by crook, before I leave the town."

"Where," said he, "will you have it? for there is no church, chapel, school-house, or room of any sort that can be got."

"Have you got a market-place?"

"Yes," said he, "but it is a noisy one, you would be much interrupted."

"Have you got a quiet square or plot of ground near the town, where I could have a meeting, without obstructing the public pathway?"

"Yes," he answered, "there is a green at the head of the town, where people preach occasionally; you might have a meeting there, if you are not afraid."

We went to view it. I saw it would do. From that I went to the town crier to ask him to call the meeting. He would not do it; saying, "Nay; I'll never cry a meeting to have no ale."

"Well," said I, "lend me your bell, and I will do it myself."

"Not for that job," said he. "It would never ring again."

So I took my rattle and called my own meeting, in the midst of insult and ridicule. When I got to the meeting, at the time appointed, several hundred persons had assembled, though it was mid-day. Everybody seemed inclined to learn what the end of the rattling job would be. I stepped on one side to ask a poor woman to lend me a chair to stand on. When she understood for what I wanted it, she said, "I cannot let you have it; for if you talk teetotal on my chair, I shall never see it again." I became responsible for damages, and on that condition I got the chair.

After singing, in which the people joined, which I took as a good sign, I proceeded to address them. They opened their eyes at the new doctrine, and their ears, and many of them their mouths also, and when I had spoken about twenty minutes, I saw a man coming up the street, hallooing and shouting, taking off his hat, throwing it up, then kicking it for falling, and performing a variety of antics peculiar to drunkards; and I talked all the faster, to get as much done as I could, fearing this man should spoil the meeting. He mixed with the crowd, and for a time I lost sight of him; by-and-by, some one disturbed the meeting, and it was this man, as I thought and as the people thought, trying to get through the crowd to insult me. I had got their hearts as well as their attention, and they kept him for a time outside, but at length he became so boisterous that I could not proceed.

So I said, "Let him come through. Let us see what he wants."

They made a passage for him, and he came to the chair on which I was standing, and I shall never forget him. Such a hat, such a nose, such a mouth. I would not have given five shillings for all he had on him. A fearful man to fight. A terror to the neighbourhood.

When he stood before me looking in my face, he said, "I'll sign."

"Thee sign?" said I.

"Yes," said he; "I will."

"Well, wait till I have done, and then we will talk about it."

"No," said he, "now or never."

"But listen a little longer, perhaps you will alter your mind."

"Nay," said he, like a man in fearful earnest, "I will sign *now*, or you shan't speak."

Well, I wanted to speak, so for peace sake I took his name in pencil on a slip of paper, and put it in my pocket.

"Now," said he, "go on; I'll take care nobody hurts you," and I went on.

Presently a big tear stole down his cheek, and another, then another, and he wiped his face with his dirty jacket. He was a beauty before I had done, and every now and then he roared out.

When I had done, he threw his arms round me, exclaiming, "God bless you, man! I wish you had come twenty years ago, I should have been riding in my carriage now."

I did not think he would have been so rich as that, but from what I afterwards learnt he would have been in different circumstances to what he was had it not been for drink.

He was a capital workman: not a man in the district could touch him as a bootmaker. A man the gentry would have been glad to employ, but he could not be depended upon. He had no credit, and if he got stuff to make up, the parties finding it were never sure to get it back again in any form; he had a wife and small family steeped in poverty, and wretched in the extreme.

Nothing would do for this man but I must walk arm-in-arm with him down the town. This I confess rather mortified my pride, but he held me as fast as if I had been in a vice. He vowed he would go all the world over with me. There had never been such a man there before. However, I compromised the matter by walking arm-in-arm with him down the town. The children followed after in procession. It was nuts for them. They sang a ditty, putting in the man's name and beating time with their feet. That was about the first teetotal procession, and I was not only in it, but at the head of it. As we went along, the people came out of their houses and shops, wondering what was to do.

Presently we got to his house, and I was glad enough to get my head in anywhere out of the crowd. But of all the homes that I ever entered, I never saw one more desolate. There was nothing like furniture in the place. The cupboard and shelves had been destroyed. He was pulling the house about his ears. There was not a chair nor a table. There was a board reared against the wall, which did duty as a table. I sat myself on the window sill. The wife, seated on a stool, seemed to take little interest in what was going on, and would have been glad for death to do its work that she might be relieved of her load. There were two or three children in dirt and rags, perhaps filthy, rolling on the floor, and as I sat there looking upon that wreck, I felt, this man is as far gone as is possible for man to go, not to be gone altogether; and when I remember that that man was saved, and lived to be respected as a citizen, and ultimately went to the grave in sure and certain hope of a joyful resurrection, I thank God for the neglect and contempt and shame that drove me into the street, without which I should never have crossed the path of this firstfruit of what has already been a rich and blessed harvest.

That was the first time I sprung my rattle, so it was not long after its reception that necessity compelled me to use it. I was determined not to be beaten, but it was no whim, it was no love of notoriety, it was no desire to be singular that drove me into the streets of that town, in the face of a grinning, insulting mob; it was the cross of my life, and a big thing to do—a stranger amongst strange people, twenty-three years of age, without education or social status, donned as I was and proclaiming an unpopular subject.

The meeting in the morning produced a good impression on the minds of the people generally, and some members of the Society of Friends, who happened to be present, offered me the use of their little meeting-house in the evening of the same day, so that I got two meetings instead of one, and thirty or forty persons took the pledge, and a society was formed. The first fruit from the rattle was there, and I found the novelty had its value, though the cross was great. There is not a town in Cumberland in which I did not use that rattle.

The town criers in that part of the country, at that time of day, as a rule, were either just getting drunk, quite drunk, or just getting sober, seldom fit to cry a temperance meeting. I dispensed with their services, and did the work myself, and the cross ceased.

The kind-hearted and noble-minded John Mawson, who subsequently met his death, in the prime of life, on the town moor at Newcastle-on-Tyne, when sheriff of that northern metropolis, while in the public interest trying some experiment as a chemist, with explosive materials, became a teetotaller in connection with that visit. He was then a handsome and blooming young man, and as good as he was handsome, and engaged as an assistant to a chemist living at Penrith. His sweetness and respectability characterized his entire life, and his teetotalism was as much of his being as the breath he breathed; a man never to be forgotten, and one whose memory is still a fragrance. Yet how sad, how mysterious his death, and what a blank it left, and what a loss it was! I am glad I ever knew John Mawson.

CHAPTER XII.

CUMBERLAND.

THE trophy picked up at Penrith, joined me in my walk part of the way to Keswick. Of this I was very glad, for it was a long journey and the weather was hot. He carried what little luggage I had, and a parcel however small, in an eighteen mile walk, is a considerable burden. He went with me several miles, and told me all his heart and life. It gave me an opportunity of giving him such advice as I thought would be of use to him.

It should be remarked that teetotalism was a new thing then, and men might reasonably doubt whether in all cases it was safe to abstain and to do it suddenly and at once. "Keep the pledge, Birkbeck," said I, "till you see me again." I told him that in all probability I should be that way again in three or four months, and if then he found it could not be done, he could give up and be free. The man had got an affection for me, and it would have made a picture in the hands of a skilful artist if put on canvas, as we looked and what we did in parting. There were only two of us in the middle of that highway, the wide expanse at our feet full of beauty, the broad heavens above our heads without a cloud, our hands clasped, and our hearts one, we called God to witness our resolve, and help us in our determination.

The record was made, the pledge kept, and the assurance given.

There was no drawing back, and within six months of that time Birkbeck could be seen in the Sunday-school on a Sabbath morning in the A B C class, teaching lambs their letters, all he could do in that direction (for he was an unlettered man), but he did it; and in his case was realized the teaching "and a little child shall lead them."

I pursued my journey in fulness of joy. At times my delight was so great that I shouted, and literally ran and jumped. The cattle started in the fields, and the men working in the ditches looked up in wonder at the sounds which saluted their ears, and occasionally I was taken aback and surprised at my own uncontrolled gladness. There are circumstances which give wings to the feet, and that was one of them; there are also occasions when labour is rest, and that was one of them. No one ever passed between Penrith and Keswick (and many have so passed), with greater satisfaction or richer pleasure then I did that day.

About four o'clock, Keswick, the city of the lake district, for the first time in my life broke upon my view. It was no doubt as beautiful then as it is now, but I was living within, and could not see it.

I knew no one, and no one knew me. A work had to be done, how to set about it I was puzzled to devise. I was happy on the highway with my own communings, and in the breath of Heaven, but it was another thing to face the multitude and mix with the people. I sat down by the wayside, and at a running stream attended to my toilet. I bought in a small cottage a penny bun and a glass of milk, and while partaking of them, my mind was exercised as to how I should proceed.

I determined, on renewing my journey, that I would speak to the first person I saw on drawing near to the town. It happened to be a miller with an empty sack on his shoulder, coming up a lane leading to the main road. He joined me. "Have you any temperance people here?" said I. "Nay, I should think not," was the reply. We were getting into the town, and I became desperate. "Have you any Christians?" "What sort?" was the reply. "Any sort; if they are Christians, they will do for me." "Why," said he, "there is an owd Methody woman lives *there*," pointing to a little haberdasher's shop, " axe '*er*."

I can see the little old dame yet behind the counter, as I entered the shop. I put the same question to her I had put to the man, with pretty much the same result. She went on to say that Keswick was a very hard place. There had been some temperance meetings some time ago, in the Town-hall, but they were only temperance, not teetotal, and they were very violent and did a lot of damage. She warned me that they would *kill* me if I talked teetotal.

"Who let's the place?" I inquired. "Oh," said she, "don't trouble; go on to Cockermouth, you will do better there." "Well, but," I said, "I have walked from Penrith, and Cockermouth is thirteen miles farther, and they know as much about me at Keswick as they do at Cockermouth."

She then advised me to get a lodging somewhere, and rest myself, for I looked tired, and then go on in the morning.

The Town-hall was refused, but I got the Wesleyan Chapel. The old lady's son was steward, and she influenced him to assist me, which he did. The following extract from an article in "The Midland Temperance Annual" for 1883, by the Rev. James White, vicar of Oakengates, Salop, will, perhaps better than I can, describe the meeting :—

"I signed the teetotal pledge in the year 1837, and have preserved my pledge and card to the present day. Teetotalism was then in its infancy, and the movement was generally regarded as utopian, fanatical, and likely to prove evanescent in its duration. Nevertheless, the announcement of a teetotal lecture invariably called together a large audience, at which opposition was very often witnessed.

"I was then residing in the county of Cumberland, 1835, and the first apostle of temperance who visited the lake district was Mr. Thomas Whittaker, now a highly-esteemed and well-to-do citizen of Scarborough, and who has occupied the civic chair of that borough. Mr. Whittaker found great difficulty in obtaining a place in which to deliver his lecture.

"At length, after much trouble, he was allowed the use of the Wesleyan Chapel. The bellman refused to cry the lecture through the streets, but ultimately consented for the usual fee to allow Mr. Whittaker to do so, letting him have the bell for that purpose.

"The appearance of a strange bellman in the streets attracted great attention. Children dogged his footsteps, and the chapel was no sooner opened than every part of the sacred edifice was filled with an excited multitude.

"Though two or three Wesleyan ministers happened

to be present (who were returning from their district meetings, and who had arranged to spend one night in Keswick), not one of them would take any part in the proceedings. The consequence was, Mr. Whittaker had to open and close the meeting himself, and deliver his lecture without the help of a chairman.

"The address produced a great effect, consisting chiefly of Mr. Whittaker's experience as a *drinker*, and the happy change which had taken place in his circumstances since he became a teetotaller.

"Simple, clear, and forcible in style, spiced with numerous anecdotes of an interesting character, perfectly original, and appropriate throughout, the lecture could not fail to amuse and convince most, and result in the conversion of some to teetotalism."

The old lady came to me at the close of the meeting, saying, "Dearie me, man, how do you live?" She knew the day's work I had done, and she, like the rest, believed in beer up to that time. My reply was, "I keep my feet warm with walking, and my tongue loose with talking. I eat when I am hungry, and drink when I am thirsty, and was never better in my life." "Well, you are a queer man, but I'll give you a shilling if you will have it."

The young Wesleyan minister, by the persuasion of the old lady, gave me half his bed, and I slept, whether he did or not; and the next day, which happened to be Saturday, I passed on to Cockermouth. The Primitive preacher who attended the meeting, the Rev. R. Lyon, signed the pledge; the young Wesleyan minister and Captain Jackson, who died last year, were also the result of that meeting.

When in Keswick in the summer of 1882, and I had

not been there for forty-seven years, I spotted the little shop where the dear old lady lived, and called upon the Captain, who gave me a cheerful and happy welcome.

There has been no labour in connection with the temperance agitation more productive and more abiding than the labours of the early years. There has been frequently much more show and far greater appearance, but there has not been the abiding faith and enduring work which characterized the morning of our life as an organization.

Saturday was not a good night for the meeting at Cockermouth, and the bellman did his work so badly, and got drunk while going round the town, so that the announcement was defective and the meeting small. We had two or three warm friends in Cockermouth, and they would not let me go round the town with my rattle. They insisted on my resting and getting ready for the meeting, for I was very weak and tired. I had had a most trying week, and had somewhat neglected myself. The meeting was held in the Wesleyan Chapel. The Wesleyan minister had a very friendly feeling towards the movement, and that was very refreshing, and some of the officials were well disposed. A circumstance happened here which I think I must relate. In my drinking days I had injured my left arm with wrestling and fighting; the shoulder had been so repeatedly dislocated that I was maimed for life, and in my speeches I was accustomed to refer to that as one evidence of the mischief in my own person through drink. This was occasionally the cause of rude interruption; so on leaving Keswick I determined never again to mention it in public, for it was certainly no credit to me. The Cockermouth meeting was the first one after that resolve. During my speech,—I must I suppose have been somewhat excited,—I dislocated my shoulder. That was terrible; I felt it was gone, and I was in great pain, but kept my counsel, but my voice failed and I broke down, and had no alternative but to make known what had happened. Of course there was great sympathy, and a rush for the doctor.

There was a gentleman living there at the time famous as a limb setter; he was unequalled in the district as a medical man in that department, but he was nearly always drunk, and all but constantly in the public-house. They found him there then. He came into the chapel drunk and in his shirt-sleeves, and handled me most skilfully and soon put matters right. Well, everybody was delighted, and I finished my speech.

Mr. Rigg, the uncle of the Rev. Dr. Rigg, of the Wesleyan Training School, Westminster, gave him half-a-crown for the job, and he stayed out the meeting, and signed the pledge, and kept it to his dying day. He soon got a large practice and attained a most respectable position. He joined the Wesleyan Society, and I believe for some years held a creditable position as a most useful local preacher.

There are two or three points about this event which have frequently begotten undetermined thoughts in my mind. Was it a coincidence? Was it a providence? That was the first meeting at which I spoke after resolving that I would never again in public refer to the subject of my infirmity in that particular, and yet in the midst of my address I was laid prostrate by it, and compelled to make known what had happened and seek help. Such a thing never happened before; it has never happened since. Had it not happened, the doctor who came to my relief would never have known me. The coming together was his salvation. I am not going to dogmatize, these are the facts. I have my own opinion about them; my readers will form theirs.

The following Sunday I took part in a camp meeting with my arm in a sling, and on the Monday held a second meeting. It was a success. It was a new thing for a man to put his shoulder out with speaking, everybody was curious to see what the article was like.

Workington and Whitehaven were visited in succession, and so was Maryport.

At Whitehaven I suffered the indignity or honour, whichever people like to call it, it matters little to me, of being (in the outskirts called The Gins) pelted with mud and stoned while springing my rattle.

In Maryport, even as far back as 1836, we were strong, and from that point my strength was renewed. It was here the following letter was written, which I believe was the second I ever did write. It was sent to Mr. Livesey, and he put it in the *Preston Temperance Advocate*, July, 1836:—

"DEAR SIR,—

"I am now in Maryport. I have never gone to bed but one night since I left Preston without having a meeting. I have to be bellman, chairman, speaker, and everything. I have been at Lancaster, Halton, Kendal, Staveley, Ambleside, Penrith, Cockermouth, Whitehaven, Workington, Ulverstone, and Maryport. These are all new places, and I generally get from ten to forty names each night. Though I am in a poor country I have set the fire of teetotalism a-burning, and I have no doubt you will shortly have very good news.

I travel from seven to twenty-two miles a day, and get up a meeting in the evening.

"Please let my wife know where I am the first opportunity, and that I am in good health.

"Yours truly,
"THOS. WHITTAKER.
"MARYPORT, *June 21st*, 1836."

At Dereham, near Maryport, lived Matthew Rigg, another uncle of the Rev. Dr. Rigg. He, like his brother at Cockermouth, espoused the cause. He was a small farmer, and a very popular Wesleyan local preacher, and he kindly piloted me through that part of Cumberland. He was a great favourite with the late Sir Wilfrid Lawson, and had ready access to him.

Sir Wilfrid at this time was staying with his family at Allonby on the seaside, and as he had taken a great interest in the Old Temperance Society, he seemed hopeful material in my case; so Mr. Rigg introduced me to him at Allonby, telling him I was intending to hold a meeting at Aspatria, the village near to Brayton Hall.

I was very kindly received, and much encouraged by my visit.

The day I left Allonby for Aspatria was fearfully wet, it rained incessantly all the way between the two places, a distance of eight miles. Both my companion and myself were drenched, and arrived as wet as if we had been dipped in a water butt.

The only teetotaller in the village was a young man, a shoemaker, living at home with his father, that father the keeper of one of the village public-houses, so that we could have no home with him.

Mr. Rigg knew a poor widow, a Methodist, living in

a humble cottage open to the roof, and from the fire, which was made from a few sticks laid on the hearth, you could not only see the whole estate, but look up at the sky and at night count the stars. And yet this was a very Bethel to us, and she made us welcome to what she had. "The poor ye have always with you," is a simple truism, and many a time have I been made to feel, even when under the patronage of the great, that "this poor widow hath done more than they all."

That cup of tea and that crackling of thorns had a blessing in them; and though the rain came still steadily down, and the people had to be notified of the meeting which was to be held that night in a small chapel, we were strengthened for the task, and turned out to proclaim our mission.

I took out the "rattle" and commenced at one end of the village, and announced as well as I could right away to the other end what was to be done at the chapel at seven o'clock. But few took any notice of me, the day and evening were so very wet. The consequence was that my meeting consisted of seven adults and a few children. This was most discouraging, and saturated with wet, and without any sign of a home for the night, I longed for the morrow as much as ever Paul and his companions longed for the day, when passing through the storm.

"Look not on things that are seen," is an exhortation begotten by infinite wisdom, and one meant no doubt to help and encourage men liable to despond when conditions are unfavourable.

This was about as small and discouraging a meeting as any I have any recollection of, and yet in its results it has perhaps been as effective as any. There was present at the meeting a gentleman advanced in life, an old family servant from Brayton Hall, one in high esteem with the late Sir Wilfrid Lawson, and who was his butler; he had been detained in the village (to which he had come on some business from the Hall) by the weather, and hoping it would clear up by the time the meeting was over (as he subsequently told me), he thought he might as well go and hear what would be said.

Brayton Hall was then no stranger to the Temperance Reformation. The Rev. Owen Clark, the travelling secretary of the "British and Foreign Temperance Society," of which the Queen was subsequently patron, and the then Bishop of London, Bishop Blomfield, president, had been there more than once, and made a convert of the late Sir Wilfrid; he had been taught to believe that *ardent spirits* were poisonous and the cause of drunkenness. That was the theory of that society, and in his zeal he cleared the house of the fiery foe by pouring his entire stock into the fish pond. The fish drank and died, and the grass on the edge of the pond, on which some of the liquor had been spilled, was also burned up, and like the fig tree cursed by the Saviour, for years it was bare and barren. When I was there it was pointed out to me as positive proof that there was "death in the pot."

It will be seen then, that this gentleman from Brayton was in some measure prepared for the new doctrine, and he was evidently much interested in what was said.

At the close of my address he begged of me to give him an assortment of tracts, with which I had been supplied by my good and never-to-be-forgotten friend, Joseph Livesey, of Preston, and of which I was making a distribution amongst the people. These tracts were taken to the Hall and read by the late Sir Wilfrid, with as good a report of the speech as the butler could carry, and from that time the home of the present Sir Wilfrid Lawson (who was then a child) became a teetotal home. He has never dishonoured the name he bears, nor forsaken the cause espoused: a braver and truer disciple we have not got.

When the handful of people attending the meeting had dispersed, then came the question what was to become of me for the night. No one had offered me a home, and the poor widow, who had gone down to the meeting, was sadly troubled; but she was equal to the occasion, and insisted upon it that after what I had done that day, it would be a disgrace to a civilized country, to say nothing of a Christian one, to leave me in the streets. I was to go to her home. She would sit up for the night, and I might occupy her bed; and not only so, but as all my linen was in a very flabby and disorderly state in consequence of the wet, she could do some washing, mending, and laundry work for me, and the night would pass away pleasantly, and she would have all clean, warm, and dry for me in the morning.

My second visit to Aspatria would be some six years after the first, and on this occasion my home was at Brayton Hall. The late Sir Wilfrid was a most hospitable and kind Christian gentleman, and the accommodation was in character with his status, and a great contrast to what I had experienced on the occasion of my first visit.

A circumstance of a very amusing and unexpected kind occurred. The first morning, before I awoke, the footman had entered my bedroom, and after emptying all my pockets, took away all my clothes, that they might (as I afterwards learned) be brushed and put in order for my use. This, however, at the time, was a new phase of life to me, and as in the interim I awoke and arose to dress, my consternation was very great on finding my public appearance out of the question.

I had then been subjected more or less to many opprobrious and offensive epithets, but I was not prepared to run the risk of being announced as a naked savage. The alarm I at once gave must have astonished the attendants.

On my first visit, when lodging with the widow, I had not a change of clothing, and that was bad enough, but now to be left without any at all was more inconvenient still.

The whole establishment was set in commotion,—bells ringing, voices calling, and servants running, and all because I was *too much waited upon*. Extremes meet. My two visits to that locality will not soon be forgotten. In each case my clothes were taken from me; in the first case by the good woman as a necessity, and for my comfort and safety; in the second, by the footman as a luxury and a service; in the one as a labour of love, in the other as a respect and duty.

CHAPTER XIII.

CUMBERLAND.

WIGTON had in it a Friends' school, and where Friends had any hold and interest in a locality, there was even then a little special patronage and help for the teetotal advocate.

They possessed a quiet power and influence which not only frequently gave us a home, but secured for us a respectful and considerate hearing. It was so at Wigton. There were printing works there employing a number of men, and the gingham weavers of those days were a feature in the town. Many of them, having much loose and idle time, fell into very bad habits. John Cluer was one of them—a fine powerful man, a capable speaker, and in political matters an influence among his class. He was taken by my visit, and signed the pledge. Subsequently he travelled somewhat freely as an advocate, and had many admirers. His home, however, never did the cause any credit; whether the fault was his, or his wife's, I know not, but he ultimately left for America, and passed through many vicissitudes.

When in the city of Boston, U.S.A., in the early part of 1875, I was present at a large conference and prayer meeting one Monday morning, and rose to make some remarks on a question before the conference. The moment I did so the gentleman who had been sitting on the same bench with me looked with amazement into my face, and when I sat down he made himself known to me. It was John Cluer. Even in his ruin and comparative feebleness he had got the old self-complacent sneer and democratic defiance in his manner, with a touch of that religious fervour which seldom fails more or less to influence those who listen. When brought face to face with the friend of his youth, the inspiration of days gone by and the memories of the land and the home far far away fired his soul. As we walked together through the streets of Boston that day, how much I was made to feel that we all do need mercy, and what tenderness and forgiving kindness frequently dwell beneath a seemingly austere if not a brutal nature.

He had not left this land with the kindest feelings towards myself, and his going away seemed to be no occasion for regret on the part of those who wished well to the cause of temperance. Still he had been true at least in that one particular, and we were both of us the better for our renewed acquaintance and happy recognition.

At Carlisle I had the name of a gentleman of influence given to me, but he was the secretary of the "Ardent Spirits" Society. I mean the society that abhorred ardent spirits but believed in wine and beer, and these were often in those days more bitter against us than the publicans themselves. He was not bitter, but he was indifferent; so I was left to help myself. That was the most formidable job I had up to that time undertaken, in some particulars. Carlisle was a large and an important city. The Primitive Methodists had a small preaching room in a low part of the town. I got the loan of that. It was Saturday, and I went through the streets of that city with my rattle calling the meeting.

The people were bewildered at the spectacle, and I was no doubt a wonder to many. The meeting was a success, and I had a patient and attentive hearing. When the meeting was over, many names were taken, and the foundation of the present society was laid.

A young man, who turned out to be the resident minister of the place, came to me and asked where I was going to sleep. I told him I did not know. He said, "Well, I am only a lodger; but if you don't object to half a bed and such fare as a poor Ranter parson can give, you are very welcome." I accepted his offer, and was thankful to do so.

It was a humble home. The room he occupied was sitting-room and bedroom. It was clean and roomy, and the housewife seemed pleased to make me very welcome. While she was getting our tea-supper ready, the young man to my astonishment said, "Would you allow me to put my hand on your head?" He was a phrenologist, and that science was just then coming to the front, but was new to *me*. After doing so, he said, "Thank you; I am not so much surprised now." I was still amazed, what did he mean? Said he, "You do not know it, but this afternoon as I came into the town (for my work to-morrow), I met you going through the streets with that rattle, I heard the remarks made, and saw the conduct of the people. How you managed to do it and continue it, I could not tell. I went all through the town and saw you at every point, even down to the meeting, and as you know I stopped there. But on examining your head it is all explained."

How he should tell what was in my head from the *outside*, was a puzzle not yet satisfactorily settled. That made me think, and I read "Combe on the Constitution of Man," a very valuable book indeed.

On my second visit to Carlisle, a few months after, the friends came to my help. Mr. Scott, the father of the present Mr. Hudson Scott, head of the famous lithographic printing establishment in that city, found me a home. And on my first visit to Ireland, twelve years ago, while in Cork, I was most hospitably entertained by the married daughter of the present Mr. Hudson Scott, and grand-daughter of the old gentleman who gave me my home in Carlisle; and while with her I nursed with pleasant and grateful memories her first child. So in that one family I have touched four generations of teetotallers; I don't care if I live to see the *fifth*.

Brampton was my next and last town in Cumberland. My visit passed off without any marked feature, except that Church and State ignored me; but a meeting was held, and some names were obtained, and I was entertained by a Mr. Haugh, a tradesman in the town who had some esteem amongst the people.

The result of that meeting was felt afterwards, for on a subsequent visit all available chapels and rooms were closed against me. A building occupied as a theatre was secured, but the lessee of that, as the time drew near, regretted his bargain, and refused to adhere to it. The town crier would not touch us, and it was thought in that way to get rid of the teaching. But they reckoned without their host. I hired a small lodge-room at the "Shoulder of Mutton," then kept by a very decent aged widow, who had a daughter living with her. The cost was half a crown. I then called the meeting myself, and some thirty people were present. I had a little interruption, but not much, and some signatures. Mr. Haugh was with me, and I think took the chair.

On leaving the place after the meeting, I passed through the kitchen. There were two or three drunken men there, some of them had been up in the room interrupting. The little bar adjoined. I stepped into it to pay for the accommodation. The old lady was very uncomfortable, and I talked to her a little.

Two days after I met her daughter on her way to Hexham to pay the brewer and give notice to leave. She told me her mother had been so uncomfortable since the meeting that she had determined to leave the place, and that she herself was glad of it. That in all probability would never have happened, had I not been driven to the public-house by the bitterness and blindness of the people.

I dwell on this case because last August (1883), I was invited to the locality again by Mrs. Howard, the lady of Naworth Castle. She and her husband, who represents East Cumberland in Parliament, are most zealous and devoted teetotallers, and as they also rule and preside over the famous palatial residence "Castle Howard," in my own county and neighbourhood, it is the more gratifying to be able to testify to this fact. The people of Brampton held a great temperance fête and gala day in the grounds of Naworth on the 21st of August, 1883, over which the lord of Naworth presided, and there was a very fashionable and large assembly. Some six thousand people it was computed were present.

The galleries of the grand old historic castle were thrown open to the public, various sports characteristic of Cumberland were indulged in, a concert by the Band of Hope was given, and a public meeting for temperance teaching was held.

During the meeting a very beautiful illuminated address, containing I think the names of eighteen hundred members of the Brampton Society, was presented to Mrs. Howard in acknowledgment of her energetic and successful efforts for the promotion of temperance in the town and district, and the day's proceedings passed off to the delight of all present. Business in the town and district had a holiday, not because it was a holiday time, but because it was the temperance festival.

Now contrast that visit of the 21st August, 1883, with my first visit in the year 1836, and it will be seen that something has been done. I expressed a desire during my visit to Naworth to see once more the little room at the "Shoulder of Mutton" public-house, in connection with which strange memories remained.

Mrs. Howard at once drove me down, accompanied by my friend Mr. J. H. Raper, that my curiosity in that particular might be gratified. Talk of the plains of Waterloo, they are to me nothing to the site of that old room! The one is a record of death and carnage, steeped in tears and burdened with debt; the other the beginning of life in the morning of a temperance day that shall know no night, the record of which is full of lasting joy and untold good. The address presented to Mrs. Howard, as well as being a well merited testimonial of worth, work, and wisdom, had in it additional interest to myself, as the execution of the work had been entrusted to the firm of Mr. Hudson Scott, of Carlisle, one of my oldest living friends, and the first secretary of the Carlisle Temperance Society.

On the platform at Naworth, sat near to me a son of the late Mr. John Slack, of Carlisle. He had come down from Carlisle to look in my face and take me by the hand. The late Mr. Slack had, after my crossing his path in 1838, on my second tour in the North of England, and while Mr. Hudson Scott was acting as secretary of the Carlisle Temperance Society, lived a most creditable life. I remember him well in the middle of the room in the Guildhall. He was a poor drunken shoemaker, and at the time I refer to very much under the influence of liquor. While I was speaking, he would respond, and the response was a disturbance, though it was not meant to be such. He was touched by the truth, and was uncontrollable in his manner, and there was a cry, "Turn him out!" Upon that he defied the meeting, and claimed his right as an Englishman—"it was a public meeting, and he would like to see the man who would turn him out." He appealed to me, "had he not as much right there as any one else?" and he "would not be dictated to." "If," said he, "I like to stop, I'll stop; if I like to go, I'll go; if I like to talk, I'll talk; if I like to drink, I'll drink; and if I like to be teetotal, I'll be teetotal." This was all addressed to me, and I saw and knew my man at once. "Let him alone," I said; "that is the man of all others this meeting is for, men who have a will and a purpose; men who can say a thing and mean a thing, and *do* a thing; men not to be put down, and who dare to be free. Those are the men Carlisle needs, and the country wants, and the temperance society is looking out for. Come, my brave fellow, and stand upon your rights; band yourself with those of us who fear the face of no man, and who snap the fetters that bind us as Samson snapped the withes, and you will never regret it; do it now, and the morrow's sun will bring you brightness and blessing."

The bait took, the prize was landed, and in that hall on that night, and in the midst of the ringing shouts of that meeting, John Slack signed the temperance pledge, and kept it to his death.

CHAPTER XIV.

NORTHUMBERLAND.

A WALK of twelve or fourteen miles took me one fine day in the month of June, 1836, from Brampton to Haltwhistle, a stranger to every inch of the road, to every face I saw. My sympathies and life-training made me religiously a Methodist, and when I knew no teetotaller, I found out some sort of Methodist, and in the end in so doing found a friend.

The little Primitive chapel up a lane at the end of the town was secured for the meeting, and I called it in the way so frequently described. When I got to the place at the time appointed, the chapel was filled, the way leading up to it was filled, for everybody who had a chance seemed inclined to see what the end of the "rattling" job would be. It was our practice from the first when a meeting was held in a place of worship to open the meeting with singing and prayer. When alone I did this myself. It was so here. I had then to be secretary, committee, chairman, speaker and everything. The society dates from that night.

A gentleman present asked me home to supper with him. I was glad to go, for up to that moment I knew not where my bones were to lie that night. The cloth was laid for supper just as we arrived. There was on one corner of the table a mug of ale, and the maid (who had not been to the meeting) was finishing the usual table arrangements.

On entering the room the host was somewhat confused. He looked at the table, then at the maid. She looked at him, and then at the table. Presently we sat down, and he took the corner where stood the beer. During supper he looked across the table at me and said,—

"Did you walk from Brampton to-day?"

"Yes."

"How long have you been going on in this way?"

I told him.

"Why it is very fatiguing, is it not? I am afraid you will never stand it, but," said he, taking up his glass of ale, "it is worth any sacrifice, any labour, if drunkards can be reformed; my *heart* is with you (all the while the glass getting nearer to his mouth), but I am afraid you will never bring the system down." Then down went the liquor!

He was, and I am afraid still is, a sample of a great many good, decent, hospitable people. The system never *will* be brought down so long as such as he keep it up. Sympathy is all very well, good wishes have their value, but if ye say, "Be ye warmed, and be ye fed," and do nothing to warm and feed, what better are we?

The Northumberland "burr" that rung in my ears from this point was a strange sound to me. I seemed in a foreign land.

I tramped on to Hexham. Beautiful for situation is Hexham, the home then of a child of tender years, and of surroundings such as have crushed out the life and blighted the hopes in ten thousand similar cases.

The father of little Joseph Parker became a teetotaller, and made the fireside and home of such a character as gave birth to thoughts and aspirations which ultimately made the man that Dr. Parker of the City Temple now is.

Oh, yes! a little spark can kindle a great fire, however big the blaze and brilliant the illumination, and in this case it is both big and brilliant.

As I approached Newcastle by way of Gateshead one hot day in June, it looked like approaching a furnace. The Newcastle of 1836 was a very different town to the Newcastle of 1884. The magic and marvellous hand of Grainger had not then remodelled and transmogrified it. It was a town of red tiles, narrow streets, and quaint buildings, surrounded by fiery blasts, belching furnaces, and busy collieries. The Tyne ran at its feet, full of life, and crowded with craft then as now, and the streets were busy with active and enterprising life.

This, in combination with Gateshead, its neighbour, only divided by a somewhat narrow river, crossed by a many-arched stone bridge, added to the numerous villages teeming with population, and not far away other large and public-spirited towns, made the metropolis of the north a very serious engagement for a poor factory lad, twenty-three years of age, to enter upon. I was not met at the station by a deputation; there had been no large bills posted for weeks about the town announcing my intended visit; there were no bands of music to head a procession with scores of flags and banners. I did not even arrive by the ordinary coach then in vogue. Nobody knew how I would come, nor exactly, when. I *walked* into the town from Shotley Bridge fifteen miles, and carried my own samples. I had the name of James Rewcastle given to me as a suitable person to call upon. He was a bookseller in the smallest of all the small shops then in what was called the "Side," a big man in a little place. I have known many similar cases. James Rewcastle was a big man, but unfortunately he did not know it, he wanted *dash*, he had no presumption, he had no self-esteem; but in brain power, in systematic perseverance, in fidelity, in industry, he was a wonder. He was the secretary of the young society, and Isaac Richardson, the Quaker currier, an upright and pure-minded Christian, was the treasurer. His hand was the first I shook in Newcastle. He happened to be in Mr. Rewcastle's shop on my arrival, and they were wondering where I should come from, how I should drop, and what I was like, when I walked into this little cabin, covered with dust and smeared with perspiration. I fear my appearance was neither exalted nor exciting. There was no enthusiasm. I was conducted to a little temperance house, and they waited the result of the meeting which had been appointed to be held in Hood Street Chapel that night. A chord was struck at that meeting, the music of which rings to-day! A fire kindled in that chapel that has warmed many a heart and gladdened many a soul in those northern regions. They are still playing the same tune and burning the same fire, so that every subsequent teacher up to the present, as far as the North goes, has *found* it was only "taking coals to Newcastle."

The new doctrine became a "sensation," and the young factory lad an attraction, partly because of the *dialect* in which at that time he dealt out temperance truths, and partly because of the unexpected deliverances which fell from his untutored lips.

The two counties of Durham and Northumberland were soon covered with this strange story, and in some of the colliery villages we seemed to carry the entire population. The Methodists of all sects had a strong hold in most of these places, and that circumstance prepared the way for our work; and it was not an uncommon thing to have the use of the largest chapel in these villages for our meeting, erecting an immense platform, bringing out the largest carpet the village could supply to cover it, and then crowd it with the horny-handed colliers, iron-workers, and glass-blowers of the district. The galleries of these places would be beaded with men round the front, who, resting their elbows on the ledge, with upturned faces looked and longed for what to them was a new life.

The hymn commencing—

"Pledged in a noble cause,"

when announced from the chair, would bring such shouts of "Hallelujah" from a dozen voices as made the chapel ring; and as the tales of experience were told, and the words of exhortation given for the leading of a better life, the mellowing influence pervading the place was such as in my experience I have never felt before nor since.

During my stay in Newcastle arrangements were made for the holding of two open-air meetings. That was a venture having about it some risk. One was held on an open space called the "Spitol," the other at what was called "Garth Heads."

These two localities were surrounded by a dense population of the lowest and most disreputable class. The committee were in some fear, and as the time drew near had their misgivings as to the wisdom of the step, and had I given the least indication of doubt or timidity, that would have been a sufficient reason for abandoning the attempt.

But I knew no fear, and urged on the attack. Temperance if not aggressive is nothing, and I have ever been a fighting teetotaller, not a milksop one.

The following account of these two meetings sent to *The Star of Temperance*, published in Manchester at the time, will speak for itself. I may say that the writer was a local preacher, and one of the secretaries of the society :—

"*Newcastle-on-Tyne.*

"In order to keep alive the interest which was created in this town in favour of teetotalism during the race week, and also to excite the attention of the lower classes of the community to the important subject, it was deemed expedient to hold a public meeting in the open-air this evening in a large area called the 'Spitol.' On the arrival of Mr. T. Whittaker, accompanied by several members of the teetotal committee, a deep sensation seemed to run through the vast multitude. Mr. Whittaker gave out a temperance hymn, which was sung with solemnity and feeling, after which he delivered an address in support of total abstinence from all intoxicating liquors, replete with sound argument, apt illustration, and affecting anecdote, which could not fail to convince the judgments and impress the minds even of prejudiced and interested men.

"It was computed that about two thousand persons were present, the great majority of whom were working men, scores of them 'the vilest of the vile ;' some were actually drunk, others a little nonsensical. On the whole the order of the meeting far exceeded what was expected.

"No real opposition was offered, nor did any one dare to dispute the plain, honest, and incontrovertible statements of Whittaker our teetotal champion.

"He with undaunted courage and Christian magnanimity bore his testimony to the cause of invulnerable truth and righteousness.

"The company dispersed very quietly, evidently under conviction of the value of our excellent system.

"Many influential inhabitants were amongst the assembly; although we only got eight names on the spot, yet we have reason to hope that the labours of the evening will be like bread cast upon the waters, to be seen after many days."

"*July* 13th.

"'Onward' being our motto, another open-air meeting was held to-day. . . .

"Much interest having been excited, and the town's talk being on the teetotal agitator, the attendance was as large as on the previous occasion. Two carts were occupied by members of the committee, who wore their medals. The Rev. D. Adam presided, and after Cook, Charlton, and Welche (three of our zealous advocates, and working men), had delivered powerful and appropriate addresses, Mr. Whittaker again stood forward with renewed energy and fervour, and whilst he spoke the stout-hearted seemed to tremble; but when he described the horrors of the drunkard, men were seen to weep, to shake their heads, to wipe the big tears from their eyes, and readily subscribed to the pledge. Desperately profane persons, who were really disgusting in their appearance, stood appalled, and some of our openly avowed opponents in times gone by were now speechless and amazed.

"The speaker was clearly under the direct influence of the Holy Spirit of God, and his soul was fired with the Divine flame of Christian charity, which drew forth the finest and noblest feelings of a regenerated mind. Such a scene as was presented to us this evening has not been witnessed here since the introduction of temperance societies amongst us.

"Not a hiss, not a word of contempt, was heard, but all was order, peace, joyfulness and triumph, which was proved by thirty-two persons signing our declaration on the field of conquest. To God be all the glory and all the praise.

"GEORGE HORNSBY."

It was at one of these meetings the following incident occurred. It has often been much misquoted, and not unfrequently misplaced.

There were many drunken men at the Garth Heads meeting, and in the middle of my speech one of them called out,—"Look here, my canny man!"

I looked there, and paused.

All eyes were turned upon him, upon which he said,—"A quart of ale is better for a hard working man than a quart of water."

And the people shouted with delight. I saw that it pleased, and was not quite ready with my answer, so I said,—"Say it again, my good man."

And he said it again.

While he did so, Thomas Welche, who sat near me in the wagon, helped me to a reply. All eyes and ears were towards me; it was a critical moment,—one step, and down we all went.

"The question," said I, "has not been fairly put. A quart of ale costs sixpence; a quart of water costs nothing. You must have sixpence in the hand with the quart of water; where the quart of ale is, the sixpence is *gone*. Now we start. Take that sixpence and go to a butcher, and ask for as nice a piece of steak as he can give you for fourpence (and in 1836 a decent steak could be got for fourpence), then call and get a pennyworth of potatoes, and go to the baker's and get a pennyworth of bread. Now you have spent your sixpence, go home. I hope your wife can cook a steak and boil a potato. When that is done, with a nice hot plate and a little salt and pepper, you sit down and eat it. Now then," said I, raising my voice so that it could touch every ear in that crowd of working men, "tell me whether a quart of ale is better for a hard working man than a quart of water."

And the crowd burst out like a thunder-clap,—"Beef-steaks for ever, Whittaker!"

The victory was won, and the triumph complete.

One Sunday morning I was present in a leading place of worship, making one of a large congregation. The preacher for the day was a very clever, good, and popular man. I was in the gallery, and in the front of it. During the sermon the minister said that "Teetotalism was a trick of the devil!" That was rather personal, and I thought every one was looking at *me*. "A man is known by the company he keeps," and he was putting me in bad company. I knew the teaching, "give a dog a bad name and hang it;" and if that preacher did not mean hanging teetotalism, what did he mean? "Satan goes about like a roaring lion." Well, I roared a good deal, and I went about; but we have to bear a good deal from the pulpit, and I bore that. On the Temperance Question that man was as blind as a bat.

A few days after, I went to Darlington. On my arrival I went to take tea with a reformed drunkard and his wife. During tea I told the couple what the good man in Newcastle had said. I have never forgotten the reply of the wife. She looked over the top of her spectacles across the table at me, as she said,—

"Well, sir, if the devil can play such tricks as these, I wish he would play two or three more with my husband."

I took care that the minister had her opinion.

Of course we were hurt and troubled by this teaching from such quarters, and we adopted a scheme which I think did something to kill it there.

In some of the colliery villages our success had been very marked—at Wallsend particularly so. I have myself in that village met in class with not less than a dozen stalwart colliers, who had been reclaimed by teetotalism and joined the Church. There was a love-feast appointed to be held in New Road Chapel, Newcastle, on a day named, and we knew that this preacher would be there to lead it. We got our men to come down, and one after another, to the number of fifteen, these men thanked God for teetotalism, so that scarcely any one else could speak. The testimony was direct and conclusive. The man who had said, "Teetotalism was a trick of the devil," listened to it, and his colleague too. They bore it very well. He who had made the attack subsequently became himself a teetotaller, and lived for a quarter of a century as such, dying in Sunderland at nearly *ninety* years of age!

One Sunday morning in the month of July, 1836, I was present in the largest place of worship in the town of Sunderland. There would be 1,600 people present. I sat in the gallery. The preacher for the day was a very good and useful man, and in much esteem, but like the one in Newcastle, on temperance in the dark.

This gentleman had five sons. It is said of him, that on one occasion he was applied to for a sermon on the "Foolish Son." His reply was, "Which of them? for I have *five*." And so he had. I knew them all; and no father's heart was ever more wrung by sorrow by more foolish sons than was his.

During the service a bill was handed up to him, with a polite note, begging that he would be good enough to announce the contents. The bill stated that during the ensuing week there would be a temperance meeting in Flag Lane Chapel, to be addressed by myself and others.

He read the bill to himself in the face of the congregation; but instead of making known its contents, he tore it up in sight of the people, and trampled it under foot! I did not throw a hymn-book at him; I have had hymn-books thrown at me, and Bibles, and Testaments, and hat-pegs, and I have an impression gas fittings too. I did not tear up the Bible as a delusion and a snare; I did not say the man was a hypocrite, or that there was no truth in religion; I did not even refuse my mite to the collection. He descended from the pulpit, and was received in the vestry by the officials, and presented with a glass of wine as an acknowledgment for the services rendered—a common thing in those days.

I walked out of that gallery a poor, raw Lancashire lad, and when I got to the door no one spoke to me a word of sympathy.

I have said before, and I will repeat it here, Had there been as much temperance in the Church as there was religion in the Temperance Movement of that day, we should have been saved from much heart-burning and much unbelief.

In rehearsing these incidents, I have no wish to be understood as questioning the honesty and sincerity of the men in question. Far from it; it is done to show the condition of things at the time. Some of them lived to repent of the deeds done, and they were after all only what the people made them, and the nation was given up to this idolatry. It must, however, be seen how we were hindered by it; and it cannot be wondered at if numbers of teetotallers were so damaged in their feelings towards such people, and such Churches, as to lose all inclination for fellowship and connection with them.

From one end of Bishopwearmouth, right away down the High Street of Sunderland, is, as some of my readers will know, a considerable journey, and what was failing in the way of notice from the pulpit on the previous Sabbath, I made up for with my own rattle and my own voice in that street.

As I approached the lower end of it, a crowd met me, headed by the town crier in his official robes, and accompanied by a little deformed man, who was the wit of the town. They were both drunk. The crier, with what dignity he could assume, forbade my usurpation of *his* office, and the little sprite of a man (whose name was Smirk) created great fun by treating me as a lunatic. I persevered and completed my task; the crowd, including these two men, accompanied me to the meeting.

One of them (Smirk) signed the pledge that night, and the other subsequently. They were both advanced in life then, but they were both true. They became members of what is now known as the Methodist Free Church, in that town, living for many years in respect, and dying in the faith.

Within three years of that visit, Mr. Smirk (who was a sail-maker by business), had a *third* ship launched at Hylton, three miles up the river Wear from Sunderland, and became a most loving and lovable man. We talk of the blood of the martyrs being the seed of the Church, would it not be quite as true to say that the trampling of that bill under-foot in that pulpit was the life and salvation of Nicholas Smirk and the town crier?

It was the difficulty, by ordinary means, of getting made known what was to be done that drove me to the extraordinary ones, the using of which brought me in contact with those two men.

I cannot express my thankfulness now for the circumstances which put that burden upon me, and that I so cheerfully and so willingly bore it.

The evening of my life is gladdened by its remembrance.

CHAPTER XV.

WIFE AND HOME.

THAT a man must ask his wife if he shall live is an axiom carrying force and containing truth, none will deny. The wife can do much to make or mar her husband, and no surroundings are more effective in their operations than the influence of home life. To nurse and bring up children with no concern beyond that of getting rid of them to any one, and in any way, as soon as can be, is murderous in its tendency, and marvellous in its inhumanity. How much this country owes to its home life no tongue can tell, and no pen can write; where would England be to-day, were it not that the home influences in our land have been an anchor to our national life and a resting-place from the whirl and worry of the outer world? I have been in homes in other lands, and seen and enjoyed much; but in no place have I felt the home life that England gives, and from which, when I returned I could not say, "England, with all thy faults, I love thee still, my country."

In the United States, there is scope, there is enterprise, there is room, there is welcome, there is wealth, there is luxury, there is hospitality, there is abundant goodness and generosity; but there is not the home, the domestic life of the mother country, and they know it, they feel it, they admit it.

There is no substitute for, as there is no equal to, an

English home; and one of the worst and most to be dreaded influences of the drinking customs is in the terrible results such customs entail on the home.

Temperance advocates, it is said, exaggerate. They do nothing of the kind; the half has not been told. I could myself bring skeletons out of the cupboard of home life that would appal the nation, the exhibition of which in public would terrify any meeting.

I met a person near the door of a place of worship not long since, at the close of a public service, during which a most impressive sermon had been preached by a gentleman who preaches as few men *can* preach, on temperance. The truths taught in that sermon were admitted, applauded, and believed by the gentleman in question, yet he to all human appearance was hopelessly gone! a man who had held the highest offices in the Church which any lay member could hold, helplessly gone, and while I am writing these pages he has gone. His house had been an open house to the preachers. The decanters and the cigar case never closed to those who cared to visit him, and they did visit him. No home could be better and more respected, was it not for the blight drink had brought.

How can I, how can any man who knows what family life is, in the face of so much threatened fatality and hidden sorrow, shut his eyes, and hold his hand?

There is a terrible reckoning one day for somebody in this case; and I am much mistaken if the preachers who contributed to the consequences which have followed in the wake of their presence, and association, and example, will not have to preach a long time before they can counteract the mischief which those who run can read and which has been done here. One of the saddest features of the business is, that men who contribute to, and live in such an atmosphere, have the recognition of respectability, and are not unfrequently stock articles as officials in the Church, and prominent figures in the social scale and on public occasions.

To be excited by drink is only to be "a little elevated," and to be indecently drunk is simply to be "overcome." If nobody knows, it is no offence at all; and if it happens in public, it is just one of those misfortunes which will now and then occur. These are special circumstances and exceptional occasions, and in that way the foul offence is plastered over, and we cry " peace " where there is none.

It will be seen then even where the home life is all that could be desired, if we play with fire we shall be burned, and if we take pitch into our bosom we shall be defiled.

John Bright tells us that when he set up housekeeping he made no provision for drinking, and there is no evidence to show that he suffered in social relationships or in public esteem in consequence.

I remember before I was as well known in the town in which I live as I am now, one evening the leading minister in the Church with which I was connected called upon me, and I naturally looked for a somewhat prolonged and agreeable visit. He soon, however, began to speak of "the preciousness of his time," and "the many calls he had to make," and in less than ten minutes he was gone. It subsequently transpired that he had gone from mine to the next door, and remained there more than three hours. The head of that house smoked and drank, and so did the preacher, and as I had neither pipes, spittoons, nor pots of beer, there was nothing sufficiently attractive to necessitate a prolonged visit to me.

My neighbour has long since gone to his rest, and so has the preacher. They were neither of them unworthy of the position they occupied; but long before the days of temperance teaching, they had, like many other good men, fallen into bad habits in these particulars, and habit as we know, is second nature, and it is hard for a man to get away from himself even in the presence of his friends. I pitied more than I blamed them, after all; but this sort of thing often isolated me and my house. The former left a family, but I do not know that any one of them did anything that improved their own position, or that was worth imitating by others.

It may, and it sometimes does happen, that the home life, which is all that could be desired in its social feeling and domestic arrangement, is not unfrequently entirely marred by the company kept and the habits cultivated. We are social beings, and we like fellowship, and it is not pleasant to be always shut up within ourselves and to be excluded from society. But it is better and safer to suffer that, than to secure friendship at the risk of what we know to be right to ourselves and safe for our children. How many families have I not known, even among teetotallers, where ruin and disgrace have succeeded the silly custom of introducing the wine decanter because "society" looked for it, and ignored those who did not practise it—and they would not be ignored.

But they are ignored now, and ignored because of the consequences which followed its introduction, and by the very people to please whom it was introduced. Better live in a cupboard, or be tied up in a bandbox, than be played with by "society" like a shuttlecock, and at last left in the mud as a thing not worth picking up.

The world wants backbone in society, and true manhood in individuals, so that when sinners entice we consent not. When I signed the pledge, nothing would do for my wife but the going to the meeting on the second night of the series, and she did so. We took our seats, not in the gallery, but in the boxes—we felt that we were part of the concern, fairly in the business; we paid for a sitting, not as lookers-on, but as interested partners. One of the speakers said that in *Preston* they did not think a man was a full teetotaller unless his *wife* joined. There was a cry from the box in which I sat. "Then put my name down," said the voice. Everybody looked, and the little woman who belonged to myself never had so many lookers-on before. That completed the business, and I was fairly in for the job. I had now crossed the gulf, and in the face of the people destroyed the bridge, so that there was no going back, or retracing my steps. I was in for the fight, and that too against fearful odds; but with a wife who lived in me and for me, a sister who loved me as her own soul, a brother who counted not his life dear that he might save me, and a mother who prayed as a mother only can pray for a son whom she knew "Satan" desired to have, I resolved to war a good warfare, and my brow became brass, and the foes were but as grasshoppers in my sight.

My home was the one green spot on earth to me; my wife the bonniest bit of all the beauties with which I began to feel the world was filled, making my life a perpetual sunshine, and my hopes full of bloom. This was indeed a new creation, and I walked in the light as

He is in the light, and not a shadow crossed my soul. The greatest luxury in the world is the luxury of doing good. That I enjoyed to the full, and though there were many things to exercise and try me, they were indeed but as dross compared with the excellency of the knowledge of God in the face of Christ Jesus my Lord.

I fear I have never had the heartiness that many whom I esteem have had, in the efforts made from time to time for the entertainment of men accustomed to go to the public-house. We all look at things from our own stand-point, and I am a thorough believer in the value of home life, and the necessity there is to cultivate that first and foremost. I like entertainment, I can enjoy a good song, but I like it as I like salt to an egg, or pickle with cold beef. If I am supplied with salt instead of an egg, and pickle instead of beef, then as a Lancashire man would say, I shall "flit."

Entertainment is not life, it may do as paper and string to wrap up life, but it is not life. People who live in and depend upon entertainment are something like a shuttlecock kept up by a battledore—miss the blow, and they are in the mud again. I cannot spend my life playing shuttlecock.

The love of home in me sometimes sends me there before I am expected, if not before I am wanted. Some quarter of a century ago now, or more, I was at Accrington for a week's work, and in the middle of my work I fell ill, I had taken cold; the winter set in prematurely, and I was without suitable clothing, so I determined to go home direct. My wife I knew to be a good nurse, and one good nurse is worth a dozen bad doctors, so I went home. When I got there, it was what the ladies call "general cleaning time." The house was upset from top to bottom, mistress and maid were in it up to the elbows. Now I like to be clean, but I hate the mop and the slop pail. That was known at home, so the following dialogue took place on my unexpected arrival.

"What on earth have you come *now* for? Why did you not send me word?"

"Well," I replied, "I will go back and write a letter if you would rather."

"Nay, you may stay now you are here."

"Thank you; we will have some tea, then, if you please."

So we had tea, but it was a very plain dish, and I could not get on. I was poorly, but maid and mistress were both too busy to spend time on superfluities. So I said to my little girl Louie, (she was just on her third birthday,) "Go and tell Betsy to make father some toast. She was delighted. Children like to be employed; they must have something to do, and what is more, they will *do* something. They need directing and helping, and those parents make a great mistake who do not frequently become children *amongst* their children. That can be done without becoming childish. Our children may be nothing to the world, but they are all the world to us. We live in them: if they do well, *we* do well; if they do ill, we do ill. "Louie," said I, "go and tell Betsy to make father some toast." Off she ran. Presently back she came, and looking in my face as a knowing, precocious, loving child can look, she inquired, "Do fathers always have toast?" "No," I said; "not always." "But they can if they like," was the response. "Yes, they can if they like," I said. Then, pouting her lips and rolling her body, she simpered, "Little girls can't." "No," I said; "little girls can't." Brightening up she responded, "But little girls can if fathers like." "Yes," I replied; "little girls can if fathers like." Then there was a long pause. After a while she began again: "If I were father, should I have toast?" "Yes, I dare say you would." "I am not father, am I?" "No," said I; "you are not father." Then she burst out, "I wish I was father," and the entertainment was over. I give this piece of domestic history for the benefit of those who want entertainment, and who cannot do without it; *children* are wonderfully entertaining, and we may go farther and fare worse.

This little circumstance gave an illustration in my public teaching which has been of immense value. Who has not heard my little girl's toast story? But for the benefit of those who have not, I give it here with its moral. What is toast? Plain bread made nice, no extra cost, a little extra trouble, that is all, to make an article additionally attractive under special circumstances. What are we men and women? In the main plain bread, some of us very plain; in other cases we have been made of very bad flour, the sins of the father visited upon the children; but what is worse still, in many cases we have gone to the wrong place for barm. We have never "risen"—sad cake, heavy bread, good flour spoiled!

It is possible that in some cases there was sufficient promise in the outset to justify our being put into the oven and baked, but the baking has been so hard that we are all crust, we are a crusty lot. Now what shall we do? Sit down and cry about it? Certainly not. Let us be toasted. Make the best of it. Never say die. There is no law in heaven, nor in this land, to keep us down because we are down, and the country is studded with men who have overcome circumstances more unfavourable, and difficulties greater than ours. Let us be toasted—toast the person, toast the home, and whatever we do, at home or abroad, let it be done in the best possible manner. Even the disagreeables of life can be mended by toasting.

On retiring from the bench one day, the clerk to the bench, who was the most courteous and most gentlemanly man I think I ever knew, had just made known to a poor wretch at the bar the decision of the magistrates, and had done it with as much politeness and consideration as if speaking to a prince. One of the magistrates said, "Well, it is almost worth while getting into trouble in a small way to have the advantage of having the sentence conveyed to one by our clerk, he does it so nicely. Were I" (he went on to say) "condemned to die, I would rather our clerk passed sentence upon me than any one else."

I began this chapter by saying "that a man must ask his wife, if he is to live." Of one thing I am certain, that many a man is driven to the public-house by a slut of a wife. I remember on one occasion, in a town in Lincolnshire, (and Lincolnshire is not a county remarkable for badly managed homes or badly managed farms,) having a little business with a good teetotaller and rising tradesman living in it, and I knew the most likely time to see him would be noon, when he came home to dinner. So I went at that time.

On my arrival I was ushered into a good sized room, well furnished. A good carpet, hearthrug, and handsome sideboard, with tables, mantel glass and everything to match. The wife was busy washing up, and putting away the breakfast things. The clothes on her back looked as if they had been thrown on with a pitchfork; there was a fine baby, about six months old, lying on its back on the hearthrug, kicking and rebelling with all fours most furiously. There were as many ashes under the fire-grate as would have filled a wheelbarrow. There were several chairs in the room and not one at liberty, and nobody sitting down either. Now here was a condition of things for a man to come to from the worry and work of life! That house wanted toasting. The wife had been gossiping all the morning with that child in her arms; and when her husband came to dinner, everything was in disorder and nothing ready, and instead of sitting down to a comfortable quiet dinner, he had to nurse the child, while his wife hurriedly threw together some sort of hodge-podge called a meal. I left that house sick at heart and sorry for the man, and I remarked to those with whom I was staying, "If that man continues," (for he had been a known and heavy drinker) "it will be a marvel." I subsequently found he did *not* continue, for after twenty years' teetotalism he went back to his cups, got into difficulties in his business and if he still lives I fear he is in poverty, if not in something worse.

That is only one sample of many cases I have known where the wife would not let her husband live.

There is a lot of work for women in the Temperance Movement, but if it takes the platform phase rather than the domestic, it will be power misapplied.

CHAPTER XVI.

FRAGMENTS.

TO "gather up the fragments that nothing be lost" was a wise teaching, the obeying of which, resulting in twelve baskets being filled, must have been an astonishing reward. That we waste more than we use is an impression begotten by the very frequent evidence given of the propensity to pass by the little and superabundant things of life. If nothing is made in vain, it follows that products and results coming from legitimate effort and natural life cannot be thrown away or trampled under foot without loss to some one. It is not always that in the great or major things of life we see the most. Their vastness bewilders us, while their generalisation destroys their individuality, and blunts their point, and weakens their power.

It is when we come down to everyday life, and speak of things which the common people understand, that we are "heard gladly;" it is then we "hold the mirror up to nature." It is there life sees *itself* in the life of others, and we stamp the image and mark the similarity.

That we are very much alike is an admitted truism; and yet there is sufficient variety and individuality in most of us to make the life-story, when told, not only valuable history, but a matter of interest to those who succeed us. The deed I now do has been pressed upon me from many sources; but there cannot be much in my belongings which is not already known to them, and that fact has restrained me, combined with the difficulty of making readable that which when spoken by the human voice seemed to be worth listening to, not unfrequently begetting unbounded joy. Still there must be millions in the land who never heard my voice, or saw my face, and at my time of life the number will increase rather than diminish. For their sake then, as well as for the families of those who do know me, and at whose hands and in whose homes I have experienced so many acts of kindness, I give these details of my private and public life.

The circumstances which forced me to the front have already been indicated, and will in future chapters be dwelt upon in detail; but that I was ill-provisioned for the work which lay before me can readily be believed; yet, when the time did come, it is surprising how ambition seemed to creep upon me, and I looked about for an opening in the great departments of life.

There is something very fascinating after all in public life, and but few men would submit to the annoyance and disappointment which must come more or less to all active and ambitious men, were it not for the return got in the way of public notice and public esteem. Members of Parliament, members of corporations, preachers, lecturers, and professionals of all sorts, go through much irritation and personal petty annoyance; and though in some cases circumstances make it a necessity that in that way their provision shall be made and their status maintained, yet in numbers more there is no such necessity, and yet it is done, and it is well that it is so.

While it is truthfully said that, "Every workman is worthy of his hire," there have been men in every age, who have never made this a condition; and not many of the great movements which have uplifted humanity and brought glory to God would ever have been set in motion had the originators and pioneers waited till some one had offered them a wage for the work.

The world is not now, and never has been, destitute of men who can forget themselves in the interests of others, and can leave home and country, and abandon ease and pleasure, and even health and life, in view of the world's good and man's welfare. These are the redeeming features of an unregenerate race, and give proof that the Divine image stamped upon our nature has not been entirely obliterated, and that there is a divinity within us, which, when kindled by the fire of patriotism and evoked by a sense of obligation, will do deeds worthy of a God. They, and they only, can compass a land given up to folly. They, and they only, will bear the brunt of contumely, persecution, hatred, and shame. They, and they only, will be found at their post, when the hireling has fled, because he was a hireling.

The book which is accepted as an authority, and is looked upon as a rule and guide for life, in all Christian lands, teaches us many things hard to be understood, and claims obedience in matters which are foreign to our taste and nature; and we may in some cases be forgiven our doubts and misgivings, and be permitted to differ from our fellows, as to the force and obligation of such claims, without being shunned as heretics and hated as heathens. But when the same authority teaches what we know to be true, and corroborates the facts and experience of everyday life (and this it frequently and almost constantly does), then to doubt is to be damned, to question is to quibble; and to seek palliation in the practice of that which conscience and common life and the Word of God combine in condemning, is to evidence a perverseness of will and a degeneracy of nature which, if unchecked, can but end in the fool's conclusion, "There is no God."

The desire for life, in its truest sense, was strong in me. Captain Pilkington, who was then travelling the country (this was in 1835) as an advocate of peace and temperance, visited Blackburn; I heard him. To my mind, he seemed one of the grandest men living, and doing a noble work.

How I longed to be like him! But he had been a captain in the army, and possessed education and social status: I had neither. He appeared in purple and fine linen: I wore a checked shirt, and walked in clogs. He shook hands with, and talked to, and rode in carriages among people I was afraid even to be seen looking at. What a gulf! So I turned away, somewhat desponding. Going home I was met by a neighbour, a member of the Church to which I had become attached, and he, as we walked together, asked me to accompany him to a cottage preaching the following Sunday evening. I did so, and took part in the service.

I have never regretted it, and I have reason to believe no one else ever did. It was a wonderful contrast to the meeting addressed by Captain Pilkington, but I was marvellously helped and wonderfully comforted in the work, and I have never despised, though I have been frequently discouraged by, small meetings since.

I have had my share of large meetings since that day, and it may be that good, corresponding with the size of the meeting, has resulted; but I have not had very tangible proof of it. But I do know that from some of the smallest meetings I have ever addressed the most tangible and glorious results have followed, and I strongly incline to the opinion that cottage and little home meetings give life and power to the Church just as home life gives character and force to the individual.

From that day I have had faith in little things, and have been "gathering up the fragments that nothing be lost."

My speeches and lectures and sermons, as most of my friends know, are nearly all about little things that nobody else would notice. They have indeed been very much like those stalls we get occasionally at fairs and markets, where anything they contain can be had for a penny. Nothing costly, but something useful; and if not used at once, the investment does not ruin anybody.

There have been times when people have put a price upon me which I never fetched. They charged for admission, sixpence front seats. It invariably fails. How can it be otherwise? Teetotallers especially are not such idiots as to give sixpence for a penny article, and one that is being sold for nothing all over the country.

I have heard of people—nay, I know of people—walking eight or ten miles on a dark night to hear me, but they will not pay sixpence for a front seat; and to make a man pay for what he can get for nothing does not accord with his notions of economy and provident habits, and would in all probability be out of harmony with my teaching. Then again the practice is so out of character with what all the early men have taught and believed—we should as soon have thought of renewing the window-tax as of taxing the people who came to our meetings. It does not pay to make light dear. "Let there be light" is the decree of Him who gave the sun to rule by day and the moon by night. It may be *professional* to make a market of it, but it is neither apostolic nor patriotic.

Possibly I have been spoiled in the making, but I have a horror of *great men*. They take up so much room, and need so much attention, while the intrinsic value is so very much below the price paid.

"Little boats must keep near to shore." That was easily learnt, so I soon got it off. "Take care of the pennies, and the pennies will take care of the pounds." Well, I could understand that. "A man could not have his cake and eat it." That was also pretty clear. The man who has saved his first shilling has laid the foundation of his fortune. I did not upon that quite see the fortune, but I could see that the end could not be reached without a beginning, so I took care of the shillings and went to work.

That could be managed, "gathering up the fragments that nothing be lost." The big things of life are, after all, few and far between, and have not half the influence little things have.

"A flea in the ear is a greater nuisance than a bull in a field." A smoky chimney will frequently give a man more trouble than a house on fire, yet a smoky chimney is a little thing compared to a house on fire. If the house be on fire, it is a decisive case, we must either put the fire out or get out ourselves; but not so with a smoky chimney, it worries our life out. A button on a shirt is a little thing compared to the shirt itself, but there have been cases when a man has got up on a fine Sunday morning and put on a nice shirt—the moment he got it on the principal button was off! It spoiled his dinner that day; it was a poor sermon, if he went to church at all. But what is a button compared to a shirt? If he had had no shirt at all, the irritation would not have been half so great; it would have been a decisive case, to which he could have made up his mind. There is no alternative, so by sundry dress arrangements he meets the difficulty, and accepts the circumstances. But to have the enjoyment of a nice shirt marred for want of a moment's kindly thought, or the putting out of a hand, "riles him." These are the little foxes which not only spoil the vine, but make us that we cannot sleep o' nights. Many a man has not spoken to his wife for a week because a button was off his shirt. The lesson taught by the loss of a nail will never lose its power, and cannot be too often repeated, and yet what a little thing is a nail. That lying in the lane was not worth picking up; and when a little further on still there was seen the half-worn-out shoe, that was not thought to be worth carrying to the farrier to be replaced; but further on still, when the horse was found dead and the owner in trouble, the calamity was seen in all its force. Then it was that the fact was realized, the entire michief came through the loss of that nail. It was for want of a nail the shoe was lost; for want of a shoe the horse was lost; and for want of a horse the man's bread was gone and the man's home a desolation.

"The stitch in time saves nine" is a wholesome axiom, and would, if acted upon, save many from flying dirty tatters and feeling bitter neglect. "Gather up the fragments that nothing be lost." A pinch of snuff is a little thing, only a pinch. A pipe of tobacco is a little thing, only a puff; yet we spend 12 millions a year in pinches and puffs, and what is our return? Soiled linen, dirty clothes, pocket handkerchiefs in rags, poisoned air, filthy mouths, and dirty spittoons. A glass of wine, or a sip of beer, is a little thing, only a sip—only a drop; and yet we spend a *hundred and thirty-six millions* sterling annually in sips and drops, and what is our gain? A harvest of pauperism and crime and lunacy, accompanied by a stagnation of trade and a waste of strength, which cripples our commerce and paralyses our power; with the homes of the people in large masses blighted, and the habitations of the land a laughing-stock and a mockery. That is our gain.

There was surely then enough, in what were thought to be little things, to occupy my mind, and give power and shape to my purposes; and I can truly say, with all this full in view, that I conferred not with flesh and blood, but obeyed the Spirit of God.

CHAPTER XVII.

MEMORIES OF MEN AND THINGS.

MUCH of the years 1836 and 1838 was spent by me in the counties of Durham and Northumberland. There were but few if any towns or villages, or even hamlets, that I did not visit and lecture in, touching also the borders of Yorkshire and Cumberland. In them were my earliest friends, and amongst them some of the bravest workers the cause has ever had. To-day there are few districts in which I am so little known and where I so seldom work. The friends of my youth are with few exceptions gone. One fact remains, and I take some comfort in it, there is no part of England where temperance teaching is sounder, nor where political influence for temperance legislation is stronger and more unanimous than there, and there is no lack of systematic and consecutive work. The men who accompany Sir Wilfrid into the lobby of the "House" on temperance questions, are in greater proportion from there than from any other part of the country, and we know how ripe is the county of Durham on Sunday closing.

The Society of Friends have been our stronghold in these parts from the first, so have the Primitive Methodists, so have the Methodist Free Churches. T. B. Young, of Sunderland, was a power in his day, so was quiet John Hills, the Wilsons, and the Backhouses. At Darlington, John Fothergill, the surgeon, with all his house gave us much help, and many of the influential Friends, the Peases and Backhouses, then, as now, stood well by us. Of John Backhouse the banker, and his brother Jonathan, I have very grateful memories. The "West Lodge" people also showed me much kindness, and did the cause good service. Jonathan Priestman, also a Friend, was our president at Newcastle, and his whole household (which was large and influential) did us lasting service. George Charlton was then, as now, a great favourite with the people; a curly-headed handsome young man, full of colour, and fresh with life. His testimony backed by his appearance was a tower of strength. A generous-hearted and lovable man was George, and an out-of-door speaker and preacher such as few could touch. He was the people's idol. I can only say, take care of George, he is almost the only one left to me of that race, and there will never be another George Charlton.

It was at Mr. Priestman's house I first met with John Bright. He subsequently married Miss Priestman. She was, I think, at the time, one of the most beautiful if not *the* most beautiful and ladylike person I had ever seen, and she was as good as she was beautiful. Her teetotalism was of the highest and most robust kind; alas! she was short lived. I cannot but think that Mr. Bright's teetotalism would have been a little more robust than it has been at times, had she lived. An incident happened in connection with my first visit to Mr. Priestman's house to dine, which may amuse my friends, though it was a serious business to me. The house was the house of a gentleman friend, he and his lady were considerate and hospitable, and the family (which was large) were then getting up in life, and had a considerable presence. Of course it was a new world to me. Of *society*, so called, I knew nothing. When asked to dine, I hesitated, and said to the people of the little temperance house where I lodged that I would rather not go. I was told it would be an offence if I did not, and it was quite an honour to be invited, and in the interest of the cause I should go. That settled it. I had done many things in the interest of the cause, some agreeable, some disagreeable, so I would do that. I went. I had always up to that time seen my dinner all at once, and usually dined off one dish. In this case it came in, as some people take in books, in numbers, and, also as in books, more numbers than I expected or bargained for. We began with soup and salmon. The soup was very nice, the lady said it was, and I went again; so was the salmon, and there too I went again, thinking that if a little sweet followed that would finish the business; I had no conversational powers, at least not for educated society, and I thought it rude to sit at the table and do nothing, so I ate. To my horror a boiled leg of mutton and capers, and roast turkey arrived, and as it seemed all this had some special application to myself, I fell in with the arrangement and tried to be agreeable. Then came sweets and game, after which followed dessert and coffee; as we took no wine, coffee was substituted.

Having engaged to meet a party of friends at a *substantial* tea in another part of the town at five o'clock, and as I was expected to do herculean service at a large meeting the same evening at seven o'clock, I was brought into trouble. When I got to my lodgings, my host was dressed and impatiently waiting to accompany me to the next party, but he never to the day of his death forgot my description of that dinner, nor the appearance of myself on my arrival. I insisted upon being excused doing any more eating that day, and remained in my room till the time for public meeting and did the best I could, but I have never been in love with after-dinner speeches from that time. I suppose education has a good deal to do with these matters as well as others, but I never go to a banquet now (and I seldom do go, for I hate them) without unpleasant reminders, and wondering how some of those about me will get over the attack they have made. I have in my time opened my eyes at "inexhaustible bottles," but I wish I could shut them to the unbounded filling of some human tubs; and the less they are, the more they seem to hold. Extremes meet. In connection with this visit, I had in my duties to go one Saturday to a place called Coalpit Hill, a place four miles wide of Shotley Bridge. Harry Wilkinson lived there: he was a small farmer and shoemaker. He had an extensive acquaintance, and was in considerable esteem, and was obliged with a meeting at his request. He lived in a lone homestead near where four roads met, and scarcely another house to be seen. On my arrival I was not pleased with the prospect, I could not see where the people were to come from. However, they came in all shapes and forms, and we had three hundred people in front of his house, and I addressed them from a cart. Harry was dead on the government, and on excisable articles. He would not take tea on that account; of course he was a teetotaller, for that and other reasons. When the meeting was over I sat down with others to tea. There were some very nice oven cakes, plain and currant, hot and cold, but the tea had been made from herbs gathered in the field. I did badly with the tea, and he said, "Can't thou drink it? If," said he, "thou art a *Christian*, thou wilt take it and be thankful; if thou art *not*, it is too good for thee." Well, I was not prepared to have my Christianity questioned, so I took it. Harry got very much attached to me, whether it was because I took to his herb tea, and ate the "crowdy" he made for supper by pouring water out of the kettle into a basin and then stirring some meal in it, or whether because of the work I did and the life I lived, I know not; we are good friends still, I never go within a few miles of that district but Harry turns up. I hope he still lives; if so, he is on for *ninety*.* Harry took a fatherly interest in me. He did not like "broidered hair," and cared little for curled "toppings." Now I always had a "topping" that curled. Of course I helped it a little. Harry used (when he came into the house after my arrival) to stroke it down, saying, "Take care of thy poor *soul*, my lad."

On one of my visits, I had been to Sunderland in the interim, and the ladies there had fitted me up with a lot of frilled and ruffled shirt-fronts, and they gave me a very handsome cloak. When I got to Harry's on this Saturday afternoon, several neighbours had already arrived, and filled the large kitchen, where everybody sat. Harry was busy finishing off some shoe work in his little shop at the end of the house. When done, in he came wiping his hands on his leather apron, before shaking hands with me; then looking in my face and at my dress he was horror-struck! I had got on one of these grand shirt-fronts, or "dickeys," as we used to

---

* Since writing this, I learn Harry is dead.

call them, and was not at the moment conscious of any speciality, for I had got used to them. Laying hold of it with his dirty fingers and tearing it off, breaking the strings and exposing my plain check shirt beneath, he exclaimed, "What on earth hast thou got here? Thou wilt lose thy soul! The Canaanitish women down yonder at Sunderland, amongst whom thou hast been, have ruined thee! Take off these 'fal de rals' and vain shows, and return to thy first love, and live in godly simplicity, and work with godly sincerity, and He who abhorreth that which is evil shall make thy brow brass, and men will be but grasshoppers in thy sight."

I was shocked and shamed at this revelation, but I survived it, as I have done many other unexpected outbreaks, and I have no cause to regret that I ever had friendships with Harry Wilkinson.

On another occasion, in the depth of winter in 1838, I was appointed to address a meeting in Shotley Bridge. I left Newcastle by a one-horse Irish car, the only passenger conveyance between those two places at that time. There had been a heavy and sudden fall of snow, the roads were hilly and the ground was heavy, the horse was lame, and in places the snow had drifted. We left Newcastle a little after four o'clock in the afternoon; the journey was fifteen miles. Ordinarily I should have arrived in time for a comfortable cup of tea before the meeting, but in this case it was nearly eight o'clock. We were four hours in going that weary journey, and I was all but starved to death.

The meeting was announced for seven o'clock, and the Wesleyan Chapel was packed by that time. Harry, who was a local preacher, had been appointed chairman. He commenced the meeting, giving out a hymn and praying, then making a short speech; still I came not. On my arrival I ran down from the car to the meeting, fearing all patience would be gone. I was faint, cold, and hungry. The chapel, however, was crowded by people waiting in great suspense for my appearance. On getting into the pulpit I said to Harry, "Select a *nice suitable* hymn, and let us have a *lively* tune, for I am almost *dead*."

They were beautiful singers at Shotley in those days, and I knew it. While that was being done, I could pull myself together and arrange my thoughts. Harry was a man of few words and great self-possession; he put on his great black-rimmed horn spectacles, thumbed over the leaves of the hymn-book, and then stood up and said, "Let us sing a verse while our friend gets a little breath," and proceeded to give out—

> "And am I born to die?
> To lay this body down?
> And must my trembling spirit fly
> Into a world unknown?"

"Oh dear, Harry!" I exclaimed, "*don't* sing *that!* do you call *that* a lively hymn? It may be poetry, but it is not truth. I am born to *live* and do something, not to die; and neither kill me nor bury me before my work is done." Harry meant well; he was always afraid I should be puffed up and spoiled, and this no doubt was done to keep me down and humble, and he kept his hold and sang what he thought proper.

Blanchland, a small mining village in Durham, hid in one of the vales lying between Hexham and Weardale, was to the front in temperance work in the morning of our life. The main part of the village formed a square, surrounded by the better class of such houses as the place contained. It was what I should call a *religious* village, and it was religion that made it a temperance home; I was welcomed there with great heartiness by a band of good men, lead miners.

The distance from Hexham must be a long way on to twenty miles, and I started to walk. When I had got about half way, I was met by a man leading a horse. He had come to help me on my way. Getting somewhat footsore, any means of motion rather than walking was just then a relief, and he gave me what he called "a leg up." I had never been on horseback before in my life. It was a thorough agricultural animal, and such a way across the back, that I had not been long in that position before I felt as if I should never be able to pull myself together again. The road was up and down, so much so that I had to get down to rest myself. I was not only footsore, but sorely troubled to know which was easier, *riding* or walking.

Life among the miners was a new life. They were men who feared God. The meeting, which was held in the open air, in the square, was very large, and the miners must have gathered from many miles round. I was very happy in my work, and the memories of those days fill me with joy and gladness now.

A second visit was paid to them a few weeks later on, after I had been down to Newcastle. On my first visit, I had spent a Sunday with them and preached to them. They wished me to repeat that sort of service in connection with my second visit, and I did so, holding the meeting on the Saturday and preaching on the Sunday. Those were days when "we had no religion." I suppose our religion was a kind of extra, a thing not in the general account, a superfluity or gratuity. The teetotallers have always been fond of extras and gratuities—something thrown in over and above, and which is never named in the account but done because it was a delight. *Now* it is bargained for and made a leading article, and fetches a good price, and is therefore a prominent feature.

During the first seven years of my public life, I have reason to believe, I addressed more meetings and preached more sermons than any man living or dead in the *same time*. I question if I had in all those seven years, putting all the time together, twenty weeks by my own fireside, and the money acknowledgment for my services did not certainly average more than thirty shillings a week, but I was never happier and never richer in my life. I had food of which the world knew nothing, and I realized the fact that "godliness with contentment is great gain."

On the Monday morning after my second visit to Blanchland, accompanied by eight or ten men, I crossed the moors for Stanhope in Weardale. We were a happy band. The sun burst upon us in all its glory, the moors were rich in heather bloom, and the wind blew balmy breezes, filling our lungs with life and our hearts with gladness.

The journey was some ten or twelve miles (I speak from memory), and we were bound for a great temperance festival, procession, and meeting to be held that day at Stanhope. Nothing of the kind had happened before in those regions, and my former visit, a few weeks before, had kindled a fire all along that interesting valley of the Wear. Stanhope was then the city and centre of that valley.

The late Bishop Phillpotts was at one time, it will be

remembered, rector of that rich living, and the theory is, that he would never have accepted the see of Exeter had he thought it would have cost him the living of Stanhope.

The following extract from a letter I sent to the *Preston Temperance Advocate*, and which appeared in the September number in 1836, will show what happened.

"Last Saturday we had a tea party at Stanhope, and after tea about one thousand of us walked in procession through the town. Several reverend and one medical gentleman, all warm teetotallers, formed a part of the procession, and I have the pleasure of writing this letter in the doctor's house. After the meeting, which was held in the open air, one of the publicans who was present, went home and pulled his sign down and opened a temperance hotel."

Can the *improved* teetotalism of this day give any more striking proof of the identity of the finger of God in the work, or of the manifestation of His power, than such facts as these convey? If so, I for one will be glad to see them. Shall I further say, that while crossing those moors, on our way to Stanhope that day, we formed ourselves in a circle on the highest point, and joined our song of praises with the lark which warbled over our heads; and then falling on our knees, when and where no eye could see us but the eye of Him who neither slumbers nor sleeps, the prayer that went up from that happy band linked our work in the hand of Him by whom kings rule and princes decree judgment?

One more incident before I leave this bee-hive of industry, this fountain of material wealth, the county of Durham. New Sheldon was a growing village near

Bishop Auckland, surrounded by important collieries, and having in it somewhat extensive engineering works. I made my *début* there one fine Saturday afternoon. It was quite convenient, and in some cases most convenient, to hold meetings on a Saturday afternoon. The Primitive or Wesleyan Chapel had been secured for my meeting. Unfortunately, at the time announced for the meeting, some strolling players, or mountebanks, were performing in the streets, and relying on voluntary help, all the world had gone to the fair, and the chapel was empty, with the exception of some half-dozen brave men. We determined to turn out and sing through the streets; in our journey we crossed the path of the mountebanks, and in the neighbourhood of that crowd I sprung the rattle. They stopped the music in amazement, and the entire concourse turned to look where the strange sound came from. I told them what we were going to do, and invited them to the meeting. Whether the performance was over or not, I don't know, but they did no more, and the company in great numbers followed us down to the chapel. The following record appears in the *Preston Temperance Advocate* for the month of October, 1836. Referring to my work, it says:—"From the 6th August to 6th September he established fourteen new societies, besides visiting and reviving a number of societies already established. At a place called Sheldon, the mountebanks were acting, so that he could scarcely get any to attend; he went among the crowd and sprung his rattle, they beat the drum, but he got a meeting, and twenty-eight signed the pledge. A wine merchant also signed the pledge, who is now getting shut of his wine as well as he can."

That wine merchant subsequently became the Rev.

Thomas Barlow, and for the last few years of his life was book steward in the offices of the Free Methodists in London, and died in the esteem of all who knew him. It was here also, I believe, where Mr. J. H. Raper first crossed my path. The grand old city of Durham took some taking, but it was *done*.

Priests, mustard, and old maids, were not considered the best materials to act upon, and these were at the time somewhat prominent features in the city. I was accompanied by a young man from Sunderland, John Candlish. He was then employed in a crown glass works of some note in that town. Mr. Alexander Wilson was also a working foreman in the same works. This Mr. Wilson also acted as minister of a little Baptist chapel in the town; John attended the same chapel; they were both teetotallers.

A teetotal glass-blower was a prize to us, because, being very *hot* work as well as heavy, beer was considered essential in such cases, and their abstinence was a refutation of the absurdity. Mr. Wilson subsequently was known as the *Rev.* A. Wilson, and died at a good old age as pastor of the little church he had served so well, while his own hands ministered to his necessities.

Mr. Wilson was the only man who ever took any pains to acquaint me with the rules of grammar. He would do it as he walked by the wayside with me. He was a most unselfish man, and full of loving-kindness; he had a fatherly feeling towards myself. John stood by me in the streets of Durham and sprang the rattle, and I announced the meeting. John Candlish became mayor of his native town, and was for many years its representative in Parliament, and few men in the House of which he was a member had more esteem and more consideration than himself; and the present member, Colonel Gourley, who for years was Mr. Alderman Candlish's colleague, had also close and intimate relationship with the Temperance Movement in early life, and both of the men have been true and valuable helpers in all temperance legislation. I name these facts not only to the honour of the men themselves, but as incentives to fidelity and true manhood in others. Temperance men, whatever their condition and position in life, *must* win, all other circumstances being equal. No man fails because of his teetotalism; some, it is true, fail in spite of it.

The arrangements for meetings had to be made with considerable care. Guisboro', then a quiet little town at the foot of what since have been proved to be the Ironstone Yorkshire Hills, leading to Whitby from Stockton-on-Tees, the discovery of which has revolutionized that district, was a place in which I soon found a home and a welcome. Mr. Smith, a Friend and chemist in the town, endured no little obloquy with his family of daughters because of their zeal in the cause; but they held on, and those of them who remain continue true to this day.

It is some eight or ten miles from Stockton to Guisboro'. Conveyances were scarce, and hiring was more than my means would admit of. The meeting at Guisboro' was fixed for the night of the market-day at Stockton. It was thought somebody returning from market *might* give me a lift. That was thoughtful and economic. I started on my way about four o'clock; that was quite soon enough for returning market-people. The days were getting short. When I had got about a mile out of the town, a gig came up with one man in it, he had a broad-brimmed hat on; it was getting towards dusk, and in remembrance of past kindnesses from the sort the hat represented, I ventured to inquire "how far it was to Guisboro'?" hoping of course the occupier would offer me a seat. Instead of doing so, he said, "Art thou going there to-night?" It is said with truth that Quakers answer one question by asking another. This gentleman never did answer my question, but asked me one, to which I answered, "Yes, I am." "Ah! thee wilt find it a long walk." Then applying the whip to his horse he left me, and I (as he said) found it a long walk. Perhaps he did not like my appearance, and as it would soon be dark, he thought the circumstances were not favourable for wayside acquaintances. Thomas Dixon subsequently gave me many a ride, for that was the gentleman's name, and he was a corn miller.

There was an old maiden lady then living in Guisboro', a minister in the Society of Friends, who soon became somewhat troubled as to Christian duty in connection with the Temperance Cause. She thought beer good, but dangerous. She was somewhat singular, but most conscientious. I was invited to dinner. There were only about three public men she would recognise, the deputation from the Bible Society, and the Tract Society, and myself. We were all privileged to be entertained by her. This was my introduction. When we sat down to dinner we were waited upon by a very proper maid, one who had seen a good many summers. On the table was a little mug about the size of a duck's egg; it was empty. Presently, addressing the maid, she said, "Wilt thou fill me that mug?" The maid took the mug down into the cellar, and then returned with it filled and placed it on the table by the side of the mistress, who said to her, "Thou canst retire: Thomas Whittaker and I want to have a little private talk." She then went on to say how much she had been impressed by what she had heard at my meetings. "Formerly," she said, "I had a small *jug* of ale brought to my table, and I supplied myself with what I wanted out of it. Now, seeing the danger attending drinking these things, and fearing the habit might grow upon me (she was getting on for *eighty*), I bought that little *mug*. I have that filled once and no more, and I only take it with my dinner, and lest I should be tempted at any time to transgress, I never even allow myself to draw the beer." "Well," said I, "but what about the servant?" "Dearie me!" said she, "I never thought of that." She gave it up that day, and I took away the mug as a trophy. She became a fast friend, and died a long way on her way to *ninety!*

The late Countess of Zetland took a good deal of interest in the Temperance Movement in subsequent years, and having a seat close by, Ann Conning, my Quaker friend, and another lady were requested to wait upon her ladyship, with a view of getting some pecuniary help. It was a long time before Ann was ready for this visit, and her lady companion got out of all patience, but Ann kept putting her off.

At length after many weeks she was ready, and off they started. On arriving at the Hall, they were ushered into the drawing-room, and there waited the arrival of the Countess. As soon as she appeared, Ann (she was a little body) trotted across the room to her ladyship and holding out her hand said, "How dost thou do, *Louisa?*" The lady companion of Ann, upon that, was fit to sink through the floor, and would have done so if she could.

The Countess knew Ann, and respected her scruples. The delay in paying the visit was occasioned, as was afterwards explained, by Ann Conning's objection to address anybody in any other way than by their Christian name, and she had been searching and inquiring all these weeks for the name of the Countess. Her objection to vain words applied not only to names and titles, but to forms and ceremony, and she was most rigid and conscientious in all this.

Her first invitation to dinner came because of her desire to show her goodwill to me, and to give her an opportunity of explaining a little incident which occurred at the meeting the night before. It was held in the Wesleyan Chapel, and was opened with singing; she was shocked and could not stand it, and left the place. People of to-day little know the difficulties besetting our path on these grounds in the early days.

CHAPTER XVIII.

MEMORIES OF MEN AND THINGS.

ROBERT INGRAM SHAFTO, of Bavington Hall, Northumberland, was a God-send. When the truth touched him he made short work of the drink business, and cleared the Hall, and the village too, of the article, turning the village public-house into a temperance hotel, and erecting a Primitive Methodist chapel. The place became a very Bethel. Many people even now, when we count our friends by tens of thousands, and cathedrals echo temperance truths, and dukes and duchesses don the blue ribbon, feel it a terrible cross to free themselves from the trammels of custom; and yet that any one should hesitate to do so, who has thoroughly appreciated what belongs to life, and has the courage of his convictions, is one of those anomalies which I suppose will accompany us to the end of the journey, and with which we need patience and forbearance.

We talk of courage, of valour, and of heroes, and we decorate with medals, and adorn with ribbons, and endow with pensions, and honour with peerages, men who never did deeds half so noble as those done by the Squire of Bavington. There is not a tithe of the courage nor a scintillation of the national service in much that commands the world's honour as characterizes such services as that rendered by Mr. Shafto.

Society laughs at the supposed folly, and the " Somebodies" sneer at what they are pleased to call meanness, and want of taste, on the part of those who have manhood enough to set at defiance public opinion and public custom, when that opinion and that custom outrage honest conviction, and exact unreasonable service. But surely so long as a "man's house is his castle" and his home his own estate, he may be permitted to rule it in his own fashion without offence, and even in the performance of the amenities of life select such means and opportunities for doing so as shall not jar upon his own feelings nor wound his conscience.

If ever there was a heaven upon earth, it was at Bavington during the life of the dear old squire, and if society could not see it and feel it, there were hosts of others who could and did.

He kept a "prophet's chamber," and lived near the gates of the heavenly city: many a weary traveller threw off the cares of life, and laid down the burden of the cross in that good old home. Personally I got to like the place quite as well, if not better, than my work; at all events Providence seemed often to call me that way. Most of us, I presume, will remember how frequently Providence does point out duties in agreeable quarters, and lay claims upon us where wages are good and surroundings attractive.

There was, I remember, a nice grey pony at the Hall, with not much to do, which was at my service at all times when at Bavington. We got to be very good friends, and I had many a pleasant trot across the country on his back. We were constant companions, so much so that he became known as the Teetotal pony, and I have much pleasure in saying, he never disgraced the society of which he was so distinguished a member.

Still he was the "Squire's pony," and always got the recognition due to his station; and as I, for the time being, was a member of the establishment, a fair share of consideration and respect fell to my lot. That was quite a new feature, and I tried to fall in with the circumstances. It is astonishing how soon we can at least *look* like gentlemen, if we are properly fitted up.

It was during these excursions that I came in contact with the family of the late Sir Walter Trevelyan. His father was then living. Wallington, the Northumberland seat of the Trevelyans, was only a few miles away from Bavington, and the village school was secured for meetings; to those meetings I frequently went. Miss Trevelyan was a most frequent attendant, and became deeply interested in the work, and through her the family became our friends.

Most temperance people know how true, how noble, and how generous the late Sir Walter was to the Temperance enterprise, when he and Sir Wilfrid Lawson and Mr. Charles Jupe came down with their thousands of pounds at a time, and did it again and again, and when in that effort they were joined by others, so that the London *Times* of that day had to admit that war upon the liquor traffic had become "a great fact."

The vicar of the parish in which Bavington stood married the widow of a brother of the squire, and was an occasional visitor at the Hall. He was a bachelor on in life before his marriage, and still retained some of his bachelor habits and fancies. He rode a shaggy Shetland pony, and had a shaggy terrier dog; they matched himself. One of the churches supplied by this vicar was a barn-like building standing in the midst of a wild and scattered district. The dog used to accompany the parson into the pulpit. One Sunday, in the middle of the sermon, such as it was, preached to about twenty people, a strange shepherd's dog strayed into the church. The parson's dog smelled or sighted him, upon which he jumped on to the ledge of the pulpit, and kicked up such a "hullaballoo" as necessitated an abrupt conclusion of the service.

I fear that event made a more lasting impression than anything the vicar ever said or did, during his many years' cure of souls in that district.

An event happened while I was staying a day or two with a very gentlemanly rector in the same county, who to his credit espoused the cause when such as he were rare birds in our nest.

While at breakfast one morning, the lady of the house was in sore trouble that she had been called upon to pay a chimney-sweep (who as I understood had come a few miles early that morning to sweep the chimney) one and sixpence. While she was complaining, a poor woman arrived with a baby to christen. At the request of the rector I went with him into the church. The ceremony was soon over, and the cost was two and sixpence. Now I thought at the time, and I told the lady so, that the rector's charge was very much more serious to that poor woman, than was the sweep's to them, and it was a cleaner and much shorter job. Sweeping chimneys did not come every day any more than babies. He coincided with my view, and I think the lady felt a little ashamed at thinking one and sixpence too much for the service rendered by the sweep and his poor boy, for he had a poor boy, and he went up the chimney, and that there might be no mistake about it, he was watched while he entered at the bottom, and never given up until he showed himself out at the top.

Who does not rejoice that that barbarism and cruelty to children has been abolished? and it is one of the pleasing memories of my life that for several months while sojourning in London I was a member of the household of Joseph Glass, the inventor of the machine for sweeping chimneys, through whose kindly nature and patient perseverance that cruel business was put down by Act of Parliament.

He was at the time a member of the committee of the society whose agent I was. When men talk of teetotallers as people with "one idea," they show their own ignorance of what is going on in the world. My experience leads to the other extreme. As a rule, they have too many ideas. They are everywhere, and in everything. Take away the teetotallers from any society that can be mentioned in Church and State, I care not what its object (so that it be good and practical), and how many active workers will be left? Sum them up, and if you are not surprised at the amount of gratuitous philanthropic, patriotic, and Christian service rendered by teetotallers, I shall be surprised at my own ignorance of the purposes and activities of life. It is that spirit and that power which makes them teetotallers; they belong not to the humdrum lot who live in the world of—" As it was in the beginning, is now, and ever shall be," but to the ever-growing tribe who cry "Excelsior!" and who have no such word as *fail* in their vocabulary.

Before I leave the north I think I must make one more record. On the 2nd August, 1838, the complete emancipation of the slaves in our colony of Jamaica took place, and the event was celebrated at Darlington with unusual rejoicings. A large tent was erected in the grounds of Mr. Edward Pease, the Edward Pease of railway history, and the friend of George Stephenson.

The gathering was no ordinary one. The Quaker Town, as Darlington was then called, came out with all its wealth and beauty and power. Mr. Forster, now the Right Honourable W. E. Forster, was then a very young man, and just gone to Darlington to get some practical knowledge of a business to which he subsequently devoted himself. He entered the tent rather late, with a young lady on his arm, who had a presence scarcely inferior to that of the late Duchess of Sutherland, while he was tall and thin, and having on his nose spectacles, and on his head the broad brim (for he came of a sound stock of Quakers), he was a very marked and conspicuous figure. The legs he had then were the same, I suppose, that he has now; and those who know the hon. gentleman, and watch his movements, will have observed with what difficulty, at times, he seems to be able to get them in the right position: it was specially so at this meeting. He was young, he was a stranger, he was late, and the tent was full.

The Friends, who could then cover a great deal with their hats, and the lady portion of them hide their faces in their bonnets, had some difficulty in keeping from public gaze their sense of what even to *them* looked funny.

He has, however, astonished many of them since. I had then, and have still, considerable regard and esteem for the honourable gentleman. He is the only son of a father who has shown me much kindness, and who was one of the purest minded and most philanthropic men

I have known, and I have known a few. The mother doted on her son, he seemed all the world to her. I knew that from conversations which took place in my presence when a guest at the house near Norwich, and I was at one time not unfrequently there.

Her humane feelings and tenderness to all living things were proverbial; and though a pet raven about in the grounds used to take great liberties with my calves, the rebuke, when administered by her, was done in such a way that the bird liked it, for it never seemed to lose an opportunity of giving an occasion for another interview on the same subject. Being a sister of the late Sir Fowell Buxton, the brewer, she had great faith in her brother's stout. She knew, as many others knew, he was a good man, and would not knowingly do a wicked or a wrong thing, and it seemed to possess her that it was an utter impossibility that anything her brother was responsible for could do any harm. Mr. Forster, the father, was very decided and firm on the Temperance Question, and Mrs. Forster seemed never to tire of showing me kindness; so much so, that I had to send for my wife down from London to partake of her hospitality.

Those were not railway days, nor days of penny post, and letters and journeys meant something.

That was a time when such friends were not quite as common as blackberries; they were therefore the more to be appreciated, and I do not forget them.

The honourable member for Bradford cannot but be a friend to temperance, whether it takes a legal or moral phase. He is in the succession, and must inherit the promise, "instead of the father shall come up the children;" and though the incidents of life, like the accidents of birth, make wonderful distinctions, and appoint great gulfs in certain cases, there will always in this case be special interest, and abiding hope and esteem.

It may here also be added that I was the first temperance teacher to visit Middlesbrough. It was then in its young life. In 1836 a few thousands numbered its people, and it was a congregation of odds and ends. There were here and there a few men who had migrated to this new and rising colony from other parts, and they knew something of temperance truths, and through them my connection was formed.

The Bank at the time was in connection with a grocer's shop, and the family occupying the premises, and who acted as agents, were soon among our friends.

Mr. John Taylor, of Tokenhouse Yard, London, a director of the Temperance and General Provident Life Office, and chairman of the executive of the National Temperance League, was then a very young member of that family. He has been true all the way up, and all the way along the line temperance has run from that day to this, as I believe has most if not all of that household, and it was numerous.

There has from that day been a strong and active temperance sentiment in Middlesbrough; but, as in all such towns, there have been times when it has been difficult to hold our own.

Great prosperity and rapid growth are too apt to beget improvident habits and foolish ventures, and these not infrequently bring in their train drunkenness and distress. Middlesbrough has been no exception to this rule, but it is a wonderful town notwithstanding, and has had in its history some noble men and enterprising spirits.

It held its Jubilee in 1881, and made a very creditable show of its power, progress and wealth. As mayor of Scarborough I was invited to take part in that demonstration, and did so; and while riding through the streets in company with such men as the late lamented Lord F. Cavendish, I had memories of men and things different from most in that procession. I have been in two processions in Middlesbrough: in the first I was alone with my rattle, the second was the one just described.

CHAPTER XIX.

MIDLANDS.

WHEN James Teare left for the west and south of England, I left for the north and the east, so that from the year 1835 to 1840 the country was completely covered by one or other of us. During those years we never crossed each other's path; indeed I do not think we met for ten or a dozen years, and yet we were continually on the move. In many cases we touched at the same point and worked in the same locality, but never at the same time.

The northern and eastern counties were mine, while the southern and western were Mr. Teare's. Before the year 1840, I had done much temperance work in the following counties:—Westmoreland, Cumberland, Northumberland, Durham, Yorkshire, Lancashire, Nottinghamshire, Lincolnshire, Leicestershire, Northamptonshire, Bedfordshire, Essex, Suffolk, and Norfolk, and was the introducer of teetotalism to very many of the towns and villages in all of them.

There were teetotallers many in all those parts, and several societies scattered here and there, but there was a wonderful quickening in connection with my visits, and results most gratifying and abiding followed the effort put forth.

London and the suburbs had much of my time and work also in the years named, and many incidents happened in connection with that work which seem to me worth a record, and which will not be without interest to all who like to know how and when it happened.

I reached London in the month of May, 1837, working my way by stages from the north. While in Sheffield in the early part of that year, accompanied by a few friends, I walked over to Rotherham to see what could be done there. We hired a small room, then used as a preaching room by the Primitive Methodists. We bought candles to light the room, and paper on which to take the names. I then turned out and called the meeting by springing the rattle. The late Edward Chrimes was then a grocer in the town, and I can see him now as he stood at the door of his shop, glasses on his nose, and his white apron in front of him. The novelty arrested him, and the boldness of the venture struck him. He came to the meeting. His teetotalism dated from that visit, and he was for years before his death (which, alas! was somewhat premature) the enterprising secretary of what is to-day one of the best and most successfully worked societies in this country.

I walked home to Sheffield the same night after that meeting, and never saw the town again till the year 1849, when on my way from London to take up my residence in Scarborough. The famous brass-works of Guest and Chrimes came out of that meeting, works which in some particulars have no compeer at this day. It is not simply that the works came out of teetotalism, but what has come out of the works. Some of the first men in that thriving and busy town date their first step in the ladder of success in connection with those works. Alderman Kelsey, who was recently mayor, is one of them; and who that knows anything of the history of the late John Guest, his refined taste, his public spirit, and gentle nature, can fail to see what a debt is due to him and to the cause (to which he never during life omitted to make known his obligations) for what Rotherham is to-day?

At Nottingham my visit was anticipated with considerable pleasure and excitement; the meetings were very crowded, and the streets leading to them so filled that I had difficulty in making my way to them. E. H. Clarke, a lawyer and Christian gentleman of much influence, had thoroughly committed himself to the movement, as had the never-to-be-forgotten John Higginbottom, the eminent surgeon. These, with many respectable and well-to-do tradespeople also forward in the work, gave me quite a status in the town and locality, and opened my path wonderfully in all directions.

Nottingham became my centre of operations for several weeks, and filled me with encouragement and joy. Mr. E. Smith was the secretary, a man saved by the society, and full of Christian zeal and great natural abilities.

The cause owes much to the medical men who are to the front to-day, but infinitely more to such men as Mr. Higginbottom, Mr. Fothergill, and Mr. Beaumont of the past, who dared to be true to science and themselves, before it was either fashionable or profitable to be so. We are glad of the medical men now, but if needs be we can do without them. The accumulation of facts, and the records of life's experience, make their opinion no more than anybody else's, when that opinion ignores facts and contradicts life's experience. The fact is, they are obliged now to admit our claim, and decency compels them to be careful in their dicta.

It was not so forty or fifty years ago, and I for one swear by the men who had the moral courage and the true manhood, frequently at great cost and sacrifice, to stand by us when friends were few.

It was here where I first met with John Cassell to know him. He had been to London, and was on his way back to the north. He called in at the business place of the gentleman with whom I was staying, and asked for me. The gentleman thought him so uncouth and singular that he hesitated to ask him to see me. He had been with Mr. John Hull, a Quaker gentleman, near Uxbridge. This gentleman was short and stout, and Mr. Cassell was long and thin, and the *clothes* made for one did not exactly fit and become the other. The trousers were too short, and the hat too big. John's legs came a long way through at the bottom, and his head went a good way in at the top. He had also on an old camlet cloak overall, and across his shoulder slung a joiner's basket with a few tools in it, with which John meant to work supposing his teetotal venture did not succeed. He announced himself to my host as the Manchester Carpenter. That was reported to me. I said, "Yes, there is such a man," so went to see him. He said he had heard that I was going to London, and he thought he would like to see me, and tell me how to go on. I thanked him, and, said he, "I were suman ruff afore I went to Lunnun!" At this my host burst out. I thought he would have had a fit. When he did recover himself, he said, "Well, I would have given a guinea to have seen you before you did go."

After that he was introduced to the sitting-room, and it was then he told me how he had heard me in

Manchester, and how from doing so he got the inspiration to become a public man. Continuing, he said, "I should like to hear thee again, Tom." "Well," I said, "you can if you go to Derby," never for a moment supposing he would think of such a thing, but he jumped at it. That troubled me, for I did not know what to do with him, and some members of the family where I expected to lodge I knew to be not so agreeable to teetotallers.

We walked together to Derby that day. At the meeting he spoke a little, and pleased the people. When the meeting was over, he said, "Can't I sleep with you?" "Well," I said, "I have no objection, but you know *I* am only a lodger." However, go with me he *would* and *did*. That was the man. When John made up his mind to do a thing, he did it, and to that feature in his character no doubt much of his future success may be attributed. The gentleman at whose house he met me at Nottingham, and who was ashamed of him, subsequently became his servant, and touched his hat to him, and John has pulled up at my own door in his carriage with a liveried servant when I lived near to him in London, which I did for a few years. But as I have said elsewhere, the history of John Cassell would be a book worth reading if anybody will take the trouble to write it.

That "it is all fish that comes to net" may be true, but that we get fish sometimes which it is a misfortune to catch, there is abundant proof. The Temperance Cause, like every other good cause, has been most shamefully imposed upon at times, and no better way of fleecing the public can be adopted, than religious pretence and persecution for righteousness' sake. We had in Nottingham, as one of our early trophies, a man a cooper by trade. He soon became a platform man, and was one of many who followed up his reformation by joining the Church. He began to whine about the persecution he suffered and the loss of work. The people in the liquor trade, said he, "would not employ him," and there was much sympathy in his behalf. The good Doctor Higginbottom had on hand a very complete set of brewing utensils, which were lying useless now teetotalism ruled at home, and he had occasionally named that fact in his speeches. He would neither sell them, nor give them to be so used as to contribute to drinking.

This cooper called upon the doctor, and said he thought of beginning business if he could get a little help. "Indeed, of what was he thinking?" "Why," said he, "if I could make a few utensils, tubs, basins, dishes, etc., and stand in the market." "Just the thing," said the doctor; "and I will give you all my brewing utensils, and you can cut them up into such articles as will be likely to sell and answer your purpose." The good doctor slept in much comfort that night in thinking to how legitimate a use after all his brewing utensils would be devoted, and at the same time help a deserving and persecuted *brother*. The doctor awoke the next morning to find that this scamp of a cooper had obtained a beer license, and had opened a beer-shop, and was using the teetotaller's brewing utensils in his trade!

During a portion of the time I was in Nottingham, I was lodged at a little temperance house. The keeper of it had seen better days, and he was put in there partly out of charity and sympathy. He could speak fairly well, and had done a little preaching in his day. He attended meetings with me and sold tracts. He occasionally, when we went to the villages, took with him a large blue bag with something special in it. I noticed that he was very much exercised to know, when he had that bag, if there would be a platform erected to speak from, and if not the bag was never opened out and the meeting was seldom satisfactory. On one occasion we had gone to a meeting in a village of some importance, ten miles away. The Wesleyan Chapel was lent for the occasion; the singing pew was a large square one under the pulpit, and a platform fixed in it. He was told before going to the meeting that there would be a platform. Upon that he opened the bag and pulled out a pair of yellow top-boots, the relics of better days, and donned them. There was a table on the platform, which he soon covered with his books and tracts. The platform was laid somewhat low, so that when he got on to it the boots could not be seen. He was not long in getting warmed up, and he sprang from the platform on to the table. The boots were beautiful: the people applauded: that carried him out of himself. He forgot the frail foundation on which he was standing, and the table collapsed, and the boots, books, and speaker lay in one confused but harmless mass on the floor of the singing pew. Of course that finished the business, and the rest of the evening was spent in gathering up the *débris*.

The speaker got so much joked about his boots subsequently, that the blue bag never figured again in connection with our meetings.

At Newark we were overwhelmed more than once by the men engaged in the malting trade. In the year 1837 Newark paid more duty on malt, I believe, than any town in Great Britain or Ireland, so that holding a meeting there was bearding the lion in his den.

Dr. Bigsby, a retired physician, and ex-mayor, kindly received and entertained me. The Old Assembly Rooms were secured for the meeting. The room on my arrival was packed with maltsters' and brewers' men. I think I never saw a meeting so full. The meeting was not only full, but *drunk*. I was received with shouts of derision. One cried out, "How bad he looks!" another, "Burke him!" another, "Set fire to him!" Several climbed on the backs of the seats; their weight brought them down and broke them. The legs and arms of these flew at my head, and the heads of those who had got on to the platform with me, so I gave in. The men then danced with delight, and jumped "Jim Crow." In the scuffle (I was told afterwards), some one managed to pin an old newspaper to my coat tail, and apply a light to it, but I suppose I had then drunk water too long to take fire very readily, for not a hair of my head was singed, neither did my clothes smell of fire.

Newark was in malt very much what Burton is to-day in beer. Great is the goddess Diana, but Diana will fall notwithstanding, and the sooner all concerned put their house in order the better. The recent silly and ill-judged persecution of the Rev. Spriggs Smith, of Burton, is only the old story and the old experience, and will burst itself as does the thrown snowball against a stone wall, the bishop's pastoral notwithstanding.

Who does not remember how the bishops of Southern America lent themselves to the iniquity of slavery in that land, and how they were the last to let go their hold? Will the bishops be the same in this land with reference to the drink iniquity? We shall see. We know where to put them, and what to do with them, if they have not sense to see the signs of the times, and the honesty and courage to sever themselves from their relations in that direction.

CHAPTER XX.

NORTHAMPTON.

MR. THOMAS COOK, the great tourist promoter and originator, then living at Market Harborough, marshalled me through Leicestershire and Northamptonshire. He was an active teetotaller then, and had already done good service in the cause.

He came to see and hear me at Nottingham, and before leaving I pledged myself to him for some meetings under his direction, when I had done with Nottingham. There were many difficulties to contend with, but upon the whole the venture was a success. They were barley-growing counties, and the farmers and those whom they employed joined with the publicans and liquor-sellers in interrupting our meetings and opposing our progress. Of course the Church was not uninfluenced by this state of feeling, and it was quite a common circumstance for the pulpit to be used to depreciate our work and beget prejudice against our persons. At Kettering this conduct had a marked influence on the meeting. The Sunday before my arrival, two of the Nonconformist ministers took occasion to preach to their people with special reference to my intended visit. One of them took for his text, "Be not righteous overmuch"; the other, "Beware of false prophets." The one went to show that we were laying obligations on the Church which the Bible did not enjoin; and the other, that nothing was happening but what had been foretold, and they must be on their guard lest they should be led away by false doctrine.

The people in the main shut their eyes and opened their mouths, and swallowed what was prepared for them. As our mental health, like our physical, is much influenced by the kind of food we take, as well as the circumstances under which we take it, there will be no difficulty in realizing the condition of things on my first visit to Kettering.

The British Schoolroom, mainly through the influence of members of the Society of Friends, was got for the meeting. It was taken possession of by the rowdies of the town, and they had the meeting conducted after their own fashion. One of the gentlemen who had preached against us on the Sunday was put into the chair, and after saying that he hoped they would hear what I had to say, he announced that at the close of my address they would be allowed to put questions, and if they did not do so he should take me in hand himself. He climaxed the whole by announcing that he hoped the day would come when every working man would have at least "two pints of ale a day." Upon that several of the men began to flourish bottles and ask questions before I could begin. The interruption was continuous, but I spoke for an hour, and I think made some impression. I have never in my life been completely put down if I once got a hearing. At length some one set fire to some loose shavings lying on the floor (some benches had been undergoing repairs during the day, and the shavings were the result). A cry of "Fire!" excited the people, and the roughs made a rush at me and jammed me against the wall. I was not quite so stout then as I am now, or the consequences might have been serious. As it was they, I think, were more hurt than myself. The meeting after this broke up in disorder. Mr. Gotch, a local banker and magistrate, was sent for, things looked so serious. He brought with him the *solitary* policeman. A Quaker gentleman named Wright, a chemist and wine merchant, who heard the men suggest my being thrown in a pond close by, came to me and said: "Thomas, wilt thou take my arm? those men mean mischief." Mr. Wallace, a farmer and maltster, came and offered his arm on the other side; he was also a Quaker. My readers will have already seen how much I owe to the Quakers. Between these two I walked through the streets of Kettering, followed by that howling mob. The magistrate headed the procession, I followed with the wine-seller on one side and the maltster on the other, "Bobby" in the rear.

The wine merchant lodged me that night, and in his little parlour, before retiring for the night, he signed the pledge and kept it to his death, and never sold another bottle of wine. The maltster also signed, and never made another grain of barley into malt; and his partner, good James Wells, also signed, and lives in respect amongst the people to-day, and is never tired of helping on the good work. I go to Kettering occasionally now. Last March the son of Mr. Robert Wallace took the chair for me, and subsequently I had a look in at the old premises of the late Mr. Wright, and saw once again the little room in which he and Mr. Wallace signed the pledge on the occasion of my first visit; and it will not be beyond the record if I say there is not a town in England of the same size as Kettering in which more tangible and marked, material and moral, progress has been made, and where that progress is more clearly and distinctly credited to the Temperance Cause.

The reverend gentleman who opposed me at my first meeting, within two years of that time became a teetotaller, and built a temperance hall, and was a most ardent and unwearied advocate to his death. During the last winter I was permitted, in company with my dear old friend, Mr. Thomas Cook, of Leicester, a man who has proved himself one of the wonders of the world, to address a meeting in the very chapel in which one of the sermons was preached to which I have alluded. The present minister of the chapel presided, and the minister of the other chapel where the other sermon was preached, to which I have also referred, opened the meeting with prayer. They are both good teetotallers. Surely our experience at Kettering in this matter has been what the experience of the children of Israel was, "the more they persecuted us the more we multiplied."

The day following the first Kettering meeting Mr. Wright drove me over to Market Harborough, and took the chair for me at a meeting in the Town Hall, and then took me back with him after the meeting to Kettering. It is ten or twelve miles. There was great interruption at Harborough, coming at one time to a free fight. The lights were put out in the midst of it. When they were renewed, having in the meantime been informed that a man who was a leader in the disturbances was a bricklayer from Preston, I took the opportunity of turning to the history of my life in Preston. I touched points familiar to this drunken bricklayer, and mentioned names he well knew, and then called upon every mother's son not to forget their home obligations, nor dishonour the name of the mother who bore them, and not only to permit the light to shine in their faces, but the truth to touch their hearts. "Talk of liberty and freedom," said I, "he who would be free, himself must strike the blow! and instead of striking one another strike off the chains that bind you, and throw down the bottle that enslaves you. It is not going from home that makes you free. It is not changing the locality that alters your life. It matters not where you go, nor what you do, if you take your old bad habits with you, the curse of folly will be your companion and the slavery of sin your shame." The Lancashire bricklayer jumped upon one of the forms, and facing the meeting challenged any man present to "dare to put a finger upon me," and finished by declaring his intention to sign the pledge at the close of the meeting; which I believe he did, but what followed I know not, excepting that we got out of the town in safety, and felt we had done a good day's work.

At Wellingborough I was pelted in the Old Meeting House with Testaments and hymn-books during my speech, and had to be protected on my way home from the meeting. From there I went to Northampton. In that town I had peace, and truly I needed it.

In Northampton I came across the path of the late Rev. Jabez Tunnicliffe, who is credited with being the founder of the Band of Hope movement. The meeting was held in the Friends' Meeting House, and my hostess was Mrs. Latchmore, a widow Quaker lady. She and her son William were warm teetotallers, and they made their home a little heaven to me. At this point my engagements were all completed, and I resolved to go to London and wait for what might open to me. I was not then the agent of any society, my connection with the Preston people having by mutual agreement come to an end. Mrs. Latchmore, on my leaving by coach for London, said, "Thomas Whittaker, I should like to beg thy rattle; thou art going to London, and thou wilt not want it there, and if thou hast no objection I should like to have it." I gave it to her. That was in the month of May, 1837, and I never saw that rattle again till September, 1880, forty-four years.

I was invited in the September of that year to attend the jubilee of the Leeds Temperance Society. I went, and as I had learned that this same rattle was then the property of Joseph Latchmore, living at Rawdon, near Leeds, I wrote asking the loan of it, thinking it would be a relic of some interest at the meeting in Leeds. I was not fortunate enough to receive it in time to be of any use at the meeting, but it came to me the morning after. When I saw it, it renewed my youth, and brought back facts and incidents long forgotten, and much of the past in this way has been lived over again by me. I have never parted with that rattle since, and as many of my readers will remember, it came conspicuously to the front on the occasion of my being elected Mayor of Scarborough. That circumstance, to those who live on the surface, was considered a little out of place, and my opponents made much of it; but I knew what I was about, whether they did or not. I felt that it was not out of place to remind the people how, twenty years before, they had done all they could to make the town so that I could not live in it. This was done by the vilest misrepresentation, and the cruellest barbarism. A number of brewers and publicans so prejudiced the fishermen and sailors against me that an effigy was made of me and hung at a ship's yardarm for half a day. It was then fixed on a crossbeam, and the beam fixed on a platform, and the platform carried through the streets headed by a band of music and followed by an immense procession; the town for the time being given up to a lawless mob, for not a hand was raised to prevent the brutality. At certain points a halt was made, and the dummy was flogged by two sailors with a "cat o' nine tails." Eventually they returned to the sands and burnt the effigy, throwing what was left into the sea.

We had a corporation then as we have now; we had harbour commissioners then as we have now; but the drink power was in the ascendant: I disputed its claims and denounced its deeds as I do now, and that was the offence. They feared my official connection with the borough, and that was their way of making such a thing impossible. But they reckoned without their host: within two years of that event I was returned to the Town Council mainly by the votes of the very men who had lent themselves to this offence, and returned too over the head of a leading publican, the most intimate friend of the brewer who was at the bottom of the effigy business, and who was a party to giving money and beer to have me thus insulted and disgraced. The fishermen chaired me through the very streets in which they had formerly attempted to disgrace me.

That then was the reason why, when raised to the chief seat in the town, I determined that the rattle, which had been the companion of my obscurity and shame, should be the companion of my distinction. I could see no use in my being mayor of the borough, if by my exaltation the cause with which my life was associated was not honoured. I therefore of set purpose and by design made it a conspicuous feature in my election. If in the procession of the Lord Mayors of London, not unfrequently there is some distinctive feature of the trade they have followed characterizing the show, then where was the incongruity of my giving the teetotal rattle a place of honour when I took upon me the office of chief magistrate of Scarborough? The history of that rattle is the distinctive feature of my life, and of which I am infinitely more proud than of the mayor's chain. That it should have been rescued from obscurity after more than forty years' burial is in itself a fact in temperance history worth a permanent record; and surely if Major Chard and his companion officer covered their names with undying fame for having rescued the colours of their regiment from the wreck and ruin of Rorke's Drift, I may be pardoned the jubilant feeling begotten by the association of this relic with my appointment to the highest office the town could give.

By what rule and under what law does the warrior glory in his sword, by which he has won his way to national honour and national distinction, though that way may have been through a sea of blood, and over the bodies of the dying and the dead, and I am to be forbidden the recognition of the insignia of what has in it my life's glory, and through the instrumentality of which life, blessing, and salvation have been carried to hundreds of homes? I know that the preaching of the Cross was, in its introduction, to "the Jews a stumbling-block, and to the Greeks foolishness," but that was because of their ignorant and blind unbelief. "The natural man discerneth not the things of God, neither indeed can he." It is now as it was then: those who already know too much to need to learn any more, with those who are more concerned about what somebody else should think than they are about what they themselves should do, see no propriety in this deed. But what is that to me? I have counted the cost, and can pay the price, and if they never before knew the value I put on teetotalism they know now. There is even now too much disposition to treat teetotalism as men treat an old glove, a thing to be done with or without, to be put on or be put off at convenience. I have not so learned teetotalism, neither do I mean that anybody else shall so learn it from me. Social status has its claims, and worldly honour its advantages, and I am not indifferent to either; but I would not sacrifice my designation of temperance advocate for any title the Queen of these realms could confer upon me.

The washy, trashy proceedings of some teetotallers as they get out of their original rut, has been a scandal to themselves and a hindrance to others, and it is high time such men were made to see their vacillation and weakness. My life is at war with all such, and I determined on the threshold of my year of office there should be no mistake about my position and purposes.

The whole system of liquordom is one huge mass of mischief, waste, and depravity, and there can be no middle course with those who work iniquity by a law. What is wanted is fidelity. We have the facts, we have the knowledge. There is no authority in politics, nor in science, nor in religion, who has a leg to stand upon in the presence of our experience and claims. Then what wait we for? The land is ours: let us go up and possess it.

CHAPTER XXI.

MY ARRIVAL IN LONDON.

MY arrival in London on the 20th of May, 1837, opened out to me to some extent a new life and a new world. True, I had then travelled freely, and had added to my experience of men and things considerably; but in many cases my arrival had been anticipated, while in others, though standing alone, there were not those overwhelming circumstances and deterring influences which the sight of London presented.

Descending from Highgate Hill on the outside of the Northampton coach that fine May morning, as I viewed the city in its extent and vastness before me, I felt what a mite in that great mass of moving, bustling life I should be; in the myriads of its population not a face that I knew, nor a locality I could spot.

The quiet Quaker home I had just left filled my mind with memories of peace and loving-kindness, while the world, the unknown world into which I was about to be cast, looked a labyrinth of streets and a maze of mobs.

It has often been said that no wilderness is more lonely, and no desert more desolate, than is London to one who can see light in no eye, and feel warmth and welcome from no heart. I had been then two years before the public, but my movements had been in a rut, and I was therefore known but in a limited circle. The public prints of that time only noticed us to ridicule us, and I had not learned, neither have I now learned, to advertise my wares, and make known my approach with a flourish of trumpets.

I was dropped from that coach in the neighbourhood of the General Post-office, very much as an orange-peel is dropped in the street by boys who have got all that they can out of what it contained. All that I knew was that there would be some important meetings during the ensuing week. They were advertised in the *Temperance Intelligencer*, and I knew that the publisher of it had a place of business in Bartholomew Close. I made for that, and Mr. Pasco (the gentleman in question) made me a shake-down for the night. He had just enough knowledge of me to realize that I was the person bearing the name I own, and that I had at least done no discredit to the cause. The next day was Sunday, and I found my way to the City Road Wesleyan Chapel, but, oh! the mockery (as it seemed to me) of the early part of that service. They read a considerable portion of the Church prayers, but during the whole of that portion of the service there was not a moment's peace. The people never ceased coming in, and there was such a want of a prayerful and devout combination that my heart was sick. On my way to the chapel the exhibition of Sabbath desecration, in open gin-shops, and public markets, and noisy conveyances, appalled me. I had never before, even in my wildest days, seen a Sunday that had in it so little of the sabbath. What would I not have given for the calm retreat of the home chapel, and the music of the village church bells, on that first Sabbath in London? We all know how much depends on first impressions. These were mine, and I fear they are only a sample of what hundreds of young men from the country feel on their first acquaintance with London life. Church and chapel-going people in London, as well as in other large centres, have much to learn and much to do yet, before the whirlpool of city life can be so utilized as to touch with loving-kindness the floating particles which life's battles cast in their way. How often the young man from the country is made or *marred* for life by his first week's experiences in town! and not less so with young women. They are very susceptible just then, and a kind word and a right direction, oh, how good it is! Do parents think as they ought to think, of what these young people *miss* and so much need at these critical times? and would it not be a most religious service, as well as a great national blessing, did we more than we do, when people are from home and amongst strangers, make it our business, to some extent, to supply the lack? I have known a few instances where this has been done, and the return has been lasting gratitude and honoured memories. I owe much to it myself, and if I lay stress on it, it is because I am speaking that which I know.

Monday, the 21st of May, was the day appointed for the first anniversary of the South London auxiliary of the New British and Foreign Temperance Society, and the meeting was held in the Assembly Rooms of "The Horns" Tavern, Kennington. Mr. John Meredith was the secretary; he was also one of the secretaries of the parent society. At that meeting I made this good man's acquaintance, and a friendship was commenced which continued uninterrupted to his death. I know no man to whom I am more indebted for moral life and religious care than the late John Meredith. We talk of "dead men turning in their coffins" when certain things are said and done; if such a thing were true, John Meredith would have turned in his coffin many a time, as people of to-day have talked of *their* religious temperance, in disparagement of the past experiences.

James Silk Buckingham, Esq., M.P., was chairman, and the Rev. James Sharman and Rev. G. Clayton were amongst the speakers. The list of speakers was full and long, and my name was not one of them, so I sat on the platform with Mr. John Wood, a Quaker gentleman from Barnsley, whose acquaintance I had made a few weeks before. He was the only one present who had any practical knowledge of me. He named me to Mr. Meredith as one likely to be of use, and acceptable to the meeting if an opening could be made for me. An opening was made for twenty minutes. I went off like a rocket! My youth, my dialect, my experience, was an astonishment to the Londoners; and the friendships then formed, and the favours then shown, have been continued to this day.

Though the friends of my youth are gone, there is no part of the country in which I am more at home than in London, and no part in which I am better pleased to labour.

The next day I was selected to second the first resolution at the great meeting in Exeter Hall. Earl Stanhope was chairman of that meeting, and my position as speaker was between the Rev. J. Edwards, of Brighton, and the Rev. James Sharman, of Surrey Chapel. Those who were present at that meeting never forgot it, and my fortune, such as it was, as a temperance speaker, was made from that time.

I became the agent of the society, and continued to be so until I left London to reside in Scarborough, in the spring of 1849. Since then I have not been in the employment of any society, but have worked in connection with all as an independent man. As such I have frequently gone through Ireland and Scotland. I have also visited the United States, and been almost incessantly employed in my own land.

When I spoke in Exeter Hall, I had never to my knowledge *seen* a peer of the realm, say nothing about addressing one, so that I was rather bothered, and did not know how to do it. The countess was also by his side, and we had a very aristocratic platform. It was the first time an earl had been on a teetotal platform, and the people "came out to see." It was a very big and a very fashionable meeting. I knew that if I once got off I could *go*, but the start was the trouble. I often stumble a little at starting, and I believe there have been cases when people have gone out of the meeting almost at once, because (as they subsequently said) I seemed as if I could not say "Bo!" to a goose. A hissing gas distracts me, a noisy baby ruins me, a giggling girl drives me mad, and a vacant stare and a listless demeanour fills my blood with wormwood and gall! I never play at temperance, it is the business of my life, and I can neither afford to be laughed at nor trifled with; hence my desire that when I go to do a work, the conditions needful for the work should be secured.

The meeting in Exeter Hall was to my mind: the people were not only there to *see*, but to *hear*. I never speak to the press, I speak to the people. I am not influenced by how I may look in *print*, so much as how I may be felt in the *heart*. When Saul was made king, we are told, "There went with him a band of men whose hearts God had touched." That is what I want, and in this particular I have not been disappointed.

I don't know if there be a man left now who took any active part in that meeting but myself. Certainly most of them have passed away years ago, and those who know me now cannot be surprised if at times I feel somewhat alone.

In rising to speak on the occasion in question, the people called out, "Name!" They meant by that, "Who is he?" for my name had been announced distinctly enough. I bobbed my head to the chairman, (very much after the fashion in which the urchin of "Hodge" bobs his head to the village squire), and then tried to forget him. To the people I said, "You want to know who I am, what I am, and how I got here,—listen. The country is divided into three towns—the *Moderation* Town, its dangers and difficulties; the *Drunken* Town, its madness and miseries; the *Teetotal* Town, its triumphs and blessings. I have lived in them all, and know the people, and what they do."

The sight of that meeting was a new thing to me. I had never before seen such a mass of well-dressed and respectable-looking people. My fears and misgivings all left me, and I held them for forty-five minutes as between my finger and thumb. The broad brimmed hat, and the plain "Friend's bonnet" stood out prominently in that crowd; the sight gave me comfort and courage. I knew enough of the people whom that dress represented, to feel that I must have many friends and sympathisers there, and my soul was fired, and my tongue loosened, as they have seldom been fired or loosened either before or since. The memory of that day lives with me now, and many have

MY ARRIVAL IN LONDON.

been the blessings poured on my head in connection with that meeting.

There were other meetings during the same week, large and influential, at all of which I spoke in company with men of note and eloquence, whose friendships I then formed, and that gave me a name and a status I could not under other circumstances have attained. The world is full of people unknown and unappreciated, and yet they have in them a power that would move multitudes did circumstances give them the opportunity. It is often the accident of circumstance which makes the difference between one man and another. The *twenty minutes* given me as a favour and an experiment at "The Horns" Tavern begot the resolve to have me the following day, and the following day made it impossible to ignore me as a teacher of temperance, and my name and work were nationalised from that moment.

The different phases of the Temperance Movement have their value in this fact, if in no other,—they bring to the front men who in the absence of them would never have been seen or heard of; true, "many a flower is born to blush unseen, and waste its sweetness on the desert air," but in no condition in life is that less likely to be tolerated than in the Temperance enterprise.

This may seem very precocious and presumptive, but it is not because of these characteristics, so much as because of the earnest purpose and determined will possessing the minds of men, who have a conviction of the soundness of their faith, and the wisdom of their practice. There can be no greater mistake than to imagine (as many do) that the Temperance Reformation is the result of infatuation and wild imaginings. Nobody could be more sober in their thoughts, and honest in their convictions, than are the prominent men in the movement. Surely the cry of "crotchet-mongers," and "impractical whims," so frequently thrown at us, can only spring from the grossest ignorance and blindest prejudice on the part of those who so deport themselves. What personal advantage can come to a temperance reformer by his public teaching, excepting so far as that teaching results in national weal and public good?

There is no law against a quiet individual abstinence, and he who so acts will get through life with more profit in his business, and more esteem to his person, than falls to the lot of him who is persistent in his teaching, and active in his exertions to make proselytes of others. Many so quietly abstain, just as many would not for their very lives have it known what politics they are, or for whom they had voted; but it can scarcely be considered true manhood so to live, nor good citizenship so to act. What are convictions worth if they cannot fructify? and what is life but the merest serfdom and vassalage, when bound by the will of others, and enslaved by the fear of offence? Perhaps there is no platform in the country from which individual freedom and truest manhood is more constantly and more freely taught, than that on which the temperance advocate stands, and I have ever felt it a privilege possessed, and a victory won, to have a footing on that platform. That is the reason why we have laboured by all waters, and compassed all lands, sowing our seed in the morning, and in the evening not withholding our hand, not knowing which shall prosper, this or that.

The post of the morning on which I write this chapter brings me a pamphlet, written by a gentleman living at Campbeltown, N.B., a pamphlet in which men are urged in most earnest and telling terms to attend to the most important things. Accompanying that pamphlet there is a letter, in which I am told that the writer heard me in 1836, in a little village near Garstang, Lancashire. He was then but a child, and was taken to the meeting by the hand of his father. Thoughts were begotten to him at that meeting, which live with him now, and helped to make him what he is.

Now I know not this man, and should not have known the fact but for the communication now before me, which comes while I write, and I therefore refer to it. These things are constantly happening to me, and they are the sunlight in my evening sky.

The Smithfield martyrs are historical, and when I got to London I must visit the scene of their sufferings. In doing so, I felt I would like to give my message on the same spot. Crowds of people were often gathered there on the Sabbath for various purposes, many of them were drovers, and men engaged in various ways attending Smithfield Market. People would assemble in small knots and groups, and listen to oracles on all sorts of topics; so I thought it would not be a bad place to have a talk on temperance. In the month of June, in the year 1837, I held on Sunday afternoon the first temperance meeting in Smithfield. That was continued for some few years by myself and others. Mr. Hart, who at the time was the keeper of a temperance hotel in Aldersgate Street, was my companion, and he worked at that business so long as the meetings were held.

On the second Sunday, in my absence, he had been interfered with by the police and locked up in the compters' prison. There was some false alarm about chartism, I think, and a proclamation had been issued forbidding public meetings, and in connection with that Mr. Hart was taken to prison, but soon set at liberty when the circumstances were explained. On that same Sunday I was holding a meeting on Tottenham Green. W. Janson, Esq., was my chairman, and good Joseph Eaton, of Bristol, assisted me as a speaker.

These two good men have long since gone to their rest, but how good and how true they were! and it should never be forgotten how much it cost men in their position to be good and true to us *then*.

The suburbs of London were about as difficult to work as any part of the country, and the disturbance and rudeness at our meetings was often most trying. We seemed to be left so much in the hands of loafers, hangers-on, and rowdies. Tottenham, Wandsworth, West Drayton, Barnet and Uxbridge, often troubled us much, and many other places which need not be named. They are very different, though, now, and have been so for years; yet it will be well for our workers to prepare for another onslaught, for we may depend upon it the drink traffic will not throw down its arms without a struggle, and if I am not mistaken in that particular we have only just begun—" the beginning of the end."

The prosperity of the country for the last thirty years has been such as to keep the drink traffic in a very active and healthy condition. Immense fortunes have been made, and increased value has been given to everything belonging to the business. While that was so, they did not trouble themselves about the little leakages made by us on their business. But it is not so now; there are fearful gaps opening out, and wasteful running away of profit; they see it, they feel it, the licenses are losing their value, and the thoughtless multiplication of drinking shops is an offence to the general public. The whole regiment of licensed victuallers have been brought to a halt by a national voice. The "stand at ease" position does not suit their purpose, and the "march forward" will not be allowed. "Shoulder arms" will soon be the cry, and "fix bayonets" their resolve; but will they fight with a nation's life, or will they die for a nation's weal? That remains to be seen.

I had scarcely got launched on the London platform in the year 1837 when I was called back home to Lancashire, to witness the death of my sweet and blessedly happy little wife. She had had much of the sunshine of a religious life since her husband had become a teetotaller, and her death was an event not forgotten by those who witnessed it.

CHAPTER XXII.

LONDON.

LONDON not only became my centre but my home; and as we had in addition to an active parent society four auxiliaries with good working executives, meetings multiplied in every direction. There was South London, acting south of the Thames; North London, taking Finsbury, Hackney, Kingsland, and Islington; East London, taking Stepney, Whitechapel, Shoreditch, Limehouse, Poplar, etc.; and West London, working St. Pancras, Marylebone, Paddington, Chelsea, and Westminster. Meetings were by the score, in some weeks by hundreds, and thousands and tens of thousands were reached in that way by sound temperance teaching.

During the years from 1837 to 1845 London and the neighbourhood was thoroughly worked, and there has never been either before or since more earnest work done in the interest of temperance than was done in those years. What we do now makes a greater show, and meets with more notice and acknowledgment, simply because we have got the ear of the public and the recognition of the press, but for sterling and enduring work, the period in question has never been surpassed, I don't know that it has been equalled. I speak now of the ordinary and systematic teaching; hundreds of men all over London made it their meat and drink to do this work. Good old Dr. Hawkins and energetic Dr. Oxley, in the north and east of London, were never weary; and that grand old man, the Rev. Dr. Pye Smith, was a tower of strength. The Rev. J. Sharman, and the Rev. John Howard Hinton, and the Rev. C. Stovel, with the Rev. Dr. Burns of Paddington, made teetotalism a feature in the pulpit, and a power in the pew.

The meetings in London proper were never much disturbed; we had from the first usually an attentive and a respectful hearing; and even in its lowest neighbourhoods, such as the Mint, the Borough, Ratcliffe Highway, Spitalfields, and St. Giles's, we were listened to with gladness. I have never been rudely insulted in London, and never robbed, and I know no people more readily pleased nor more quickly influenced than the residents in the metropolis; and I think I am correct in saying that my labours in London have even been more immediate in their returns and more pleasing in their results than in any other part of the country. They have often been in out-of-the-way places, that is to say if anything can be out of the way in London, but they have invariably been near enough to some one to beget a response.

I remember walking one thick foggy night across London from Hoxton to Pimlico (this was in the winter of 1837), over what was then known as the wooden bridge in Pimlico. In a room made out of two cottages for a preaching place near the water that bridge crossed, I addressed a meeting. There would be about fifty people present. I stood on the floor on a level with the audience. In front of me was a man, rough in manner, and cursed by drink; he had on a dirty flannel jacket, his wife clinging to him and trying to keep him quiet. He got as near to me as he could for my nose, and kept putting questions and making remarks. In my speech I spoke of the value of a praying mother. This man had had one whom he had long forgotten and dishonoured. That night his home was a single room, and his bed shavings. The rags he and his children wore by day were their covering by night, and the gaol and even worse consequences threatened him. He signed the pledge, and never wavered afterwards. That man was James McCurry, the Chelsea bricklayer, and who does not know what a life he subsequently lived, and the work he did? I walked back to Hoxton after that meeting through a fearful fog, for it had thickened during the evening, and I know not how I managed, but I must have been more than two hours on the road, for my host had given me up as lost.

In subsequent years, when I at times felt somewhat depressed, I would walk across the park from St. John's Wood to Pimlico to take a cup of tea with James and his sunny wife, in a good and respectable house, one of a row of substantial buildings, his own property. Then it was we would count up our mercies, and talk of the time when we first met in that humble room over the wooden bridge. What a contrast was here! What light and blessing came out of that dimly lighted preaching room, through that densely foggy night, on the 8th of November, 1837! and no man felt it and acknowledged it more than did James McCurry. In his heart was a well of water springing up to eternal life, and he never to the day of his death forgot the pit out of which he had been digged, nor the hole of the rock from whence he had been hewn. If there be such a thing as life from the dead (and some of us think there is), surely it was here. There was no restraint between Mr. McCurry and myself, we talked freely on all subjects affecting the body and the soul, our hearts warming within us by the way. He has closed his account. After living for many years in comfort and respect, he died at a ripe old age—eighty-four, having done for the last forty years of his life a noble and generous work. The meeting on a Sunday afternoon at White Styles, Chelsea, carried on for many years by him, was a Bethsaida to many. There was a plainness at times about the utterances of Mr. McCurry which made one feel as if walking on the edge of a precipice, but no one who knew him could fail to see how transparent and honest and pure minded he was. His earnestness led him into great warmth of expression at times, and when he got on to the religious side of his life, his exaltation of the Saviour knew no bounds, and the Bible was a book beyond all price. That we have infidel teetotallers, and always have had, there is no doubt, and that these in many cases have been among our firmest and most abiding friends is an indisputable fact. It is therefore false in theory, and contrary to truth, to teach that teetotalism cannot live and thrive apart from the grace of God. Men might as well say that food will not nourish the body unless sanctified by the word of God and by prayer, as say that teetotalism is useless without religion.

There are the laws of life as well as the graces of the Spirit, and he who acts in accordance with the laws of life, will, at least to that extent, be saved.

On one occasion Mr. McCurry was a speaker at the anniversary of the Westminster Broadway Society. One of the committee of that society was not what is called orthodox in his religious views, and Mr. McCurry during his speech had laboured to show how much the world was indebted to the Bible. The sceptical member, who was on the platform, took exception to this teaching, and went on to say, "that in his opinion the man who had invented *gas*, had done more for the world than the man who had circulated the Bible." Of course that was a firebrand in the crowd, and produced much uneasiness, and threatened to beget disastrous results. My friend Mr. G. C. Campbell, who was on the platform, and was in his day the idol of the London temperance meetings, and never failed to arrest attention, and please an audience, rose to pour oil on the troubled waters. In doing so he said, "Now, my friends, don't get excited, but calm yourselves. It is simply a difference of opinion, and you know the sentiment, 'May difference of opinion never alter friendship.' My friend Mr. McCurry is a religious man, and believes the Bible. My friend Mr. —— is not a religious man, but he is a good teetotaller, and believes in *gas*. If Mr. McCurry were dying he would send for a minister, if our other friend were dying he would send for a *gas-fitter!*" The effect was electrical; the meeting was convulsed, and harmony and good-will were restored.

The following letter, dated London, 10th July, 1837, will give some idea of how my time was then occupied; and it will be seen, that even so far back as *that*, I had made the acquaintance of the Mint in the Borough, and done some work in it.

Preston Temperance Advocate.

"Dear Friend,—

"During the last week I have held nine meetings, and distributed 2000 tracts; and large as London is, I hope before long there will not be a soul in it who has not heard of teetotalism. The following is an account of my last week's labours:—On Monday, after giving out 400 tracts, I held a meeting in the Association Chapel: Mr. Gilbert in the chair. On Tuesday, I attended a meeting in the British School, Red Lion Square: John Hull, Esq., chairman. After this I had a most excellent meeting in Harp Alley, the very seat of the enemy. Wednesday evening, I spoke in Providence Chapel, City Road. Thursday, a crowded meeting in Providence Chapel, Southwark, Borough; Mr. Charlton, from Bristol, and myself spoke, and Mr. Gilbert presided. On Friday, I held a meeting in the Mint, and distributed a quantity of tracts; several drunkards joined. On Saturday morning, distributed 400 tracts on the Margate steamer; and in the afternoon, accompanied by several friends, went to Greenwich. On our way in the steam-boat we preached up abstinence, and the consequence was, no intoxicating liquors could be sold, although they cried out 'brown stout, ale, and porter.' We held the first teetotal meeting ever held in Greenwich Park, and a good one it was. Returning home I distributed tracts, and gave admonitions at the dramshops. On Sunday, an open-air meeting was held at Tottenham, addressed by W. Janson, junr., Esq., J. Eaton, Esq., from Bristol, and myself.

"We have begun to hold out-door meetings in London; at one of these, two of the speakers were taken to prison, but were immediately released by the magistrate, who gave them every encouragement, and declared they could hold their meetings there at any time.

"T. WHITTAKER.

"LONDON, 10*th July*, 1837."

It was during this time that I made the acquaintance of my friend Mr. Thomas Hudson. We were thrown together in a private hotel in the city of London, both young men, both active teetotallers. I do not now know another man, who came so near to me as he then did, who still lives. We have journeyed on very much together, in mutual esteem and warm friendship, from that time to this. There is much of oneness in us, though very dissimilar, and in each case, I think I may say, tracks have been made in the path of life, from which others taking knowledge, would take heart and find safety. He is a most social and entertaining man; in speech most chaste and correct, in life most honourable and trustworthy; he has done a steady, useful, and graceful work on the temperance platform: his selections and quotations are conscientiously rendered; he is no trifler, but a sound logician and sensible speaker. In a word, he is an instructor of the people.

That he is at times most witty and full of humour none will deny, but in his fun there is no nonsense, and he abhors vulgarity as he does dirt. Some, who know him not, think him pedantic. That is not so; he is careful and precise, and would have been better known and appreciated had his audiences been a little more advanced in book-lore and classic taste. Personally I owe him much, for he has a faultless diction and a well-stored mind.

On one occasion he had before him a respectable and very appreciative audience in the Assembly Rooms at Uxbridge: John Hull was chairman. Mr. Hull was somewhat peculiar in his habits, and he had a detestation of late meetings. Sentiment he had none, of matters of fact he had much.

The meeting was after Mr. Hudson's heart, and he waxed very eloquent, which when circumstances were favourable he could well do; the peroration was one of his best, and full of beauty, working up to an exciting climax. Mr. Hull, who was a very stout man and full of colour, in the midst of this peroration, jumped up, and taking out his watch in the face of the audience, and touching Mr. Hudson on the shoulder, exclaimed, "That will *do*, Thomas; if I were thee, I would not fatigue myself!" Nothing could be more ridiculous, and the chairman, whether Mr. Hudson did or not, made an impression which has never been forgotten.

On the Saturday night I closed the week's work to which the letter just quoted refers, by visiting the district of Ratcliffe Highway, taking stock of the public-houses, dramshops, and dancing saloons, which abounded in that neighbourhood. Two gentlemen were with me, one of them a Quaker, dressed in the true orthodox style. In one place, the other gentleman and myself found our way into a long room filled with sailors and women. The drinking, the dancing, the language, the singing, made it a pandemonium. We were shocked. Coming out, we described what we had seen to our Quaker companion. He expressed a strong desire to see for himself, but the style of his dress was so marked and singular that he would be sure to be noticed, and he knew not what mischief might follow. But he was bent on going in, so I went with him down a dark lane, and made sufficient exchange in our clothes to, in some measure, destroy the peculiarity of his appearance.

It was a success, but he was horrified, and when he came out trembled from head to foot. He had never seen anything like that before, neither had I. Poor man! I am not sure that it had not some influence on his mind, for it seemed to lose its balance after that. We were at the same hotel together, and I occasionally joked him on the virtue of the Friends, saying, "Ah! when you go into doubtful places, or do anything wrong, you borrow other people's clothes, and save the credit of the society."

Mr. John Meredith, of 3, Durham Place, Lambeth, of whom I have already spoken, was one of the most remarkable men I ever knew. He had, some little time before my arrival in London, retired from business, and was devoting his life, to an extent I never saw in any other man, to philanthropic and Christian work. The days, and months, and years, which he gave without fee or reward, to "do good and communicate," was a feature in his life few men could understand, and consequently not always appreciate, but no man could more diligently work for profit in any business than he worked in the Temperance Movement. Early and late, night and day, did he consecrate his life to this work. His house was a receptacle for the helpless and forlorn, and not unfrequently for those who had a passion for drink, but who were otherwise refined, educated, and respectable. I have known cases where ladies of high connection have sought the shelter of his home, and the piety of his household, that they might break the trammels that bound them, and they have lived under his roof for months, and have subsequently walked in sobriety and freedom as others. Those were days when no special provision was made for such, as is the case now; yet John Meredith saw the need and did the work, when the facts and possibility were unknown, save to those who were immediately concerned. He had also a prophet's bed, and men from all climes, and in pursuit of all sorts of benevolent, patriotic, philanthropic, and Christian work, found a resting-place and a welcome there. He was unbounded in his resources, and marvellous in his ministerial abilities. He was punctilious to a fault, and his rule of life, to strangers severe, was never broken. There was no such thing as "no time" for family devotions night and morning in that establishment. I was seldom permitted to go in or come out (and no man did it more frequently) without an audible and tangible acknowledgment of God. With him the gates of heaven were always ajar, and he was ever in intimate relationship with the inhabitants thereof. He spoke to them in the unseen world, as a man would with a familiar friend. There was no irreverence, there was no presumption, in all this; it was his daily bread, his native air, and he literally carried out the injunction, "In all thy ways acknowledge Him, and He will direct thy steps:" he believed it, and acted accordingly.

There were times when this sort of service seemed out of place; but knowing the man as I did, I seldom failed to be benefited by anything that was done. On one occasion, an important meeting had been appointed at Highgate, and a well-to-do gentleman living there, and a relation by marriage to Mr. Meredith, invited a somewhat fashionable party to meet at his house to tea. I was late in my arrival, having to come up from the country, where I had been holding some meetings. Several handsome subscriptions had been given to me for the society, including a cheque for twenty pounds from Mr. Grant, the banker of Leighton Buzzard. This was a very unusual sum at that time, and when I got into the drawing-room amidst the blaze of light, and surrounded by a posse of ladies and gentlemen mostly strangers to me, Mr. Meredith introduced me, and in doing so announced what I had been doing, and what I had brought back with me, and called upon the entire company to fall down on their knees and thank God for my success. They did so.

On another occasion, a great gathering had been held on Kennington Common, one Sunday afternoon, in connection with Father Mathew's visit to, and work in, London. After the meeting some dozen ladies and gentlemen returned to tea at Mr. Meredith's. After tea it had become too late to attend any place of worship, but Mr. Meredith was equal to the occasion. After reading and singing, every one present was asked to say a prayer, beginning at one corner, and in rotation going round the room. This was a terrible ordeal for some of them, and I knew at least two ladies who were present, who mutually agreed while on their knees to resist the claim; not that they were less religious, but more conscientious than some of the rest. Surely the religious condition of the heart, and the earnest purposes of the mind, are not to be judged by our volubility or readiness to confess. Confession is often after all hypocritical and unreal as was Topsy's, and prayer is not unfrequently most prevailing when consisting only of "the falling of a tear, or the heaving of a sigh."

Mr. Meredith was a great rule maker; but though fixed in his habits, he had great variety in his proceedings, and the morning and evening household devotions were frequently most interesting and profitable.

I remember at one time before reading, every one present, parents, children, servants, and sojourners, had to relate some kind act or deed done to somebody or thing during the day. It will be seen how the thought would sometimes beget the deed, and when some ten or a dozen persons had made known how in some way they had served their day and generation, the combination gave variety of expression in prayer and produced mutual sympathy and goodwill. I don't know that I should go into these details, were it not for the flippant utterances occasionally made on temperance platforms concerning the spirit and work of such men as the late John Meredith and his compeers. "The rut" in which they ran, if not baptized with blood, was bathed in tears and sanctified by the word of God and with prayer, and it is but a lame excuse at best for the Church of God and the ministers of Christ to seek to cover their past neglect of duty and scandalous indifference to the Temperance Cause, by seeking to point out the imperfections and shortcomings of the men who did their best, while *they* themselves slept. Mr. Meredith was one of the officials of Park Street Chapel, Southwark, when Mr. Spurgeon was invited to take up his abode in London, and had religion enough to be a teetotaller before the famous and honoured preacher had learned the A B C of the question. I went with him to hear the boy preacher, who was at the time on the Temperance Question as dark as midnight.

CHAPTER XXIII.

THREE "GEORGES."

THE three "Georges" who proved themselves men of mark, and did good service to the movement, owed much to Mr. Meredith, G. C. Campbell, G. Howlet, and G. Cruikshank.

Mr. Campbell was a very young man, of attractive appearance, and active business life. Living south of the Thames, he was constantly in connection with Mr. Meredith, and in our early days no part of the metropolis was so thoroughly worked as South London, and that characteristic continues to this day.

There is now more moral and religious power and political influence on that side of the water (as we call it) than can be found in any other part of London, on behalf of temperance. That John Meredith laid the foundation for all this, no one in possession of the facts will question. Dr. Ellis, the Rev. James Sharman, and others, contributed to this result, there can be no doubt. George Howlet, the coal-heaver, came to land early, and did genial and lasting work, and he, with his companion and friend Mr. Campbell, filled South London, and many other parts as well, with gladness. The two "Georges" were like twins, for years inseparable, and their spirit was most unselfish. To know them was to love them. There are many men we like, but there is a difference between liking a man and loving him. There is often much that is purely selfish in our likings; but when we love a man, we give as well as take, there is a reciprocity, a oneness, a fellowship. George Campbell knew everybody and everything; he always knew where to go, and what to do, and in his presence London was never dull. He could get sunshine out of a London fog, and be merry as a cricket on a warm hearthstone, when plodding through the pelting rain and floating slush of a London street. To meet him was to meet a sunbeam, and to talk with him was like a summer's day that knew no night. No man left such a blank on the London platform, and made such an aching void at his death, as did G. C. Campbell. My last companionship with him was in the gallery of the House of Commons, and the vote taken that day on some temperance question troubled me much. George was amazed at my excited condition, and went home and wrote a very witty and humorous paper on the circumstances. I think it appeared in *The Temperance Star*, and was remarkably clever. Poor fellow! that was the last paper he ever wrote.

George Howlet, as may be supposed, having been a coal-heaver on the Thames, and having fallen into the habits common to his class, was a wonderful power in our meetings. He had an experience which told well, and rising subsequently to the position of coal merchant and van proprietor (which he did), that put him beyond the reach of the oppressions of the trade, and gave him an influence with the masses few men possessed. George had great physical power, and was withal comely and genial, so that *usually* he kept his audience in the best of tempers.

One day, at the Obelisk at the end of the Blackfriars

Road, a point where at one time our meetings were constantly held, a man in the crowd kept up a running interruption. He was a big bullying fellow, and as speaker after speaker had very little power and not much presence, the man got very offensive and defiant. Mr. Howlet at this point took charge of the meeting. The man continued his silly interruption. George turning to him, said, " Now I will have a little private conversation with you. In the first place," said he, "if you have any sense in you, and will come this way like a man, and let it out in the face of the people, we will listen to you; but if you will neither do that nor be quiet where you are, I have a shot in my right arm which, if fired, will settle the dispute in a minute."

The man continued his interruption. George beckoned the crowd to make way for him to where the man stood. They did so. He descended and faced him. "Now," said he, "as I cannot drive sense into you, I will knock you down!" The man squared up to George, but he was heels over head in quick sticks. He pulled himself together again as well as he could, and sneaked away from the grinning crowd, and George went back to his stand and finished his speech.

That was muscular Christianity, of which George made modest profession, but in which, if needs be, he could do creditable practice.

If bishops consecrate fighting colours, and clergymen lead their congregations in thanksgivings when our arms have been triumphant, though death and desolation follow in their train, there cannot be much objection to our expressing our gratitude for occasional success such as that rendered at the Obelisk.

Mr. Howlet kept a good horse and a smart trap, and

never objected to give a neighbour or friend a spin round the park, or a drive into the country, if he felt it would cheer their spirits, or improve their health; and if persons so circumstanced would more frequently think of some one to whom such a service would be as a fresh May morning, how much gloom and sadness would be lifted from many a heart.

George Cruikshank had a face never to be forgotten. He was not only a caricaturist, but a character. In looking at him when in good form, there could be seen, not only his *own*, but nearly all the faces and figures he had ever sketched.

He was a most versatile and industrious man. The work he did in his own profession was marvellous, while his pleasure in it, and application to it, seemed to be marrow in his bones. That he was a valuable trophy to our cause none will question, and few, if any, when fairly won (which he was), have been more sincere and more indefatigable.

It was no easy matter for a man in his line of life, and with companions and associates such as his, to break with the customs of his class, but he did it, and he could "a tale unfold," and in safe circles occasionally did it. What a history he had of professional wrecks, and of blighted geniuses!

George Cruikshank was for many years a constant figure in our movement, and a welcome light at our meetings. He was so juvenile too. At eighty he could dance a hornpipe with vigour, and amazing elasticity. That he did not do so, was simply because, when the humour was on, there was no room on the platform to do justice to the subject.

There was a strange mixture at times in his teaching,

but he was ever tolerated. When he took the clergy in hand, and ventured on the wine question, then it was one felt as if dragged to the edge of a precipice, and we had to hold on with both hands. His theology was peculiar rather than profound, and his orthodoxy more muscular than merciful. To see him describe the clergy in their treatment of the Temperance Question,—for he never got below a full beneficed parson, and not often below a bishop, or a dean,—was a thing to be remembered.

I remember him once in Exeter Hall doing so. He had them in the character of a number of jackdaws hopping round a trencher, which had on it something looking like food, and of which they were anxious to partake, but afraid. They waited for one another, they were very suspicious; he threw his body into the exact attitude one would suppose birds in such a case, to be. The meeting was convulsed. I can see him yet; the picture is as vividly before me now, as anything he ever in pencil drew. Nobody ever heard this "George" urge the people to sign the pledge. He had not done it himself, but he was as true as those who did, notwithstanding. When he got on to the question of pledging, his views were very novel, if not astounding. He would draw himself up in an attitude of self-reliance and aristocratic dignity, then placing his hand on his heart, would appeal to Heaven and say, "I am pledged to the Almighty on the faith and honour of a gentleman." Of course, against that arrangement there was no appeal. These were the three "Georges" of whom I meant to write when I commenced this chapter. They had each though very unlike, much similarity. There was an individuality about them, and such marked characteristics, that no temperance gallery would be complete in which they were not. The social gatherings and annual soirées of the National Temperance League, which even now are very attractive, and much appreciated, to many of us are but skeletons, in memory of the presence of these genial spirits, and pleasant faces; but it must be so, as time gathers in from our ranks those who have served their day and done their work.

We are not by any means destitute of workers now, notwithstanding the fearful gaps in our ranks in some cases. "The Georges" especially, even on the old battlefield, are to the front as of yore. South London never was, and I hope never will be, in the rear, but always to the front, in this battle; and it is no little consolation to myself, that from the early morning of the temperance day I have had a part and a share in the work. The seed has been put into good ground, and has taken deep root. It has grown steadily, and is therefore strong, not turned by every wind, nor washed away by every flood. Those who have been touched by "The Bitter Cry of Outcast London," should talk to the Rev. *George* Murphy, the Rev. *George* W. McCree, *George* Howlet (the second), *George* Ling, of the Central Hall, Bishopsgate Street, and *George* Thorniloe, of the Barbican.* These men know something of the slums, and these "Georges" have done, and are now doing, a work amongst the people who have landed, and who usually *do* land in such quarters, the records of which, if properly set forth, would take the breath from the panting, poking parsimony of much that just now

* Poor George Thorniloe also gone before my ink is dry. A great loss to the cause is his death.

seems to astonish and puzzle the people. The complaint is *not* the house, nor the street—these are secondary causes, these are *effects*, they are the ordinary results of a wasted life and abused means. The cure, as Professor Huxley has said, *must* come from *within.*

Of course, the secret traps and blazing ginshops contribute to and keep alive this festering mass of misery and squalor; and no people can possibly rid themselves of the intolerable filth, and foul indecencies, which visit these poor wretches, who have no resources but the rags and dregs of a cursed life, and a crushed existence. There must therefore be a hand put forth from without, and while the "Georges" are touching and training the hidden world, and the inner life, we must demand the surrender of these citadels of death out of the hands of liquordom and landlordism. Men *must* be taught, that the money that buys beer will buy bread, and that four or six shillings a week (or even more than that) *now* left at the "pub," if put on to the *rent*, would soon give them a better home, a lighter and sweeter dwelling.

The writer of this sheet lived in a hole at a shilling a week. He was then a drinker; he is now a teetotaller, and can live where he likes. No one ever left him a fortune, he has had no special advantages, and he is not clamorous that Government should do something for him, but rather that Government should cease asking him to do something for them.

I do not say, do not emigrate, but I do say, do not go mad in that direction; for we are quite as likely to send away that which is of national value, as to get rid of what is a national trouble. The papers just now are drawing attention to the doings of an emigration committee in the East of London, of which the worthy Vicar of Stepney is chairman; and one lad, it seems, has been living on "dry bread and onions" all last year, to save a pound, the amount wanted to entitle him to get the aid needed to get away. Surely there is stuff enough in *that* lad to make a man, and such a man as the country may be proud of. No, no! I do not like such to leave the country, we need them here, and need them very much; and when the houses are properly furnished as well as properly built, and the children properly clad as well as properly fed, there will be no need for any man, who can and will work, to either leave the country, or remain in idleness in it. If men like to emigrate from choice, or venture, or enterprise, I say, God speed them. There is much to be admired, in the man or the family, who let go the bonds that bind them, and battle the world for foothold and bread; but that men indigenous to the soil, and families with heart treasures, should be perforce and of necessity driven to strange lands, is to my mind a scandal and a shame to any country calling itself Christian, and to none more so than to ours, possessing such vast resources as we do.

Recently it fell to my lot to take part in committing to gaol for a month a woman not fifty years of age, who made her *sixty-first* appearance before the magistrates, for drunkenness and other offences in connection therewith. These are the sort we keep, and the lad who lived a year on bread and onions, that he might save twenty shillings, we send away.

Any other business conducted in such a way would be ruined. Then why should we escape because it is the work of the nation? The woman I have referred to, when she returns from gaol, will in all probability be locked up again the same night,—it has happened again and again,—and the following morning the magistrates will repeat the old farce.

Mending the houses in which the people live, will no more mend the people than does going to gaol mend that woman. When the *people* are mended, they themselves will mend the houses; and the people will not be mended, so as to completely cure the mischief complained of, until the machinery by which they are broken and marred be sent to the ends of the earth, instead of the people it ruins.

We can do a little, it is true, but national sobriety, national purity, and national prosperity, so long as the liquor traffic lives, is an impossibility.

Of course this is "Utopian," this is "impracticable," but it is true. Father Mathew in his day did a mighty work. I was with him much. He was received as a saviour, and looked upon as a heaven-sent messenger. People fell before him in thousands, and repeated his pledge, and devoutly and solemnly resolved to abstain. The Blue Ribbon Movement is nothing in comparison with it, and yet how little of it remains! *There* was not only religious fervour, but priestly power. I have been in the carriage with Father Mathew when in procession through the streets of London, when the lame, the halt, and the blind, beset the carriage and besought his blessing.

The anxiety depicted on the countenances of these afflicted ones, in combination with the wailings of a distressed mother, holding up her sickly child, that he might only pass his hand upon it, was a sight to touch the heart, and open the hand.

In Cumberland Market, in Bishop's Fields, Paddington, on Kennington Common, and other parts, many thousands in a day took the pledge. Ireland for the time being had (so to speak) been regenerated, and we in England welcomed the instrument of all this good with joy. On the 11th of May, 1840, the Bishop of Norwich, the late Bishop Stanley, said, "Father Mathew has done more for the peace and happiness of Ireland, than any person for the last hundred years."

The following was Father Mathew's prayer:—"May God bless you, and grant you grace and strength to keep your promise," a very sensible and sufficiently religious sentiment, one would think, for anybody. The pledge I myself (though then an old teetotaller) took from Father Mathew, on Kennington Common, in company with the late Earl Stanhope and the late John Meredith, and have now in my possession a silver medal, which the worthy priest gave to me in recognition of the deed. That was in the year 1843.

Father Mathew counted his disciples by millions, and Daniel O'Connell (the liberator of Ireland) was carried away by the stream of popular enthusiasm, and took the pledge, as did many of the nobility and great in the land. Ireland for the time being was positively regenerated, and there has never been in the history of the world so near an approach to a "nation being born in a day" as occurred in connection with that wave of well-doing; and yet, in the beautiful city of Cork, the home of Father Mathew, in one of the main streets of which is a very handsome statue of him to-day, at the corners of that very street, and in some cases shamefully and insultingly near to this memento of a godly man and a noble work, are planted the fountains of death, in the shape of gin-palaces and whisky-shops, laughing to scorn the image set up, and trampling down the people Father Mathew's life and fortune were given to save! That men for gold will do such deeds, and that in the doing of them they suffer no loss of social status in the world, and but little respect in the Church, is one of the most disheartening features of society.

From whence came the collapse of Father Mathew's movement? and from whence will come the collapse of the Blue Ribbon and Gospel Temperance Movement? The want of true life in the Church, and sound morals in the State. If the Church gave itself for the people, as Christ gave Himself for the Church, and the State made it easy to do right, and difficult to do wrong, instead of encouraging the reverse, the task of the temperance reformer would be easy, and the work he did much more abiding.

Why, in the name of all that is sacred and honourable, was not Father Mathew's labour supplemented by prohibition of the sale and manufacture of liquor in Ireland? and why did not the Church of the living God in that land stand, like Aaron of old, "between the living and the dead," that the plague might be stayed?

The nation knew the work, and admitted the advantage, from the Lord Lieutenant, the Marquis of Normanby, down to the lowest in the land. Gaols were emptied, revenue increased, order was established, religion revived, and prosperity secured, and this to the entire country. Surely that was the time to spike the liquor gun, and dismantle the drink fortress. It was an opportunity lost, and a fearful retribution has followed.

There is something in knowing the times and the

seasons, and if the Government neglect the opportunity to strengthen the present temperance sentiment in our own land, and fail to put in such checks to the power of the liquor traffic as we feel and know to be needful, they will put back the national clock an indefinite period, and paralyse their own hands in many much needed undertakings.

It is not meant by this teaching to discourage any moral or religious effort now in operation, but I am bound to admit our inability to grapple successfully with our national vice, so long as the State sells the drink, and the Church blesses the cup. "Have no fellowship with the unfruitful works of darkness," is Heaven's call, and the response to that call is our *demand*.

CHAPTER XXIV.

MARRIAGE.

"IT is not good for man to be alone." No one ever felt the force of that truth more than did I at the loss of my little and happy wife. She, poor thing, had had but little of mutual joy with me, for, as has already been indicated, I was, soon after my joining the Temperance Society, called upon to take a prominent part in the new crusade, and that involved an almost constant absence from home. Those were days of stage coaches and carriers' wagons more than are these, and getting about was much more difficult and expensive than is the case now. My twenty shillings a week would not admit of many special costs, and as there was no provision for anything beyond a walking distance from town to town, it will be seen how impossible it was for me to look much in the face of my wife, or feel much of the joy of my own fireside.

My journey to London from Preston had been by stages; all along the route holding meetings and making friends and converts, occupying six months in the programme. My London experience and reception increased the demands on my time, and within a month of my arrival there were more calls for my help than could be responded to. In the midst of all this came the message for my return to Lancashire, my wife was in dying circumstances. She who had lived in me so lovingly from her girlhood, and who, as my young wife, had clung to me in the darkest hour of my existence, and who, when the light of day broke in upon our little home, filled the atmosphere surrounding it with buoyant hope and blessed aspirations, was now, at twenty-three years of age, panting for her own life. I must break from my then surroundings, and at all costs go down and see her die. I had not seen her for seven months. We had lived in hope. My work and success filled her with gladness, and my own constant employment and agreeable duties made the time pass pleasantly away, and we looked with longing desire to the day when that fulness of mutual love, and that realization of oneness of heart, which alone comes from a complete satisfaction in our lot in life, should have its completeness in the presence of each other.

Life has many lessons, some of which are hard to learn, and there are circumstances occurring to us all, the wisdom and reasonableness of which it is im-impossible to see. That we may get good out of that which at the time seemed to betoken evil and only evil, has again and again been proved by most of us, I dare say, but it is a lesson not easily learned, and a mode of operation seldom appreciated. The death-chamber of her whom I had loved in all the freshness of her youth and beauty; and who, in the wisdom of her womanhood, would in my wildest manhood lay the devil that was in me by the sweetness of her temper and the fondness of her heart; and who, when the way of life was opened to me, with a glad heart and free, joined me in the resolve to live a better life and do a noble deed; and who also, when in the providence of

God she was asked, when her own cup of joy was full, to pass on that cup to others, that they also might be partakers of like precious faith, with tears, and prayers, and blessings, bid me war a good warfare;—such a wife could not pass from me without leaving a sad blank and a terrible vacuum. Yet I never was so near heaven as when standing by the bedside of my translated wife. She did not die. Nobody in that room felt themselves to be in the presence of death, it was more like the mingling with the angels of God, and she sang herself away, as the hymn puts it, "to everlasting bliss." Her face was as the face of an angel, and the people in the room, for the neighbours had come in, lifted up their hands in amazement and literally shouted for joy. All this, I fear, will seem weak and foolish to many, but it is very true, and the minister who had come from Manchester to Blackburn the night before to occupy the pulpit of the chapel in which we usually worshipped, and who on the morning of that Sabbath on which she passed away looked in and beheld the scene, took with him from that chamber into that chapel an influence and a power as from the throne of God, and which none who were then present ever forgot.

This was another crisis in my warfare. Fortunately for me, I was in full harness and bent upon the work of my life, and within three weeks of the time of leaving London to see my sick and dying wife, I was back again at my post, having been on the top of the coach travelling between Manchester and London for twenty-two hours, and of course throughout the entire night, which at times was very cold. I remember when in Leicester about midnight, and in which town supper was spread for the passengers and I alone took water, the rest set up a great horse-laugh, and the waiter could not or would not understand what I meant when I asked for water. He kept saying "porter?" At three o'clock in the morning some of my fellow-travellers, who had fortified themselves with fiery liquids at Leicester for the rest of the journey, began to chatter with their teeth and shiver with the cold, while I was comparatively comfortable. I had taken a little solid food as well as water, and that had made blood, and blood is the life and health of man, hence the warmth.

When I returned to my work, there was a loneliness in my life and a wandering in my thoughts which interfered with the fixedness of purpose which I was anxious to maintain. The little homestead, which since my teetotalism had been the one green spot on earth to me, was now gone, and the woman with whom my oneness of life was complete was also taken away. At twenty-four years of age I was a widower, with one living and two dead children, and I had but little outlet for the pent-up feelings of my nature. Though but little in the presence of my wife when living, we had frequent communications and hopeful expectations. These kept our hearts light, and were wings to our feet; but now, in the midst of multitudes I walked alone, and there was no one to whom my inner life was known and in whom I could trustingly confide. Admiration is not food, popularity is not life. At least, they are only food in the sense that confectionaries are, and everybody knows how unwholesome and dangerous these are to live upon.

I got on pretty well while labouring in and about London, and I had also the good fortune to become domesticated in the house of the late Mr. Joseph Glass, who with his good and motherly wife took the greatest interest in me, and manifested the greatest care for me. Their house was an oasis in the London desert, and sanctified by the word of God and prayer. Mr. Glass had a big heart and a tender soul. He it was who in sympathy for the poor little climbing boys invented the machine which now sweeps our chimneys. For many months as a widower I was under their roof, and our friendship and mutual esteem continued to the end of their natural lives.

The late Rev. Robert Aitkin was then a great sensation in London,—I speak of 1837 and 1838,—and people from all parts of London and of the country flocked to hear him. The large chapel in White's Row, Spitalfields, was crowded at every service.

I had not at the time any settled place of worship in London, so I went there and sat with Mr. and Mrs. Glass. To my mind, Mr. Aitkin was the most powerful preacher I had ever heard. I think so still. I was charmed and blessed and fortified by his deliverances. They were at times overwhelming, and begot in me strong resolves and a true sense of the duties and purposes of life. I never missed hearing Mr. Aitkin. In the spring of 1838 it was arranged for me to make a second tour to the north of England as far as my old quarters, Newcastle-on-Tyne and Sunderland. As I said before, I got on very well while in London, but I knew enough of human nature and of public life to feel the danger of a journey such as contemplated, as a disengaged young man.

All public men are more or less attractive, because of their public position; and those who have anything like popularity are especially so. At twenty-four years of age I had a fair share of esteem and favour and was nationally known. "Great men are not always wise;" it cannot therefore be wondered at if men who are not great occasionally make fools of themselves. I confess I was afraid. The women, too—God help them!—how they rush at a conspicuous figure, just as the moth rushes at the lighted candle, and not unfrequently with the same results. They like to get those whom everybody admires. It pleases their vanity, but not unfrequently blasts the life not only of the woman but of the man as well. Oh! the mistakes and heartburnings that I have known in this department! All public men in my judgment are best married, but *few* women are fit to marry *public* men. It is a great risk to run on their part, and whether to pity the public man who has no wife, or the woman who has a public man for a husband most, I am undetermined. When the selection is wise, and the connection mutually helpful, the relationship helps and gladdens both. Believing this, I determined, though not prepared to marry at once, before I left London on my northern tour, to fix my purpose and set my heart.

I had learned from inquiry the history and character of a lady who had business connections with the family at whose house I lodged. They had, unknown to myself, persuaded her to attend a meeting held near her home in the City, at which I was the principal speaker. She had then never seen my face, and knew nothing of my life, and was in total ignorance of the society whose agent I at the time was, but she was one seeking to know, and willing to do, what was right. She signed the pledge, and I saw her face for the first time that night.

From that moment I looked upon her as one to be desired, and I determined, if certain evidences were satisfactory and nothing happened to prevent, she should be the future companion of my life. I watched her for weeks; I saw her industry; I admired her deportment; I was convinced of her integrity and high principles, and I loved her person. All this was going on unknown to herself, and my opportunities were numerous, for she was in business in the City, and I could easily pass the place and see what she was about and what were her surroundings.

"Marriage is honourable in all;" and my knowledge of life teaches me that no young lady need go from home to find a husband: when men want them, they know where they live,—I mean the men who are worth having,—and they will find them out. This walking about to be seen, this dressing to catch "flats," this constant parading in places and in company which manifests its own purpose, will seldom take the eye or touch the heart of a man worth having, and he who is so touched and taken often finds he may have got an admired woman, but he has not found, in the truest and best sense, a wife. Marriage is not simply an interesting and pleasing event, the honeymoon does not complete the business, and the introduction to certain connections and the congratulations of neighbours and friends, will not make the pot boil nor domesticate the home. There is, in all probability, a long and serious future, bringing with it responsibilities and obligations of a sacred and binding kind; and the question comes, can we and will we help each other to bear and to do? This is true oneness, this is true life. It is not what other people think, or public opinion or public custom may require; it is, what will the partner of my life do for me? Shall I, though nothing to the world, be all the world to him or her? If so, then my life shall be blessed and my home shall be glad. Many a noble ship, after a prosperous voyage and weathering many a storm, has been wrecked near home; while many a life, with noble purpose and attractive appearance and promising future, has been wrecked *at* home. I knew this then, and I know it better now. The world was before me then, and I was busy with life's struggle; it is behind me now, and I look back upon the field of contest and see the slain. The lady in question was constant in attendance at public worship. I saw it; I admired it. She gossiped not by the way, nor tarried as she went; her demeanour was becoming, and she walked like one who had resources within herself, and she had but few of the frivolities and tattle common to young life.

The last moments of the year 1837 were spent by a very large congregation in religious exercises in the chapel in White's Row. The lady I had in my mind was one of that congregation, so was I. She was on one side of the chapel, I on the other. After midnight had passed, Mr. Aitkin, who had conducted the meeting, in a most solemn and earnest manner asked the men who were present and who intended to serve God during the year upon which we had just entered, to stand up. A host of men did so, and I amongst them. The same question was then put to the women. At that moment I said in my heart and before God, "If that young lady stands up, I'll have her." She did so, and that settled the matter as far as I was concerned. At the close of the service I asked her if she would allow me to conduct her home. She did not object. When we were near her residence, I proposed a walk round The Circus, near her home. That was a test question, for it was nearly one o'clock in the morning, and I concluded if she consented I might venture further. In that walk I opened my heart and explained my purpose, telling her I might be ten months out of the twelve from home, and giving her two weeks to consider the question, for I had no time to spend in courting. I went the next day down into Essex for two weeks, and on my return called for my answer. The rest is explained by what followed; and though we both knew it might be twelve months or more before I could sit down by my own fireside, as it proved to be, we pledged our troth, and were one to the death.

The following account, recorded in "Memorials of Temperance Workers," by my dear friend, the late Jabez Inwards, will perhaps best explain the rest.

"The late Mrs. Thomas Whittaker's maiden name was Palmer. She was born at East Harling, Norfolk, on the 3rd of November, 1810, and died at Scarborough, January 9th, 1875. Her father and family connections were, sixty years ago, proprietors of several of the coaches then running between Norwich, Bury St. Edmund's, and London. They also held several of the principal inns and hostelries on the line of route. Reverses came to the family, and the subject of this sketch came to London at sixteen years of age, to seek her fortune. She took a situation in a business house in the City, and at twenty-five years of age was proprietress of the same business. She joined the Wesleyan Society in connection with Spitalfields Church, and was a teacher in the Sabbath-school. In the year 1837 she attended a temperance meeting in the little Baptist Chapel, South Place, Finsbury, at which Mr. Whittaker was the speaker. She there signed the pledge, and became the wife of the lecturer by marriage at Hoxton Church on the 6th of August, 1838. She bore him six children, four sons and two daughters, none of whom ever knew the taste of liquor. The daughter, the youngest born, died in her 25th year in 1877; and her remains now lie with the mother's in the Scarborough cemetery. Three others died in infancy, and were buried in London. In 1849 Scarborough became her home, and it is now the home of her surviving husband, and of her two sons.

"The history of the Temperance Cause has yet to be written, and much as it owes to the early men, it owes more to some of the early women, and to none more than to the late wife of Mr. Whittaker. She was a modest, retiring, ladylike woman, minding the duties of her own house, and watching with undying affection the best interests of her family. Her husband has been from home in early days more than twelve months at a time, and frequently six and nine, yet she never murmured. The remuneration he received would not admit of needless travel; neither did it suffice to maintain and educate his family in a suitable manner. This necessitated her devotion to business, which was continued to the hour of her death. A more self-abnegatory and self-sacrificing life has seldom been lived.

"Mr. Whittaker had for thirty years proposed a visit to America, but circumstances seemed to forbid it. At length, however, in 1874, the resolve was made. Mrs. Whittaker had been in delicate health three or four years. In the early attack of her illness things looked so serious that her life was despaired of. Their daughter, who was at school in Prussia, came home in the depth of winter, expecting her mother's death. She, however, survived that attack, and seemed to recover so nicely; that in 1874 she appeared better than she had been for years. Under this condition of things, by mutual consent, the venture was made, and Mr. Whittaker at the end of September looked upon the face of his never-to-be-forgotten wife for the last time, and departed for America.

"While in the city of Boston, just launched before the public, and with a large number of important engagements before him, on the 9th of January (1875 ?), the Atlantic cable brought the following message:—'Father, come home, mother is dying.' In two hours later another message:—'Mother is dead! gone in peace.' That was a dark day for Thomas Whittaker. The companion of his life and helpmeet for thirty-seven years gone; and gone, too, while he was in a strange land. But she lives in her children; and her two sons, whose obligations to such a mother can never be overlooked, to her lasting credit bid fair to do as great a service in their day and generation as their father and mother combined have done.

"We have only now to add that Mrs. Whittaker's teetotalism, like that of her husband's, was of a robust and enduring kind. She did not believe in drink for any purpose whatever, and further, she had no faith in what are called substitutes. Substitutes for bad things are not desirable, and she believed drink to be a bad thing. She was a pure-minded and God-fearing woman, living a spotless life and dying a Christian's death. Her two sons and her only daughter and her sons' wives stood by her bedside when she passed away.

"After leaving a message of love for her husband, and expressing her confidence in the abiding love of Christ, and the goodness and mercy of God, she looked her children in the face and said, 'Be just! fear God!'

"She was buried by the Rev. Mr. Briggs, M.A., Wesleyan minister; and on her tomb in the Scarborough cemetery is placed a very handsome granite monument, on which is the following inscription:—

'In loving memory of
LOUISA,
The faithful wife and true helpmeet of
Thomas Whittaker, Temperance Advocate.
Born November 3rd, 1810;
Died January 9th, 1875.

Having served her day and generation by the will of God, she fell asleep, leaving as a legacy to her family that which had been the pole-star to her own life—

BE JUST! FEAR GOD!'"

CHAPTER XXV.

THE EASTERN COUNTIES.

IN January, 1838, my first connection with the eastern counties was formed; it began at Chelmsford.

Mr. Francis Marriage, who was then a young corn merchant, had inherited an old established corn and malting business. Previous to settling down to it, he took a tour in the north of England, visiting Newcastle-on-Tyne and other places; it was while out on this journey he crossed my path.

Attending a large meeting at Newcastle, he was very much impressed, and from that time he determined not to touch the malting business. He was a very fine, handsome, intelligent man, and belonged to an old family of Friends, and was much respected.

It is well in these days for our friends to be informed how, from the first of our agitation, persons whose business and profits were identified with the liquor traffic here and there got troubled, not so much because they feared the ruin of their *trade*, but because they feared the ruin of *themselves*.

Those were days when temperance teaching stirred the heart and touched the conscience, and when men so connected were made to tremble in the presence of temperance truth. When we contrast the conduct of many men, who then abandoned profits rather than wound their consciences, with the conduct of many

Christian men of late years, who, as grocers and confectioners, have for the sake of gain gone into the liquor trade, we feel there must be an awful degeneracy of religious fervour and high principle.

What a testimony was that of Joseph Sturge of Birmingham, when he gave up even selling barley for malting purposes, and did it too at a very great sacrifice! and what a rebuke to men who seem to have no scruples, and indeed no conscience, on such matters to-day! The iniquity of the system is not less now than it was then, and the obligations of consistency and righteousness are quite as binding, I presume. But we run with the "ruck," and the lack of fidelity in the pulpit has filled the pew with all manner of filthiness of the flesh, and sordid and unholy gain. Why are *not* the money-changers scourged from the temple as of old? and why do we not denounce and rebuke the men who paint the outside sepulchre, while within it is full of rottenness and dead men's bones?

Francis Marriage turned his malting-house into a meeting-room, and my first address in Chelmsford was given in that building. That sort of thing was repeated again and again, and under his direction and guidance I did a lot of temperance work in that district.

In the years 1839 and 1840 I did much work in Essex, Suffolk, and Norfolk, returning again frequently in subsequent years. At one time these counties were regularly and systematically worked by appointed agencies, and monthly visits at least were paid to most of the towns and many of the villages in them. As these were barley-growing as well as malting districts, it will be seen that we had not only appetite and custom to contend with, but powerful vested interest. The farmers were almost as bad as the maltsters and brewers in their feelings against us, and the labourers of course were readily influenced to do mischievous deeds.

The difficulty we had to obtain places to meet in, was in itself a trial. When we did get them, the people had no hesitancy in taking great liberties with us, knowing as they did that the leading people, and even the Church, looked upon us as a danger to the State, and a trouble to the Church.

The common mode of annoyance and interruption was to let off sparrows, and these poor things would fly about the meeting in all directions, not unfrequently bobbing against the candles and putting them out. Occasionally we were favoured with a crow, and sometimes fireworks! It was not an easy matter in such a condition of things to get an attentive and appreciative hearing. I strongly incline to the opinion that this sort of persecution in many cases did more to beget *abiding* and determined friends, than our teaching would have secured.

It was plainly seen from what *source* all this sort of thing sprang, and the motives which prompted it were clear enough to discerning minds, and many from that reason alone were inclined to look at the matter, and determined to battle with such unfair proceedings.

At Harlow, in Essex, the most serious riot and disturbance took place. That was in the winter of 1840. The large British Schools had been lent for the meeting, but as the time drew near the committee of the schools felt it best to withdraw the offer, and we had to fall back upon an old building standing in the middle of a field, which had in years gone by been used as a schoolroom. In the upper part of this was a long room, the lower part was let off in tenements. The Nonconformists and Methodists of the place had been frightened by threats from the maltsters and farmers, who had declared that if the schools were so used their future subscriptions would be withheld; and as to the Established Church, proceedings which had to be taken not long since against the old vicar, which were such a scandal to the cloth, will show how things were in that circle. The room was taken possession of by a drunken mob, and they conducted themselves in such a way that it was impossible to have an intelligent utterance. The first signal was the flying of a sparrow, and then another, and another; at one time there must have been nearly twenty sparrows flying about. Then a can of beer was introduced, followed by fireworks—squibs and crackers! This of course made great confusion, and almost suffocated the people. They then broke the forms, and began to dance and jump on the floor like wild Indians. Outside, in the distance, was heard the sound of a horn; this was blown by a "gentleman" (so called), who seemed to have no better occupation than drinking and treating others. He brought with him an additional mob; on their arrival the windows were broken, and the people inside became more frantic than ever. The floor of the room was somewhat rotten, and not considered safe, so the people in the dwellings below began to remove their furniture. I opened a window close to the platform and waited the result, having resolved, if the floor *did* give way, I would throw my body across the window ledge, and wait till some one took me down. At length the parish constable arrived, and offered to conduct me through the crowd which had assembled outside the building. They opened an avenue through which I had to pass, it was some distance from the room to the main road ; the fields on each side of the road were filled with turnips ready for gathering, and the crowd gathered them and threw them at my head: I was tripped up twice, but recovered myself. At length I got a good start, and ran like a hare, and they followed me like a pack of hounds! However, I got to cover, as hares occasionally do, and reached the house of my host, Mr. James Barnard, a respectable and well-to-do farmer.

The house was more than half a mile from where the meeting had been held, so I had a pretty good run for it. It was a lone house standing in its own grounds, and a considerable stream of water ran along at the back part of it. Subsequently the constable arrived, and the Baptist minister, and Dr. Lovell, who had come over from Brentwood to help me. We sat down to supper, and got rather amused at what had happened, but in the midst of it there was an awful yelling up in front of the house. Some sixty men armed with sticks and other weapons, having been further primed with beer, were instructed to " demand my body," and insist that I should not be lodged in the parish. It was impossible that I could escape, for they formed a complete circle round the dwelling in conjunction with the stream flowing round the back part of the premises. They rang the bell, and broke the windows; they then burst open the door, and two of them came into the house, and demanded my body. Poor Mrs. Barnard fainted, and I was very much troubled on my own account, and on behalf of my host and hostess. It seemed so like bringing them into trouble with their neighbours, and I thought at one time the lady would have died.

I ran upstairs, and the men made an attempt to follow. I knew not what to do, nor where to go. In my excitement I sought to escape by the chimney, but I could not manage to climb it, and I was for the first and last time in my life put in great "bodily fear." I lost all power for the moment of life and limb, and I lay flat on the bedroom floor unable to move or stand. While I lay in that condition, the two men who had entered the house were *recognised* by the constable who was present, and that fact cowed them, and they ultimately dispersed.

That affair cost us an assize trial at Chelmsford, and myself a journey outside the coach up and down from Bristol during the night in very cold weather. All the accused pleaded guilty, and we exercised mercy, for we never got hold of the real offenders in the business, though it was pretty clear who they were.

Sawbridgeworth and Bishop's Stortford had also been fixed for meetings in connection with Harlow, but they were alarmed, and the meetings were not held. It is worthy of note that Mr. John Barnard, who was uncle to my host, and the largest maltster in the district at the time, was so annoyed at my treatment and the conduct of the people, that he cleared out one of the maltings for a meeting for me, invited me to tea, and I think lodged me for the night, declaring that if the business would not stand argument and fair-play it must go. I had a very good meeting in that malthouse, and several signatures at the close of the meeting, so there was a redeeming feature even in that cruel business.

I spent nearly a week amongst them, but when I did leave Harlow by the coach for London, a crowd of people gathered near the inn, and pelted me on the coach as we drove out of the place.

An incident happened to me at Colchester about the same time, which may help to account for some mistakes made, and silly stories told about us. The meeting was held in the Bible-room, Lion Walk, and we had a very nice respectable company. There was present, however, *one* man much the worse for liquor. I told the meeting an anecdote about a man who attended a meeting I once held at *Plaistow* near London, and in my introduction to the story I was saying that "some time ago I held a meeting at Plaistow, a place seven miles from London." At this point the man alarmed the meeting by calling out, "Glasgow is in Scotland." I replied, I knew *Glasgow* was in Scotland, but I was not talking about Glasgow but about *Plaistow*, and "I say *Plaistow* is a village seven miles from London."

The man became furious about my "ignorance," insisting upon it that "Glasgow was in Scotland," and it was a disgrace to anybody, who was so ignorant as to say that "Glasgow was a village near London," presuming to lecture to such a meeting.

Well, he could not be made to understand, and the result was he had to be put out of the meeting, and as he retired down the walk he kept declaring that the "Teetotal lecturer was telling the people that Glasgow was a village seven miles from London."

No doubt he would go straight to the public-house and tell the story, and if he be living now, may be he is telling it yet; and that is a sample of the intelligent conception of many people who attend our meetings and make reports of what they hear. Essex was simply terrific in that way, and Suffolk was very little better.

The long walks I had, and the want of home comforts with which we had to put up, was a thing not easily forgotten, and yet there were cases in which we had fulness of joy, and most hospitable treatment. Thomas Smith, of Woodbridge, was a grand man, and he with his household made us most happy and welcome. Mr. and Mrs. Clodd, of Framlingham, never wearied in their friendly help, and that old homestead has in it memories which live throughout the entire ranks of the temperance hosts.

That was the home of that splendid specimen of true philanthropy and Christian character, James Larner. He was for years the man of Suffolk, the moving power, the undaunted spirit, the unwearied defender; and when it is remembered how special were the difficulties, and how numerous the foes, the way in which he brought the whole district under his influence, and even to treat him with loving respect, it is the more remarkable. When he died, the heart pulsation seemed to stop, and the town he had so well served, and the district he had so honestly and so disinterestedly worked for, mourned his loss, and to-day miss his manly form and genial presence. There are some men who never die, and though their bodily presence is neither seen nor felt, their spirit and their teaching and their work *live*. It is so with James Larner. We cannot forget him, he is ever in our memory, and though there are vacant places, and aching voids, because of his material absence, there are hidden springs of life which come up, and hopes of future reunion that are gradually but surely throwing down the "wall of partition" that separates, and one day shall be levelled to the ground, when we ourselves cross the border, to the brighter and the better land, in which there is fulness of joy and life for evermore! That dear old mother of his held on her ninety years, and was cheerful in spirit and companionable in soul even to the last. Not so with James, he suffered much, and died sadly too young, but he did a big work, and left a name that shall live so long as goodness has a record!

Sir H. Thompson, who has made a name in his profession, was a native of Framlingham, and his signature is in the old pledge-book kept in this homestead. He was identified with the movement in his native town when a young man and a student of medicine.

He attended Mr. Larner in his last illness, and showed much interest, and manifested great kindness in connection with that sickness, but, alas! the work was done, and no medical skill could avail much.

Sir H. Thompson knew all about the science and practice of teetotalism long before he sent that letter to the press, a few years ago, giving in his adhesion to our truths; and welcome as that letter was, and respected and honoured as his name is, I cannot but feel that he and many others, who have worked their way into the front ranks in their various professions and departments, owe more to the Temperance Cause than they have yet either admitted or paid.

Framlingham was badly off at one time for places in which to meet. The chapels and schools were all closed against us, and my first meeting in the town was held in a cottage. The Wesleyan chapel was not tied to Conference as most Wesleyan chapels are, and Mr. Clodd was a *trustee*, and other officials were warm friends to the cause. They determined to use for the town's good the building which they felt belonged to them. The resident *minister* would not permit it, hence many unpleasant circumstances, and some *ridiculous* ones as well. On one occasion, Mr. Clodd, a slim, active little man, opened the chapel doors and began to light the *candles*, preparatory to a meeting: the minister, a stout heavy man, blew them out as fast as he could. Mr. Clodd "topped" the pews and relit them. The race between light and darkness became quite exciting. The preacher ultimately had to puff for breath, instead of puffing out the candles. The race was won by the man of light, and we used the chapel regularly for years, but it resulted in destroying Methodism as represented by the Conference in that town. A little wisdom and forbearance on the part of the resident ministers would have avoided that. I hold that there is no Church in the country that has suffered more than the Methodist Church, because of the folly of some of its ministers, and the blindness of the Conference in reference to this question.

They are recovering wonderfully, and no one rejoices in that more than myself, but there are some things it is due the people should know, and that is one of them.

In the little town of Eye we were sadly punished for the want of accommodation in the way of meeting-places. On one occasion I had to hold my meeting in a bakehouse after the oven was drawn. Of course it was a hot one. On another occasion the meeting had to be held in a sawpit. These were trying circumstances, but we have ever had in our ranks men equal to any emergency, and the baker and the wheelwright in question, who utilised their premises at some cost and trouble to themselves, had in them stuff that would either face a foe or make a martyr. The truth has often to walk in untrodden paths, and the way has to be made as we go along, and the time was when teetotallers had not only to teach the truth, but to make the way for it to walk in. They were often very poor, so much so that we could not always put our hand upon a man who could stand the entire cost of entertaining an agent during his visit, and the responsibility would be divided. We would take tea at one house, and supper and bed at another, and next morning go out to breakfast at a baker's, and help off the stale bread. As to dinner, we walked at dinner time to the next appointment. This, I remember, was specially so, in the beautiful village of Yoxford.

Luton in Bedfordshire was bad to work; no chapel or school. Mr. Hiram Higgins fitted up a hay-loft in his yard, and the public had to climb up a ladder to the meeting, and they *did* it, and in great numbers too. The late Henry Brown did that. He had inherited a malting and brewing business, and had built himself a very handsome pretentious mansion, standing in its own grounds, quite in character with his position and business prospects: he had a young family. He never felt quite comfortable in the connection that business gave him with the publicans and brewers, and his visits to my meetings in that hay-loft settled his malting business. He gave it up, sold his house, and built one of more modest pretensions, thinking it wise and prudent so to do, as the malting department was a profitable source of income, and he had given it up. He turned his business premises into a timber yard and saw-mills. They are there to-day, and have been a success. Mr. Henry Brown died in the modest villa he built, about two years ago, at a ripe old age, having lived in the esteem of the whole town; and his eldest son was chairman for me at one of my successful mission meetings the winter before last.

The late William Drewett also came to that hay-loft, and for many years subsequently was the active secretary of the society. He has left behind him a large family, most if not all of whom are active and useful teetotallers. The homestead is to-day a very "Bethel" to many who visit Luton in the name of humanity and of God.

CHAPTER XXVI.

THE WEST OF ENGLAND.

IT was not till the winter of 1839 and 1840 that I was introduced to the west of England. Bristol at that time had assumed a supervision over many of the western counties, and from that centre, Gloucester, Wilts, Somerset, and Devon were worked. South Wales also was benefited by the band of men who in Bath and Bristol had identified themselves with the movement. Joseph Eaton, Robert Charlton, and the Thomases were names very familiar, and as they were men of social status and wealth, as well as mental power, their adhesion was most valuable. The Cotterells of Bath, the Saunderses of Market Lavington, and of Bath, were also useful acquisitions. Samuel Bowly of Gloucester, and Josiah Hunt, the intellectual and eloquent farmer of the same county, had not only presence but power on our platform. The giant Nonconformist minister of Ebley, near Stroud, the Rev. B. Parsons, was a scathing speaker, and swept as with a whirlwind the gauze of excuses and cobwebs of philosophy advanced in the interest of drink. His work "Anti-Bacchus" (which as many think ought to have obtained the prize of one hundred guineas, offered in 1838 by the new British and Foreign Temperance Society, for the best essay on total abstinence) was an able production. Dr. Grindrod was, however, the successful competitor in his valuable work "Bacchus;" but Mr. Parsons's, for the time being, was by far the more popular work with the public, and was very largely read.

"Bacchus," as an historical work and as a book of reference, will no doubt be more enduring; but "Anti-Bacchus," for food, fire, and heart-stirring appeals, was infinitely more powerful. Dr. Morgan, a physician of good repute in Bath, and the famous Rev. W. Jay, the "Prince of preachers." (as he was called), were early in the field, and with such men as the Foxes of Wellington, F. T. Thompson of Bridgwater, and the Clarkes of Street, we were, in the western counties, in clover as compared with many parts of the country.

In addition to these we had the clergy freely with us. The Rev. Thomas Spencer and the Rev. W. H. Turner were specially active, as well as many substantial farmers. The late Dr. Gale and his two brothers were also located here, so that the Western Temperance League, which was organized in connection with my first visit to the West, and which has had an uninterrupted and useful existence down to the present day, and of which Mr. Thornton is now, and has been for many years, its painstaking secretary, had a most formidable and presentable start.

The men at its head were Christian and philanthropic, their lives spotless, their motives pure. Intellect, time, and money were freely and joyously given. There was no question of character, no doubt as to motive. All this helped me much in my work among a people slow of heart to believe, and terribly prejudiced in favour of cider.

It was not so much "barley and beer," here, as " apples

and cider," with which we had to contend. There were many difficulties special to the district, and we had at times rough work and rough usage. Ilminster and Ilchester, Langport and Stogumber, stood out from the rest in violence and opposition. James Teare was the apostle of teetotalism to the West, and had covered portions of the district before my acquaintance with it was formed.

He had very violent opposition in more than one instance, but down in Cornwall his career was more a triumphal march than anything else. Cornwall was a Methodist county, and James was an effective local preacher in that body. The followers of Wesley, who were true to their founder, had no difficulty and no prejudice to overcome on this question, so they received him with open arms, and he went from house to house with gladness, eating his meat with a merry heart, and, as the early records of the work down there show, his name was a household word with them.

Many as were the difficulties in some parts of the West my home comforts and sunny spots have left pleasant memories. Alderman Saunders of Bath, the Vicar of Banwell, the Tanners of Sidcot, F. T. Thompson of Bridgwater, and the Rev. W. W. Robinson of Yeovil, with the Clarkes of Street, may be specially mentioned.

Of course, in all these cases, and in others of a similar kind named in these pages, there were *ladies*, and if they are not mentioned, it may be taken that while words are silver silence is gold. The ladies have charmed my life and comforted my heart all the way along, and I would not like to be a wanderer or a sojourner in any country, nor on any mission, where there were no women.

In preceding chapters I have more than once referred to the conduct of ministers. They were in all cases either Methodists or Nonconformists, not that they were worse than others, but that circumstances brought me nearer to them. In Somersetshire I had an experience which I think I must mention. This was in the year 1840. The Rev. W. W. Robinson, who had then charge of the important parish of Yeovil, invited me to spend a week with him in that town and neighbourhood: I went. During the week he invited the ministers and clergy of the town to dine with me at the vicarage on a day named. Several came, among them an Irish gentleman, his curate. After dinner and social intercourse, the time for the public meeting drew near, and it was suggested by Mr. Robinson that we should kneel down and pray for God's blessing on the meeting. While we were thus engaged, and Mr. Robinson was most devoutly asking (for he was a very devout man) for a blessing on the meeting, and especially naming myself as an object needing help to advocate teetotalism, the curate jumped from his knees in *indignation*, and protested against what he called the blasphemy of asking God to bless anything so unscriptural, and so contrary to His Word, as teetotalism was! He left the room in a rage, and slammed the door.

Now we sometimes hear of the silly things teetotallers say and do. I have known many teetotallers, and heard not a few, but I never knew any one say or do anything so unseemly and unbecoming as this clergyman. Does anybody judge the church or the chapel by what this or that man may do? It would be an evil day for both church and chapel were it so, and it is an unmeant compliment to teetotalism to expect *it* to live in circumstances in which religion itself would *die*. The fact is we have taken a great deal of killing.

Take another sample. Stogumber, a small town in Somerset, had in it in 1840 a large brewery, and Stogumber ale had a name and a place amongst the people. The brewery was the authority and power of the locality, yet we ventured to question, at the very seat of the enemy, the supremacy exercised.

The Watchet and Williton friends accompanied me to Stogumber. The Baptist chapel was secured for the meeting, and in due course we commenced operations.

The chapel stood in its own grounds, and the pulpit was fixed against the wall in one corner, between one of the front windows and the gable end. The pews in the body were filled with people; I occupied the pulpit. Presently we heard in the distance strains of music. A band, having just been refreshed at the brewery, commenced its march in the direction of the little Baptist Chapel. The strains became more distinct, interspersed with wild shouts of an approaching foe. Presently the seat of action was reached, and the storming of the citadel commenced; stones flew through the windows in rapid succession, some of them coming unpleasantly near our heads. I crouched down in the pulpit, and told the people to do the same in the pews, and I would talk to them though I could not see them, and so I did. The cowards outside having spent their rage, returned to the brewery for a fresh supply of courage. I rose, and the people rose, and the meeting resulted in considerable *success*.

An effort was made to upset our conveyance on leaving the place in the dark, but we escaped without any serious damage. An attempt was made to bring these rioters to justice, but we were only laughed at by the magistrates sitting at Dunster Castle.

At Ilminster the old workhouse was utilized for a meeting; Mr. James Clarke (who I am happy to say still lives) accompanied me from Street. We were pelted with eggs of unpleasant flavour, and as these flew about during the delivery of my speech, it was somewhat risky opening the mouth, for one or two of the men who fired at us were not bad shots. There have been in more recent times several attempts to break up meetings bearing on the legislative aspect of the Temperance Question, but for years the country has been at peace on its moral aspects. The only exception that I have known is in the town of Hitchin. Even now while I write these pages, a lawless terrorism is being exercised, and the authorities are either unable or unwilling to lend such help and protection to the friends of law and order as justice demands and common decency calls for. I am specially interested in this case, and I cannot but think, that though some of the leading and most respectable citizens of the town are interested in the liquor trade, that will neither be held to be a justification for withholding the rights of citizenship from others, nor in any way deter those who have the best interest of the people at heart from persevering in their work of redemption among those given to folly.

It is forty-six years since I gave my first address on temperance at Hitchin. I had a very respectful and considerate hearing, and formed agreeable pleasant friendships, and though most of these friends have gone, they have left pleasant memories, and I think there must have been fearful degeneracy in the people, for a town of the character of Hitchin to have its moral power paralysed and its fair name dishonoured in such a way. I have had but few opportunities of visiting Hitchin for many years, but if anything could renew my youth, and again put into me the spirit and fire of a war-horse, it is the knowledge of lawlessness on the part of the people, and imbecility on the part of the constituted authorities. There should never in any community be a withdrawal from moral standpoints, nor a giving in on questions of civil rights, and if Hitchin does not speedily set itself right on this business, it will be time for some one outside of themselves to see to it. That there have been in recent times, in several instances, a renewal of outrages practised in early days, may be one evidence that the steps now taken to secure legal power for the suppression of the liquor traffic are telling upon the business, and the struggle is one for life. Be that as it may, flour bags hurled at the head of a bishop will not settle the question, and the refusal to hear a man of such honest intentions and genial nature as Sir Wilfrid Lawson, will not harmonize with the sense of fair-play which has ever characterized our people.

There can be but one issue now, the declaration is made, the resolve fixed, and that issue the triumph of right and truth. We think we have that right, we believe we hold that truth, and all whose interest and practice lie in an opposite direction must sooner or later succumb.

CHAPTER XXVII.

THE WEST OF ENGLAND.

DURING the years from 1840 to 1846, my labours in the West of England were very extensive, and at certain periods constant and consecutive. From Gloucester down to Plymouth on the one hand, and from Reading on the other, there were few towns and villages I did not visit in the counties of Berks, Wilts, Dorset, South Devon, Somerset, and Gloucester. Cornwall I never touched before the year 1874, and Worcester and Hereford were practically unknown to me. With these exceptions, before I was thirty years of age I had covered the land, and no man dead or living can have felt more than I the blessedness of having borne the yoke in his youth.

It is impossible, from the platform on which we now stand, to conceive the condition of things as they then existed, and though in living my life over again, which I have done while penning these pages, I have frequently broken down as I have passed by the homes and called to mind the names of men who were my familiar friends and brave companions, and who have fallen by my side, at times the sunlight has burst through the cloud which these memories beget, and filled my heart with joy and gladness.

I have many times in public meetings declared that

I would not be without my share in this work for all the world calls great and good. This, to those who listened, might be thought a mere flourish of rhetoric, or an excited outburst of the moment, but not so; it is the calm and fixed feeling of my heart, and the glory and determination of my life.

From Exeter down to Plymouth the word went like fire amongst dry stubble, and though Devon does not rank amongst the excitable and enthusiastic of our people, teetotallers were much more numerous than raisins are said to be in their dumplings.

At Kingsbridge, my meeting was held in a malt-house; the owner, Mr. Kingston, a gentleman with a conscience and a Christian character, abandoned the malting business, and turned the premises into a meeting-room, and entertained me most hospitably. The chairman of that meeting was the late Richard Peek, Esq., proprietor of Hazelwood, an estate some seven miles from Kingsbridge, and the founder of the famous tea-house known as "Peek Bros." There and then he identified himself with the movement, and became a liberal and ardent supporter, and continued such to the day of his death. His acquisition was an immense gain, for he was held in high esteem and was known as a true philanthropist and Christian gentleman, not only in Devon, but throughout the kingdom.

His history is one worth knowing, and I give it as I had it from his own lips. He was the son of an agricultural labourer, and he himself tilled the soil and followed the plough up to manhood. During the war with France, he was cast in the ballot for a soldier. He had even then a horror of war as he had of slavery and of drink. He resolved he would not be a soldier, and as he could not get a substitute for less than forty pounds, and could not at the time command forty shillings, he fled from the district and tramped to London, getting an occasional lift by carriers on the road. On his arrival, his means were nearly exhausted, and for some days he was much exercised to know what to do. He made several applications for a situation as a labouring warehouseman, or street porter, and ultimately succeeded at Saunderson's, an old-established and well-respected tea-house. His wages were a pound a week. He was diligent in his duties, and became a confidential working man. First to business in the morning, last there at night, trustworthy and reliable, he was soon felt to be an essential part of the business. He was taken into the counting-house, then sent on the road an occasional journey, then becoming their principal and most successful traveller; indeed the right hand of the house. At this point he felt justified in claiming an interest in the business. This the firm refused, which they no doubt subsequently much regretted, and he commenced on his own account, and laid the foundation of a tea business second to none in the trade. "Peek Bros." has been known now for nearly half a century as one of the first houses in the city. Sir Henry Peek, one of the members for Surrey, is nephew to and one of the successors of this wonderful Devonshire lad.

Richard Peek was elected Sheriff of London the year after the Reform Bill of 1832 was passed. He was the first Reform Sheriff, and the office was held by him for two years in succession. He was an intimate acquaintance and frequent associate of the kind-hearted Royal Duke of Sussex, and was most persevering and energetic in his efforts for the liberation of all our colonial slaves, and lived to see the British dominions clear of that foul blot.

Shortly after the term of his shrievalty, he saw in the *Times* newspaper, Hazelwood, in South Devon, advertised for sale. That was the estate on which he was born, and on which he had followed the plough, and on which his father's cottage stood, and in which the old man still lived. He bought it, retired from the business he had made, and with ample means built as near to the site of the cottage in which he was born as could be conveniently fixed upon, a mansion in character with his position, took his father into it,—for he himself was never married,—apportioned a nook in it for his special use in his own way, and in that nook I more than once visited and talked to the old man, for he lived to a great age.

Mr. Peek himself was put in the commission of the peace for the county, and the first case which came before him in that capacity was a case of poultry stealing committed by the man who as boy drove the team on that very estate when Richard Peek held the plough. "Look on this picture and on that." Richard Peek never was a public-house man, and when teetotalism was brought before his notice he at once saw its necessity and advantage, and without hesitancy, or quibble, or excuse, committed himself to it. That was the man —all through life he saw the right and did it, conferring not with flesh and blood.

The other man loafed and louted and grumbled, and thieved and drank; and as men reap what they sow, there was no exception to the rule in this case. The remains of Richard Peek lie now in Hazelwood, not many yards from the cottage in which he was born and the mansion in which he died.

He took me to see the spot in which he meant his bones to lie when life's work was done.

He was a Nonconformist, and had no faith in consecrated soil, and did not change his religion or his politics with his circumstances, as too many people do. It is life that sanctifies, and not the soil, and in Richard Peek there was a oneness and an entirety which is refreshing to look upon.

In his case was exemplified the teaching, "a good name is better than precious ointment." The effort some men make to be recognised by society, and to obliterate all knowledge of their origin, would be amusing if it were not contemptible. They not only leave localities, but sometimes country too, hoping to secure this result. And what is it worth when they get it? And they seldom do get it after all. It is character that lives, not reputation, and when we go hence all that we can take, and all that we shall take, is character. There are lots of men with reputation but no character, and many with character but no reputation.

No one ever heard anybody say that Mr. Peek was "a good *sort* of man." No, it was always positive and certain that he was a *good* man, the *sort* was left out. Good *sort* of people is a very open and indefinite designation. It may mean anything or nothing. Usually it means people who are all things to all men. They are never disagreeable. They would not trouble your conscience for the world, and their own conscience never troubles them. They are ever sunny, but never sure. They belong to everybody, and yet nobody is sure of them. It is their marketable commodity; on it they trade; by it they live. They are both church and chapel, and yet they are neither. They are neither conservative nor radical, they are as the wind happens to blow where they chance to be. They are agreeable and that is all, and that only lasts till they are found out, then they are simply contemptible.

I prefer a disagreeable man to such as these. With him I know where I am and what to do, but with "*good sort of people*" it is a bewilderment. "It is better to obey God than man;" and when obedience to God comes in collision with the will and wish of man, there will, there must be conflict.

Expediency is a convenient word, but a potent spell with some, and an awful mockery and fearful sham to others. How much temperance reformers have been hampered by it, what a loophole it has been for "*good sort* of people," and what crowds of them we have at times had hovering about us! What adds to the annoyance and difficulty, is the parade and the virtue they make of *this* principle. For myself, I never could see any principle in it. There may be policy, but principle I see none.

To talk of expediency in matters of life and death, or of what may or may not be required in cases of moral welfare and national salvation, is a misapplication of words, and an assumption of virtue and superiority for which there is no just claim. Do the thing because it is right; if it is not right, don't do it. It may be expedient to be honest, it may be expedient to get married, it may be expedient to be religious, but what true value is there in such honesty, what true love is there in such marriage, and what true inspiration in such religion?

In such cases, that which is expedient to-day may be inexpedient to-morrow, and then, where is our honesty, where our marriage, and where our religion? The basis is unsound, the foundation rotten. The thing, if done, must be done because it is right—right personally, right relatively, right nationally, right for time, right for eternity. Against temperance there is no law, and there is no true temperance where the laws of life are violated, and our obligations to others ignored.

I remember Mr. Peek giving me a note of introduction to a gentleman living at Ivybridge; he had rendered some service to the church with which this good man was connected, for Mr. Peek spent the end of his days going about doing good, and out of respect to Mr. Peek I had found me a comfortable home, and secured for me a nice little meeting.

My host did not accompany me to the meeting, but came on subsequently. I saw him hanging about the door as if in doubt whether it would be becoming and respectable to go inside. At length he did decide to sit down just within the door of the little preaching place. This was a very common expedient in early days; lots of people have come to our meetings under the impression that there would soon be something so outrageously untrue said that they would have to leave, therefore it was always well to be near the door.

This gentleman stopped. The meeting being held in a place of worship, and knowing as I did in this case that the ignorance was great and the prejudice strong, there was more of a pronounced religious character about my address. Several members of that society at the close of the meeting signed the pledge, and my host got sufficiently interested to walk from the door to the communion rail to see them do so. When all was over we left together. Putting my arm in his, and pressing me warmly to his heart, for I felt it, he remarked, "I fear you will not think me a Christian." "Why?" said I. "Because I have not taken the pledge." Well now why should he have had such a thought? I had none such. Was it not that his *own conscience* was troubling him? And he thought it was mine that was exercised about him. May not this explain the many mistakes men make about what we say and think?

Richard Peek of Devon, Charles Jupe of Mere, and the Quaker banker, Mr. Fowler, of Melksham, were never described as "*good sort* of people," and consequently they never troubled themselves about what *other* people might *think*. They stood transparent and free in their own manhood, and were more concerned to be right with their own conscience than they were to be *thought* right by other people. That was the feeling which prompted the generous help so often bestowed by Mr. Jupe, and the self-sacrifice and honest bearing of Mr. Peek, and the kindly consideration of Mr. Fowler.

These men did their country and their God a quiet and lasting service in their recognition of the Temperance Cause when such friends were few and far between, and it is because I was personally made to feel and to enjoy it that I make this record.

The same applies to the house of the good Quaker of Melksham. That John Fowler, the son of that house, should, after founding a splendid business in Leeds, be prematurely struck down, was a terrible blow in many ways. How I remember his blooming manhood and noble form, and yet docile as a child and tender as a mother. He stood by me when a very young man in the British School in the town of Melksham, and was not ashamed of my bonds.

His brother, one of the members for Cambridge, and his cousin, this year London's Lord Mayor, and also one of the members for that city, will not, cannot, be unfaithful to the family traditions; and the influence they have attained, and the power they possess, can surely be reckoned upon in support of the interests cherished in the homes of their childhood.

CHAPTER XXVIII.

HISTORY.

IT is reported of John Wesley, that when troubled by men who were continually suggesting improved methods of management, he replied, "Don't mend my rules, but keep them."

Without going so far as to say that no improvement can be made on the original plan of operation as adopted by the early teetotallers for covering the land with temperance truth, and stamping out the evils of the liquor traffic, it will be admitted at least, that so far as their theory has been put into practice, and their example of personal abstinence followed, success, if not complete, has been most encouraging. The genuineness of the article may be ascertained by the circumstances and conditions under which it is manufactured, and an examination of the materials of which it is composed. That the people speaking our own tongue and in many instances allied to us by relationship of blood and faith and fellow-feeling, living on the other side of the Atlantic, should have been aroused to action because of the havoc made amongst the people of that young republic by the constant and deadly use of spirits, made us think at home whether or not something could not be done to deal with the same mischief at our own firesides; and it was under that impulse that the Rev. G. Carr, of New

Ross, in Ireland, John Dunlop, of Greenock, in Scotland, and Mr. Forbes, of Bradford, in Yorkshire, in the years 1829 and 1830, took action and vitalized a movement for the suppression of intemperance in our own land, and that too on the lines which up to that date had proved so very successful in the United States. They got, as is well known, a considerable following; but as that fatal and mistaken measure, the Beer Bill, came into operation the same date, a neck and neck race ensued, and we all know now at what disadvantage the friends of temperance were placed, and how shamefully they were beaten. The race is not always to the swift, I know, but in this case it was so, and the multipiied facilities for the sale of beer, and the increase in the number and size of public breweries all over the land, not only more than counteracted all the temperance teaching of that day, but made desperate and terrible havoc in virgin soil, and among the rising youth of the land. Nobody who has any true knowledge of the origin of the Temperance Movement, either in this land or America, can question the spirit that prompted it, nor doubt the motives which actuated its founders. They were philanthropic, patriotic, and Christian, and the names and lives of the men immediately concerned put doubt and misgivings on these points out of court at once and for ever. To talk as some men are doing now, of the godlessness and the prayerlessness of early workers, is one of the most unjust if not wicked circumstances in connection with our history, and that is saying a good deal, for we have had many unjust and many wicked things to survive and live down.

The Beer Bill and the beer power was the Goliath of that day. It defied the armies of the living God, and struck terror into the heart of the king, and men's hearts quailed for fear. The spirit pledge, which had been so effective in America, did not touch the root of our disease, and the friends of temperance were paralysed. They were at their wits' end. The people believed in beer, to touch beer was to touch the life of the nation; beer had been made cheap and beershops had been multiplied and brought near to the homes of the people by Acts of Parliament, that they might with the greater freedom and less difficulty possess themselves of the water of life. The Church said Amen to this deed, and prophets prophesied falsely. By these means the priests bore rule, and the people loved to have it so, and thus it was that in the nineteenth century a wonderful and horrible thing was committed in the land. Now the elder brethren, the rulers and leaders in the Church and the nation, were all to the front, they were there just as David's elder brethren were there in Gath, when the Goliath of old challenged and defied the hosts, and like them they did nothing but look on. But as soon as somebody else came to the front, also like them they began to move, but it was in the wrong direction. They questioned the propriety,—such people are always questioning somebody's propriety, they are doing it to-day, were it not so, I do not think I should have troubled to write this chapter,—they questioned the propriety of David's presence, and doubted the suitability of the weapon to be used. Of course nobody knew how to do it but themselves; it is always so with people who themselves do nothing, and they fold their arms under the fond delusion that people will have to come to them, they cannot be done without. But the people do *not* come to them, and that is the trouble; so at length, when they see that the thing will be done without them, they rush to the front, and like the limekiln soldiers, with flying colours exclaim, "*We have done it.*" Yes, they have done it, and it would be interesting to know how, and where, and when. Oh, yes, history repeats itself, and there is nothing new under the sun. Putting a new cloth into an old garment is not a commendable practice. Cannot our friends see the folly? We have had rents enough already,—don't make worse; and no rent is more ugly and more to be deprecated than a religious one. It may be an anomaly, but it is a truism that "No war is so bitter and so bloody as a religious war," and if temperance workers begin to fight about faith, farewell to their good works. As a temperance reformer, my concern is not with their faith so much as with their works. The signing and keeping of the temperance pledge is a deed, and one that *can* be done by *any* honest and honourable man, whatever he may believe, whatever he may think. That is not only our theory, but it is confirmed by practice, and to deny and doubt that is to deny and doubt the most established and irrefutable facts. Indeed, if we have had an especially weak place in our bulwarks, it has been the point watched and officered by men whose position in the Church might fairly have been supposed to have secured for them an abundant amount of saving and self-denying grace.

We suffered so much from this source that there were years in my history, as a temperance advocate, when I never applauded the signature of a minister; and if I am not mistaken I have somewhere in print a letter written more than forty years ago, in which I avowed that I had recently come across so many broken-down teetotallers among ministers, that personally I felt inclined in future when such a one presented himself for membership, to demand security for his fidelity from two other respectable citizens; and I am sorry to say I am not alone in that experience. Well, now, is it not preposterous, in the face of such experience, to talk of nothing but the grace of God helping a man to keep the pledge? I am utterly opposed to anything so unreasonable and, shall I say, unscriptural as this kind of teaching. We blame the devil for much of the ills of life, but pray let us not be guilty of charging upon the Almighty the responsibility of our infirmities and shortcomings. The guilt is not so much in the one direction, nor the failure in the other. The whole business is with ourselves, and the sooner the world and the Church in the world understand that and act accordingly the better.

The spirit pledge was worked in many localities with a good deal of zeal. The Queen lent her patronage, and bishops preached temperance. It would have been a marvellous thing if they had not done so. The people of Preston were not idle in those days; the conviction had been brought home to great numbers in our midst that drunkenness was an evil, that it was desirable to remove it, and the sooner it was done the better. Sir Astley Cooper and other leading physicians of that time spoke very pointedly and very plainly of the poisonous nature of ardent spirits, and a considerable feeling was begotten against their use. But wine and beer grew in favour, and the lips which denounced gin as poison, were frequently, while doing so, moistened with alcohol in the shape of wine and beer. Talk of " putting the devil out at the door and letting him in again by the window," here it was being done with a vengeance. The whole thing became demoralized. For a few years they struggled on, and by the aid of the Rev. Owen Clark, who was their paid and travelling secretary, they retained a name to live while they were dead. His mission seemed to be to fight the teetotallers, but he got the worst of it. The people ceased to subscribe enough to pay his salary, and when that happened the thing was buried. But in its day it did a good work, and helped to make a road on which and by which truer temperance could be taught and a more permanent and consistent work could be done.

There was no rush to what in early days was designated the teetotal pledge, the nation believed in beer, and every church and chapel vestry kept its wine. Teetotalism was therefore no whim, it was no wild fancy; it was not then, and is not now, a crotchet. Men who believed in the responsibility attached to life, felt that something must be done. Many plans were tried; amongst others was one which allowed those who signed it to have one pint of ale a day, seven pints a week. It was thought that if men would adopt and strictly adhere to that rule it would in some measure suppress drunkenness. That was thought a capital pledge, and they got many to sign. Some who did so, there was reason to believe, had not been in the habit of getting above a pint or two during the week, but they signed under the impression that they were entitled to seven, and they acted up to the pledge to the very letter. For a while things looked promising, but one Saturday a gentleman, who had taken special interest in that department, met a man in the street drunk who had signed that pledge. He was charged with having done so. "Well, yes, sir," he said, "I did, but I have been so busy all the week I have not had time to take my pints regular, so I had a little time on hand to-day, and I took them all together, but (hiccoughing) I have only had seven, I assure you."

Another pledge was one allowing those who signed it to have only "one glass at a sitting." Well, a great many signed that. The early men tried hard, I can assure those who may care to know, to cure the curse and keep the cause of it; and I firmly believe that if the plague-spot of drunkenness could have been wiped from our country's brow by what men called the "moderate" use of strong drink, it would have been done. Amongst the signers of this pledge was a relation of my own. What were his motives for signing I cannot say. He was a strange character named Moss. He was a wet moss; he worked hard all the week, on the Saturday got his wages about noon, went to Lancaster and called at fourteen different public-houses and got fourteen glasses at different sittings, quite in accordance with his pledge. When he got to the fourteenth place he did not feel disposed to go any further, and climaxed the whole with a violent and disgusting drunken bout. All this was very discouraging. If our Church friends can do any better, none will rejoice more than myself, but they must not imagine that they have found out some *new* and royal road to a nation's sobriety.

We have had platforms quite as broad as theirs, and we have abandoned them, if not in disgust, in despair, feeling convinced that there is but one cure,—and that consists in clearing the stomach, clearing the homestead, and clearing the Church of everything, by whatever name it may be known, or in whatever colour it may be shown, that can intoxicate. When that is done, the nation will do the rest and the land will be free.

During the operation of these various pledges, two men were reclaimed in the town of Preston,—Swindlehurst and King. The committee learned from these men that ever after signing the moderation or ardent spirit pledge, they had acted upon what is now known as the teetotal principle. Though there was no such pledge in existence at the time, they had abstained entirely from *all* intoxicating liquors and from the public-house, and had consequently never been overcome since. That practice in all probability had been begotten by the teaching of William Pollard, of Manchester, and James Teare, who not infrequently in public meetings in the town of Preston declared there was no safety but in entire abstinence. For this the committee more than once called Teare to order; but from all I can gather, James struck the key-note for remodelling the machinery, and Joseph Livesey embodied and crystallized it in that wonderful pledge written in his memorandum book, signed by John King himself and five others, dating from September, 1832. *That* was, and *there* was the fire kindled which has warmed many thousands of hearts, and brightened many hundreds of homes in these three kingdoms, and in other lands as well, and no power under Heaven will ever be able to put it out.

It will be seen then that it was no plot on behalf of bad and revolutionary men, as some said, to ruin the country and beggar the Chancellor of the Exchequer; neither was it an insult to God by perverting Scripture, and rejecting His blessings and despising His mercies, as the Church taught; but a benevolent desire to save men from death, and an earnest wish on the part of comparatively humble and unknown men once again to renew the song, "Glory to God in the highest, and on earth peace and goodwill to men." In that resolve they made no mistake; in that hope they have not been disappointed. The cloud little as a man's hand, which for years could not at all times be seen, and was not infrequently hid and sought to be blown away by men who ought to have prayed for it and blessed it, has gathered and spread so as to be seen by all people and scatter blessings on all lands. At this point many interesting details could be given, but that would be going beyond my purpose and occupy space wanted for other matter, which perhaps if I do not mention nobody else will.

The first teetotal pledge, it should never be forgotten, was an experiment, and was only an adjunct to the pledge already in existence. The working and experience of it was, however, so far above and beyond all hope and expectation, that in twelve months' time it became, so to speak, the substantive motion, and the original was decently buried, and has never been resuscitated, except the Church of England Temperance Society may be said to have done it. Should that be so, they may have put back their own family clock to suit the time of day in which they themselves are living, but it is not Greenwich time, and only shows how late they themselves are in rising.

The period from the year 1832 to 1842 covered the great battle-field on this question, a handful of men braved, as one of our early hymns says, "the world's unpitying scorn," and faced a grinning insulting mob; and while that was the condition of things out in the open field, in the inclosures of the Church, though the fighting was neither so furious nor so coarse, it was often more persevering, disastrous, and fatal. That this contention and strife was in the main founded on sincere belief I do not question, but as numbers do not determine right, so neither does belief make the truth. A thing that is right is right apart from and independent of opinions; and that which is true is not true because it is believed, but true whether people believe it or not. Circumstances may alter cases, and often do, and never more so than has happened in connection with temperance teaching, but no circumstance and no power can alter facts. In that fixed law has been our strength, and though there have been times in our history when we have fainted, we never lost hope. The force against us more than once came with overwhelming might, and in its presence we staggered but did not fall. Then it was we were made to feel the appropriateness of the language, "If it had not been the Lord who was on our side, now may Israel say; if it had not been the Lord who was on our side, when men rose up against us: then they had swallowed us up quick, when their wrath was kindled against us: then the waters had overwhelmed us, the stream had gone over our soul: then the proud waters had gone over our soul. Blessed be the Lord, who hath not given us as a prey to their teeth. Our soul is escaped as a bird out of the snare of the fowlers: the snare is broken, and we are escaped. Our help is in the name of the Lord, who made heaven and earth." No kid-gloved hand could use the weapons then in use, and no drawing-room assemblage could stand the assaults made upon our ranks.

The work of the time had to be done by men fitted

for it, and if ever the finger of God could be seen in the uprising of any people it was seen in this work. While it is true in the main that "there is nothing new under the sun," it is also true that some things can never be repeated. There has been an individuality and adaptation suited to the times, in connection with our history, which marvellously manifested unerring wisdom, and a guiding care not common to ordinary life. Where shall we go for a second Joseph Livesey, a duplicate James Teare, a copy of Edward Grubb, a likeness of Henry Anderton, and a second F. R. Lees, and others whom the readers of these pages will have no difficulty in bringing to mind? They were made for the work, and the work was made for them. They were men born in due time, and well their part was acted, and "in that the honour lies." Should any one tarnish their names or reflect on their work and spirit in my presence, I will thank somebody to hold my hands.

The assumptions and parade, the presumption and pride of the temperance platform to-day, are but the confectionaries of the establishment, and will need watching and doctoring just as children do after the parties and feastings at Christmas-tide.

That we should rejoice in our abundance is but becoming, and that the sheaves when ripe should be gathered in is a wholesome and proper arrangement; but where is our next crop to come from if our workers have no implements but mowing machines? And what will become of the crops gathered, if they are not properly housed and utilized? Harvest time is a time of joy and rejoicing, and we have not been denied the ordinary results of a well-worked and a well-cultivated soil; but it is a shabby thing to forget the needs of the gleaners, and when sitting down to the feast to ignore the tillers of the land and the sowers of the seed. The fact that the revenue derived from the sale of drink was at its lowest point for very many years past, during the years 1880 and 1881, and that since that time there has been a tendency upwards, ought to moderate the claims of certain men who are apt to confound things that differ, as well as ignore things that exist.

I should be sorry to say that the increase in the revenue derived from drink, during the last two or three years, was because of the Blue Ribbon Movement; but it would be as true to say *that* as it is for the men who have made themselves conspicuous in the decoration business to say that the diminution which previously took place was because of their presence and work, notwithstanding they were not in it at all.

The fact is there are at times other causes at work apart from ourselves which affect the barometer of the liquor traffic. It will, nevertheless, always be a gain to our side if only one man be induced to leave off drinking who drank before. Counting heads for show is very misleading, and parading figures and calling them facts, when realization proves them fiction, is only in character with a bankrupt who cheats himself into the belief that he is solvent, by putting his own value on his effects. There is another side to all these things, and he who neglects to look on that side will sooner or later come to grief.

To speak of the thousands who have donned the blue ribbon as converts to what is called Gospel Temperance, is a delusion, and is contrary to fact; they have in very many cases, as in my own, accepted the insignia as a happy and innocent protest against a silly and obnoxious practice, as well as a proclamation of a received and valuable truth. These were converts before; and what with reckoning up such as these, and counting thousands who in many cases thoughtlessly, and in some I fear wickedly, took the ribbon in sport, and in many cases several times over, that is to say attending every meeting during the mission, and at each meeting thought it fun to let the lasses pin on the blue, certainly a show is made, but it is an egotistical blaze of assumption to think that *that* is the thing which has touched the liquor traffic at the core, and made the Church and the nation combine to break the yoke that binds us. Brain power and moral life come not like a flash of lightning, nor by magic, they are the result of patient plodding and personal discipline, and patient plodding and personal discipline are neither hothouse plants, nor begotten by a meteoric life.

CHAPTER XXIX.

OUR MEANS AND MEN.

THE love of fight and the disposition to strive for the mastery must be very strong in us, for long before we had settled the business with our foes, we began to quarrel with our friends. The first Temperance Society (that is the one imported to us from America) had scarcely been put to rest, when a very serious quarrel and dissension took place amongst leading friends in London.

The Preston teetotalism, the original article, undoubtedly enjoined on all its adherents not only personal abstinence, but also forbade the giving and offering of drink to others; that means of course neither buying nor selling, nor keeping it in our homes, nor giving it to others, except purely as medicine. The providing for friends and putting it on the table has been a great difficulty with many from the first, and is so still. In the main, the men who founded the society and laid the basis were not amongst those who cared much for public opinion, nor were they strongly tied by social customs, and consequently their moral sense had healthy exercise, and in this particular it developed itself in a complete separation from what was felt to be an immoral business.

Not that they of necessity thought the men engaged

in it immoral or irreligious, but to themselves it did take that form, and they acted accordingly. Well, that of course narrowed our sphere of operation very much, and vast numbers who were morally certain of the correctness of our theory had not the courage to put in force our practice. Still they were our friends, gave us money, found us homes, and in other ways rendered most acceptable and needed service. In that way they gradually became a power, and agitated as to the propriety of continuing this rigid rule of excluding from us those who could not withhold it from their friends.

Lord Stanhope, and others high in the social scale, were willing to be personal abstainers, but could go no further, and there was a giving way to embrace in our organization all such. The executive of what was then known as the " New British and Foreign Temperance Society," were divided in opinion as to the course to be taken, and it resulted in one portion forming another society, calling itself the " Society for the Suppression of Intemperance," with Earl Stanhope at its head, and opening its doors to all pledged to personal abstinence ; the remainder keeping to the old lines and the old name, with William Janson, Esq., a banker in the City and an influential underwriter at Lloyd's, at its head. The amount of ill-feeling begotten for a time was very pitiable, and proved to demonstration that teetotalism was not "everything." Certainly it was not, it was neither charity nor brotherly kindness : separate offices, separate committees, separate periodicals, and a separate body of agents. In the press and on the platform frequent bickerings and misrepresentation took place. The periodical then known as *The Temperance Intelligencer* was the organ of the separatists, and was edited (and often in a very bitter spirit) by Mr. G. W. Green, a very clever but a very irreconcilable man.

The original party had as their organ *The Temperance Journal,* which was under the control of the honorary secretaries, of whom Mr. Meredith was one—a man of marvellous perseverance and wonderful tact, with a singleness of purpose most unquestionable. A better, a more upright and more devoted worker I never knew.

It is possible that upon the whole good came out of this separation, provoking and unpleasant as it was in itself. The two societies strove for power and influence. To secure this they had to find money and do work. Many in connection with them were most sincere in their feeling, and energetic in their efforts; but for several years the separation and contention was a very disturbing element. Still the work went on, and great progress was made during these years, from 1838 to 1845 especially.

There are always more offices to fill and more places to be had in two societies than in one, and when there are men fit for office, who think they ought to be in office, and are kept out, from whatever cause it matters not, it will not be long before they begin a new society on its own merits, or because of the shortcomings or incapacities of the old. This is always happening. It happened then, it is happening now, and it has happened many a time in the interim and will happen in the future. In business there are companies and companies, and in the societies there are societies and societies, and in each case there are always designing men and easy dupes.

Teetotalism does not change our nature, it only alters our circumstances, and that which is unpleasant amongst us must not be debited to the thing but to the management of those who have charge of it.

Now religion is credited with illuminating the nature, and yet even nature in its improved and regenerate state does some fantastic tricks. Then why not teetotalism? And if all these disagreeable things happen in our improved condition, what a mess we should have been in had we never been improved at all!

After all, in the case in question, better counsels did in time prevail, and for nearly forty years now we have heard nothing, or but little, of "long" and "short" pledges, and people are left to settle these details as their own consciences and circumstances may dictate, and no one presumes to interfere.

The National Temperance League, with its late marvellous president, Mr. S. Bowly, and its incomparable secretary, Mr. R. Rae, many years ago healed that breach, and has ever since been carrying on a temperance work which is perhaps more enduring and farther reaching in its results, than is the work done by any temperance organization in the country.

The Weekly Record, the organ of the society, which has taken the place of the periodicals which in the past were issued by the two societies, is a very exceptional serial, and a vast advance on much of the temperance literature of the past, and scarcely equalled by any of the present day; at 337, Strand, London, will be found the offices and book depôt of the League. They may be visited by all workers in the temperance world, and what is perhaps better still, without offence to taste, prejudice, or principles.

The British Temperance League, the executive town for which is now Sheffield, is really the parent society, and dates back to 1835. It was organized in Manchester in that year, and was the first national teetotal organization in the country. It has continued to this day, and is at present more vigorous in its operations than it has been for many years past. It has never departed from its fundamental principles, and has been thorough in its teaching all the way along the line. Its agents are sound in the faith, and the platform on which they stand is immovable as the granite rock. They are the real inheritors of the Preston faith, and the most true and triumphant defenders of its doctrine. Mr. W. Gregson is now the senior agent, and is but one of many of the most self-denying and disinterested labourers, by which this sadly too little known society has covered the country. James Barlow, J.P., Bolton, is the president, and the Rev. C. H. Collyns, of Sheffield, the secretary. If Mr. Barlow were as well known nationally, as he is in his own home and neighbourhood, he would be about the most esteemed and best loved man in the land. So far as he is known, that esteem and that love he possesses. His teetotalism dates back to an early day, and he is a wonderful example of what piety, probity, and business application can do. Mr. Collyns is of more recent times, and has only for a few years held the office he now fills; but he is at home in the work, and has helped very materially to give new life to an old organization, and manages with great patience to keep in good form the societies and agents which are under his special care and direction.*

---

* Mr. Collyns is deceased since this was written.

The *British League Temperance Advocate*, which is the organ of the society, is really what was originally *The Preston Temperance Advocate*, commenced by Mr. Livesey, and is the oldest teetotal paper in the world. It has been very much improved under Mr. Collyns's supervision and direction.

The great drawback to the nationalization of the League is in its localization. The head-quarters have always been in the north, and its executive is a movable body. There is more difficulty in circulating its literature from the country than there would be from an office in London, and a local executive is a disadvantage in comparison with a London one. That will explain how we came to have a London centre, and a national executive resident there; that was felt to be needed very early in the movement, and no one can doubt its wisdom. The two societies work in harmony, so that, as the land is covered and the work done, there is no necessity for complaint.

The United Kingdom Alliance, as everybody knows, is an organization with a political purpose; it dates from 1853. The original intent was by an imperial act to put down the liquor traffic.

The State of Maine had passed such a law, and the results were of such a character as to beget the desire to secure something of the same kind for England. Nathaniel Card, a Quaker and a Manchester manufacturer, became quite an enthusiast in the business, and he managed to surround himself with a few warm-hearted sympathisers in that city. In 1852 he came to London, with papers and proposals to a temperance conference to be held in Exeter Hall. He lodged at an hotel where I happened to be staying. On the morning of the conference, he was ill in bed and could not be removed. He was in great trouble, he had come on purpose to do a work which his state of health forbade him to attempt, and in his emergency he sent for me into his bedroom, and begged that I would take charge of his papers, and submit them, or get some one else to submit them, to that conference. I did so. They were simply a recognition of the good work done in Maine, and an expression to the effect that some organization should be set on foot to secure similar results here.

The conference gave its assent, but took no practical steps. Mr. Card returned to Manchester, and in the year following the first conference having that definite object in view was called. I was present. It was a very influential gathering; some very stirring papers were read, upon which interesting discussions followed. The affair was fairly floated then; the conferences have been annually continued in the same city, at nearly all of which I have been present, and they are undoubtedly the most influential and enthusiastic gatherings (in combination with the *public meetings* in the Free Trade Hall) held in this country, in any place, and on any subject. The object of the United Kingdom Alliance, as already said, is a political, not a *party* one. Persons of all religions and of all shades of political feeling, may join, and *do* join it, as do teetotallers, and non-teetotallers. Politics are taught, religion is taught, and teetotalism is undoubtedly taught; but it would be a violation of the fundamental principles of the society, and a departure from its practice, to use its platform or its press for sectarian purposes, or political partizanship. In that respect it is the same as the temperance platform pure and simple.

We are not faithful to our trust if by act or deed we make our platform uncomfortable to any citizen of this country. We are emphatically the friends of all, and the enemies of none, and the Alliance it must be admitted (considering the critical position it holds politically) has been marvellously clear of blame in this particular.

A large amount of true temperance teaching, and of good, sound, general, moral, and political sense come also from the same platform. It is therefore a valuable acquisition to national life and health, as well as a wonderful combination of national power.

"Some men are born great, others achieve greatness, and some have greatness thrust upon them." Without saying anything here on the first and last conditions just mentioned, I may be permitted to say a word or two on the second characteristic.

I speak more especially of what the Americans call the "hub" of the society, its working, its moving power. Did ever anybody know such a secretary as Mr. T. H. Barker? Talk of doing the work, why he would *die* if he did not do it, and what is more, he would die if he could not get somebody else to do it as well. He is never without a job, neither is any one else who goes to see him; indeed, I have given it up, I never go to see him. He does not talk, he works, he has "achieved greatness."

Then look at Mr. William Hoyle: what a wonderful man that quiet Rossendale lad has become! Why, he is a power in the nation, and in some particulars we bow at his feet.

It was said of Paul, his "letters are powerful, but his bodily presence is weak;" what shall be said of Mr. Hoyle? In life and in letters he is a marvel. He is seriously in earnest. He walks like a man among the dead, and cannot rest because of the iniquity of the land. How much of sober thought, how much of self-denial, how much of mental application it has cost him, no tongue can tell.

The result is, however, he stands a giant before us to-day, he has "achieved greatness." Like the secretary, he is buried in his business, and unless what you say or do bears upon what he feels to be the burden of his soul, namely, the national loss and the national waste by drink, he becomes restless.

Jocularity and mirthfulness he thinks is trifling, and any one given to that in his presence, may see written on his forehead " no room for mirth or trifling here." Those of us who would "laugh and grow fat," are sometimes, I fear, a trouble to him; but he should understand that people who are accustomed to condiments with their mental as well as their physical food, will only do badly if they cannot get their accustomed appetizer.

Mr. James H. Raper, who does not know him? What would the Alliance be without him? Who could spot a man fit to take his place? Racy, ready, and at times refreshing, and we do now and then need, and actually take refreshment like other sublunary mortals. Our good friends, Messrs. Barker and Hoyle, may be able to go on for ever without, but some of us cannot—do let us have a recess, ten minutes for "refreshments."

"Raper is up"—everybody else sit down—up just in time to prevent an explosion, or dispel a gathering cloud. With what skill, what careful manipulation the unseen is revealed, the contradiction made to harmonize, and the difficulties of the situation made to contribute to firmer resolves, and more united action;

x

the peroration and climax, if not lifting the roof and bringing down the house, raising the people from their seats, and sending their hands down into their pockets to a depth that even brings sunshine into the faces of our two serious friends, and joy into their hearts. In council, in conference, and on the platform Mr. Raper stands unrivalled, and has therefore "achieved greatness."

Once again, and I leave this department: Sir Wilfrid Lawson completes the quartette. He is the most wonderful man of all, our own Sir Wilfrid as we call him, the people's joy! The president and leader of the Alliance hosts; coming to us a slender, unpretending, delicate young man, what a promise he made, but what a power he has become! He is not the people's tribune, but he *is* the people's trust; he is not the greatest power in the House of Commons, but he has the biggest heart and the most unlimited soul, and the influence of these will be felt and seen when most of the glory and greatness of the present will be, if not forgotten, repented of.

The favour with which he is looked upon, and the respect in which he is held by all parties in that House, is a testimony to his merits and ability which has but few comparisons in the history of that congregation of gentlemen. He has in the best of tempers and with becoming deportment, led in that House what many looked upon as a forlorn hope, for nearly a quarter of a century.

Again and again, when friends were few, was he equal to the occasion, when not successful, still not defeated, and though the story was a twice-told one, he never failed to obtain a respectful, and often a joyous hearing. The House believed in the man before they believed in what he advocated. They knew it was an unfailing test of sincerity, when a man gave his money and himself in support and in defence of his principle.

They therefore at length admitted the justice of his claim, and for the time being Sir Wilfrid is triumphant even in the House of Commons. Having then carried his resolution in the House, he has "achieved greatness." The House has now taken the responsibility off his shoulders and must deal with this question. It is for those who have pushed the battle to the gate to watch that there be no outlet from the city, and to see that there be no traitors within it; making fair allowance for time and opportunity, but to keep sentinel until the ground gained is fairly realized and fully possessed.

CHAPTER XXX.

MANY, BUT ONE.

THE British League, The National League, and The Alliance, are the three great organizations in this country for the promotion of temperance among our people and the suppression of the liquor traffic.

Ireland and Scotland do battle in the same direction, Dublin and Belfast being the working centres in the one case, and Glasgow in the other. The fiery spirit and burning tongue of Mr. Russell of Dublin is equal to the conflagration of any nation, and no wonder that a land like Ireland should be in an occasional blaze with such a fire running through its dry stubble. The speech he made in the Alliance Council, October, 1883, will not soon be forgotten. We were ignited ourselves, and had we not been steeped in cold water for nearly fifty years, we should have been consumed. That that pale face and attenuated form should have underlying them a persuasion and a power at times overwhelming, is one of those things "no fellow can understand." *How*, we may not understand; but that it *is*, we see and feel, and with such spirits in any land, backed with a sense of right, there can be but one termination, and that termination means, freedom from all moral and social wrongs, and from every political injustice and religious fraud.

While Dublin carries sail, Belfast attends to the ballast, and is careful with the ship and rigging, and in combination keep the country hopeful in a temperance point of view.

Our Scotch friends have ever been to the front. It is well known that at times attempts have been made to show that they are not all they seem to be; but did ever any one happen to be present when a Scotchman's claims to pre-eminence were disputed, and he did not make them feel that at least it would have been as well if nothing had been said about it?

They are not only soon awoke, but they are bad to put to sleep, and it will not surprise me if even now whisky-drinking Scotland shows the way in local option and national sobriety, as it has done in Sunday closing and the excellent organization of auxiliary work.

The publication department of the Scottish Temperance League is certainly second to none, while their agents in character and labour are beyond praise. Ex-Provost Sir W. Collins is a most intelligent and painstaking president, while W. Johnston is a most unwearied and efficient secretary.

George Easton—grand old George!—stood head and shoulders above his fellows physically, while he was no dwarf mentally. He did a noble work, was, until his recent death, senior agent of that League, and his name was a household word throughout broad Scotland.

David Lewis—Ex-Bailie Lewis—is only one of many men who in Scotland have done herculean work, and left their mark upon a thoughtful and an appreciative people.

With such interest as North Britain possesses, there is not much fear of her holding her rank with honour amongst temperance reformers.

I cannot of course mention a tithe of the names deserving record in connection with temperance work in a production such as this is meant to be; but there are certain men it is difficult to get away from, and it is only those photographed on my brain, and who are ever with me, who come out at my finger's end.

The Rev. J. A. Johnston, Springburn, for instance, is one of many spirits which cannot be laid, and with which the temperance cause is blest—I say blest. Some of my readers may question this, and say, "Why, Mr. Johnston is in temperance legislation what John Bright said the Americans were in reference to patents, he has always got a bill in his pocket." Just so; John Bright's reference to the characteristic of Americans was to their credit, and I for one think this reference to Mr. Johnston is to *his* credit. He has an eye to business; he can see the signs of the times, and provides accordingly. That is true wisdom, and Scotland need be proud of the Springburn parson. He is indefatigable, and works with an honesty and sincerity, combined with great ability, such as is seldom seen. He is spring-*born*, and may he long well up the life and force he puts into what he does.

The societies which may be called the inner circle of the movement, and have sprung out of it, are the "Rechabites," "The Sons of Temperance," and the "Templars." The Rechabites and the Sons of Temperance are beneficiary societies, making provision for their members in cases of sickness and death, and well deserving the patronage and support of all teetotallers who have the good sense to see the necessity and feel the need of such forethought and provident habits as these excellent institutions beget and foster.

The Templars is one of the many importations with which we have been favoured from America. It has no doubt its good points, but whether they are worth the time it takes, and the money it costs to keep the machinery going, is a very questionable matter. It has certainly brought to the front a number of men we should never have heard of had it not been for it, but it has shut up and buried alive a great many more who ought to have been, and who would have been, much more valuable to the cause had they not spent so much time in dressing and undressing, and in discussing what templarism means, instead of what teetotalism does. The charter is not worth the paper on which it is printed, and yet thousands of pounds have been spent to know who shall hold it, and miserable jealousies are begotten, and exclusive prejudices cherished, which are a disgrace to our intelligence, and a grievous hindrance to the work of temperance.

Good Templarism has always seemed to me to be a society set on foot to put little men into big places, and as there are so many little men, they cannot all be provided for, and hence the scramble, the disappointment and dilemma. The advantages supposed to be gained by signs and from words and grips are too ridiculous to mention. The simple bit of *blue* is worth more as a testimony and a recognition than the whole paraphernalia of the "Grand Lodge," and then it is so cheap, and can be "donned" and used without the ceremony of a lodge. That many of our oldest and best friends and workers have been taken and carried away with this speciality and superfluity is admitted, and that there are no more sincere and honest workers in the cause than many of them are, is not the less true; but the whole machinery is out of gear with the habits and tastes of our people, and there is not now, and never has been, and in my judgment never can be, an equivalent for the money spent and time wasted in what is called "the working of the order."

Temperance in this land is the child of Christian charity and pure philanthropy, and all our native national organizations have been instituted and worked by bodies of men who have given their time and money in promoting them. Not so in America. Organizations in that land are run very much as they run stores, and the rulers have their money interests in the one as in the other, and this does not fit our figure, nor harmonize with our national tastes.

There is no blinking the fact, that in all the American importations in connection with temperance, the almighty dollar has sooner or later been a prominent feature, and the "starring" system is as purely professional, and as much of a venture, as any stage performance or theatrical enterprise in the world.

This sort of thing may exist, but it cannot thrive among men whose business is to call sinners to repentance, and who count not their lives dear that they may save some.

Perhaps there is no feature of the Temperance Enterprise more pleasant to look upon than is that of the Band of Hope. The thousands and hundreds of thousands of children now under temperance training in all parts of this land is one of the soundest and safest temperance investments extant; and there is this advantage in it, nobody objects. The publicans themselves say, "save and bless the *children*." They are virgin soil, and no one is hurt, but every one blessed by our gathering them, and they like it themselves.

When we take the drinking adult, it is butter out of the dog's throat. It is difficult, and the dog barks, growls, and bites; but with the child it is different. "What the eye does not see, the heart does not grieve at." The publican has not yet seen them, so he does not grieve at their loss. The child has nothing to lose, nothing to give up, and a child without the example and lesson to drink will no more think of doing so than does the domestic cat or dog.

It may be thought that there is but little in young people taking the pledge, for as a rule children do not under any circumstances drink much. That may be so, but is not "the child father to the man"? and have we not in all parts of the country to-day men and women who have now themselves families of children, who have sung from early days in our concerts at the Crystal Palace and other places, and who even yet take interest and part in these gatherings?

I travelled myself with a carriage (I might almost say a train) full of them from the midland counties last summer on their way to the fête. Our good friend, the Rev. G. W. McCree, in his day has done good and enduring work in that as well as many other departments, and our energetic F. Smith is doing it now, and doing it well.

The London Band of Hope Union is a healthy and hopeful work, and our Yorkshire and Lancashire friends are not a whit behind them. Both Mrs. Carlisle of Dublin, and the Rev. Jabez Tunnicliffe of Leeds have left their mark in this work, and Mr. T. B. Smithies of London, with his wonderful tact and beautiful publications, did lasting and loving service in this way. These have all passed away. We heave a sigh and drop a tear over many a grave in penning these records, but we gird our loins and brighten our hopes as we think of the work they did, and the memories they left.

The Temperance and General Provident Life Assurance Office is another outcome of the Temperance Enterprise, and so also is the London Temperance Hospital. These two institutions were born in due time; they were the wholesome and legitimate offspring of temperance teaching.

When it was attempted to charge a man an extra premium for insurance, because he was, as they then believed, *shortening his life* by teetotalism, it was time to take steps in self-defence, and to demonstrate to an ignorant and prejudiced public that they had much to learn, while we ourselves were prepared to ratify our belief in our principles with our lives.

That was the foundation of the *Temperance* Life Office, and though the risk was great, so was our faith. The country was not then so ripe for temperance talk as it is now, and people *did* doubt then if teetotalism was always safe and practicable, hence the risk.

The progress, for a time, was slow; but we held on, and the guaranteed fund, secured to us by Mr. Robert Warner and others, vitalized our confidence, and stimulated to perseverance.

The office has had forty-four years' experience, and will to-day compare favourably with any similar institution in the country, indeed in some particulars it is unapproachable, and has now an annual income of £400,000, and an accumulated capital of nearly *four millions*, while the lives of teetotallers have been proved to be not only equal to the average lives of the people, but very much superior.

That has settled the question as to whether teetotalism onduces to length of life or not, and the *Temperance Life Office* has not only succeeded in a business sense as but few offices have done, but it has also been the great factor in the production of evidence indisputable as to the value and practicability of teetotalism.

That in itself is a gain to our agitation, and a weapon in the hand of the advocate of temperance, by which can be slain the entire hosts who believe in the teaching, "Skin for skin, all that a man hath will he give for his life." I am glad I joined this office in its morning, and that my confidence in it has grown with its years.

No more striking proof of the valuable service of this institution could be given than is contained in the fact that several other life offices have recently opened special departments for the insurance of *teetotal lives*, and promising it too on terms something cheaper than they charge the ordinary public, while on the other hand a great number of offices refuse to insure a publican's life on any terms whatsoever. What a change! People who forty years ago were charged extra because of what they were, are now charged less because of what they are. The change is not in us; the change is in them. We are teetotallers now when the charge is cheap; we were teetotallers then when the charge was dear.

We wish success to every effort that goes right and works straight, but our friends will do well to look before they leap in life assurance matters as well as in many others, and no office, by whatever name it may be known, can do more for its teetotal members than can the good old, well-tried *Temperance Provident*, and very few so well.

"Honour thy father and thy mother, that thy days

may be long in the land," is wholesome and commendable teaching, and all temperance men will do well to remember this in connection with insurance. There is something due to age as well as to past service.

What a lesson the positive refusal to insure a publican's life contains! These offices will insure sailors, pilots, fishermen; they will insure coal-miners, engine-drivers, stokers, and railway guards, and indeed almost anybody and everybody, especially if they pay a little extra premium to cover any little special risk they may run, but they will not have a publican at any price. Why? There are more storms in the public-house than at sea; and there is more destruction in the bottle than in the winds of heaven. That is the reason why. Then why does not Government insist upon every public-house carrying a life-boat? and why do not doctors who recommend drink supply their patients with life-saving belts?

Perhaps the experience of the Temperance Hospital will do for teetotalism, in matters of surgical operations and hospital treatment without the use of strong drink, what the *Temperance* Insurance Office has done for it in matters of health and life.

That the past ten years' experience of that hospital has so far gone in that direction is pretty clear. We have long since driven the advocates of these drinks (as a necessity to health and the ordinary duties of life) out of court. They have not a leg to stand on, and we are now running them into a corner in matters of medical treatment, and in cases of severe surgical operations. Dr. James Edmonds, the head of this hospital, is filling a place and making a name that will not be forgotten.

Everybody who pays any attention to the management of our public institutions knows with what freedom, if not extravagance and thoughtlessness, liquors in them are used, and so using them under the high authority which is supposed to exist, this practice leads the country and influences the lesser lights.

To speak of withholding beer from the pauper brings down upon the proposer of such a deed contempt and scorn, and it is but rarely indeed that there is sufficient support given to such proposals to secure a trial of the experiment. The common clap-trap of "cruelty to the poor," is a powerful weapon in a contested election for guardians. The people never think how very few of such poor as our workhouses contain would have any existence at all as such were it not for the drink they or their connections had taken, and yet we are so blind as to nurse the delusion and encourage the cheat even in the minds of those who are pauperised by it.

However, men are moving, and the light is dawning on even the minds of guardians and vestry-men, and in cases where the experiment of expelling the drink from such places has been tried, the results are in character with the results following in every institution, of whatever kind and object, in which they had the good sense to be guided by facts and common sense.

That beggars should be choosers is an absurdity, and that medical men should be tolerated in a baneful and unnecessary expenditure, is an injustice to the ratepayers and a mischief to the paupers. All that temperance people want is fair-play, and we hold that in asylums and hospitals, as well as in workhouses and infirmaries, the people, all other things being equal, are better *without the drink*. This is not only our theory, but it has been realized in practice, and it is persecution and bigotry on the part of those concerned to shut their eyes and stop their ears, and deny us the ordinary rights of citizens.

We claim, however, to know about what we talk, and demand to be heard at the bar of public opinion. Closed doors and secret conclaves may succeed for a time in hoodwinking the people, and retaining power, and even beget a cry among the ignorant and malicious and revengeful such as was uttered in the court in which Pilate sat, "Not this man, but Barabbas. Now Barabbas was a robber." He was one then; he is one now. But now, as then, many of those who so cry will regret when too late their blindness and folly, and it will be seen how utterly impossible it is to put out the light of science now, as it was the light of truth then.

Agitation for the suppression of the sale of intoxicating liquors on the Sabbath, and the closing of the public-house on that day, is another child of the Temperance Reformation. All who take an interest in that movement do not work on the same lines or for the same reason as teetotallers; they act as Sabbatarians, and on purely religious and sacred grounds. This is all legitimate and welcome help, but the origin, and life even, of this wholesome and much-needed reform, belongs to *us*, and no better proof can be given of that fact than to show how the Church slept on this business, as it has on many others, until somebody from the outside thundered at its doors. Then who did this thundering at the Church? and who first intimated to Parliament the need for this step? The Temperance League (founded at Manchester in 1835, its headquarters is now at Sheffield) led the van, and they have been joined by the London League, and all the other temperance organizations throughout the country, and by none with more earnestness and practical results than by the "Alliance" people.

The marvellous petition of more than half a million Methodists in 1883, under the direction of its president, the Rev. C. Garrett, was after all but the putting forth of the temperance power in that community.

The patience and perseverance of Mr. Edward Whitwell in connection with this phase of temperance work is beyond all praise. Sir Wilfrid for the prohibition, Mr. Whitwell for Sunday-closing, Dr. Norman Kerr for medical teaching and medical reform, and Mr. Robert Rae for an intelligent and popularizing teaching of teetotalism, are each and all marvels in their way. They are unique. We care not from what quarter the foe comes, these men in their several departments are prepared to give him battle, and belong to the class who "never say *die*."

Nobody would ever dream of Mr. Whitwell drawing a sword, or floating a banner, or rolling a drum. But there are more ways of fighting than one, and the most triumphant fighter is the man who will not die, and who never gives in: the man who folds his arms in the face of the storm, and stands unmoved as the rock in the tempest, knowing no rock is more sure than the Rock of Ages, and no weapon more powerful than that of truth—such a man is Mr. Edward Whitwell of Kendal.

CHAPTER XXXI.

GOSPEL TEMPERANCE.

WHEN any agitation attacking a national vice, or seeking to bring about a national blessing, obtains sufficient hold on public feeling to command something like general approval and respect, then it is that men start up, in some cases, to write a history; in others, to make a purse; and in others, to keep a footing. These are generally from the ranks of those who see the signs of the times, and who know how to utilise events, so that they themselves shall not be lost sight of in the hour of triumph and the day of victory.

Worldly wisdom is no crime, and may (if influenced by a spiritual understanding) be of immense value in a moral and religious sense. That there is in such often a large amount of what the world calls "go," and, may be, no lack of confidence, ought not to disqualify, but rather commend, them. We have at times been slow enough and mean enough in our movements to make any impulse, from any source, and with any motive, a refreshing and welcome circumstance, and I am not yet sure that this Gospel phase and Blue Ribbon bloom may not be a God-send to our dull and decaying natures.

It is quite true that the history of the past tells us of some terrible impositions and fearful collapses under the cloak of religion; but it is nevertheless true that, though the preaching of the Cross be to the Jew a stumbling-block, and to the Greek foolishness, "it is to them that believe the wisdom of God and the power of God." If there be " tongues in trees, books in the running brooks, sermons in stones, and good in everything," then why not in the circumstances now influencing much of the Temperance Enterprise? That it may be a policy rather than a principle, this putting on of a religious aspect, is true; still, if that proves to be the best way of getting the article down we want the people to swallow, the swallowing of which is essential to health and life, what harm?

There is nothing new, and I don't know that there is anything wrong, in exercising a little policy, for the apostle commends the catching of people, even by guile. I know my mother practised it in giving me medicine. I would not take it in its bald and disagreeable form, so she put the physic in a spoon and covered it with jam. I jumped at the jam, not knowing what was under it, but got the physic, and the end was answered.

If the Church, with childlike simplicity, jumps at the American jam and gets the physic, it is all right; it has done them good, and we are no worse. There is a little bitterness now and then, when the taste of the medicine is left in the mouth, and the jam is somewhat costly—very much higher in price than the home-made; but then if there be a market for it, and we are free-traders, surely the manufacturers are not to be blamed. Things *will* find their level, and nothing does it sooner or better than *water*.

How deep, how genuine, how enduring all this parade and show may be, time will prove. In the meantime there is no need to swallow every dogma presented;

and those who know the country and believe and understand the truth will not bate one jot or tittle in their work.

That past histories and sudden transformations may beget doubts and misgivings, especially when the old tricks of the stage are not forgotten, and there is much more of the shop than of self-sacrifice in the mode of procedure, is not to be wondered at; but we must not forget that there are sudden transformations which are real and permanent, and that there will be mighty upheavings among the peoples of the earth from time to time, we are taught to believe and expect, but I have yet to learn that any blessing must of necessity come through a church window or in at a chapel door, or be regulated by a noon-day prayer meeting.

When it takes fifty years to make the world, and the Church in the world, feel how much the Temperance Movement is dependent upon religious influences, and how very little of that sort of influence has been at the base of past operations and influenced its prominent promoters in their long and persevering labours, it says little for the Church of God in our midst, and less for the prominent leaders of that Church. The Temperance Cause has a history, as has also the Church of Christ, and every one who will take the pains to compare these two histories will, I think, have no difficulty in seeing how much of that which begot the one gave life to the other. To speak as some modern teachers of temperance have done, of the absence of religious influence and religious power in the operations of temperance teachers in early days, is not only to ignore palpable facts, but to propagate that which is contrary to truth. It is marvellous to me that such men do not see the self-complacency of such proceedings, and the shameful presumption of such conduct.

They enter our meetings and cover our platforms, filling our front seats, taking the very words out of our mouths, reprinting our teachings, and calling by their own name that which their fathers spoke long enough ago to have been forgotten now. They, while riding in carriages and walking in well-trodden paths, seem to forget that there would never have been a road on which to ride, nor a path in which to walk, had not *somebody* made them. Where were these men of ribbons and roses, of right honourables and riches, of righteousness and religion, when the roads had to be made?

The Temperance Movement, like its prototype the religion of Jesus, has always had the poor with it, but also like the Religion of Jesus, not many of the rulers believed in it.

The very persecutions and neglect and shame to which the early men were subjected, one would have thought, was in itself enough to arrest the attention of the Church, and bring it in its full strength to our side; but so far from that being the case, its ministers denounced us, and closed its doors upon us, practically giving sanction to the persecution and siding with the enemy.

Many of the most influential members of the Church in all its branches were largely engaged in the traffic. The families of these married and intermarried the ministers and medical men in connection with the same Churches, and there will be no difficulty in seeing how naturally such people came to see how vulgar, how unscientific, and how unscriptural teetotalism was. We were snubbed at every step; the bills of our meetings looked upon as a desecration and an outrage on the property of the Church, and if occasionally posted were not unfrequently with indignity and violence torn down.

Now I suppose the religion of that day was very much in its obligations and claims what it is now, and so was teetotalism. Then what has happened? Teetotalism is and teetotallers are now what they were then The change is somewhere else, not in them. Teetotalism is not more religious, neither are teetotallers. The change is in the Church, and in church-going people. They are more teetotalised and less prejudiced and blind, and the consequence is a oneness and a brotherhood and fellowship which had no existence in the past. But is it not a grievous mistake to infer, as many men do who are caught with the designation "*Gospel Temperance*," that there was no gospel in the movement till it was baptized by that name? I have heard of an American colonel who came to help Mr. Booth stating to a large temperance meeting in Bristol that until the advent of the gentleman named we knew not the truth, and were in fact spiritually dead. It was done in this wise: quoting from the 19th chapter of Acts, he said: "Mr. Booth's visit to this country reminded him of Paul's visit to Ephesus, 'and finding certain disciples, he said unto them, Have ye received the Holy Ghost since ye believed? And they said unto him, We have not so much as heard whether there be any Holy Ghost.' Just so in this case," said this gentleman; "we had not only not received the gospel, but had not even so much as heard that there was such a thing as gospel in connection with temperance." And the people positively applauded this misrepresentation of truth!

Where was the spirit of the sainted Robert Charlton, and Joseph Eaton, and the Rev. W. W. Robinson, and a thousand others whose lives and labours give the lie to such teaching.

Of course we are all more or less familiar with the feeling which possesses people when they are in special joy and blessedly pleased. "No time like the present," "Never had such a meeting as this," "Never heard such a sermon as that," etc., etc. This can be explained on *this* if no other ground: nothing is so near to us as the present. But we should not entirely forget that the past was once near, and the future will also one day be near. Therefore do not in the joy of the present quite forget the past, nor neglect to provide for the future.

Peter was a member of a large family. It will be remembered that Christ took Peter and John and James on one occasion up into a mountain to pray; but they fell asleep, and when all was nearly over they awoke and saw that something good had happened. Then they were in a hurry to do something, and "Peter said unto Jesus, Master, it is good for us to be here; let us make three tabernacles, one for Thee, and one for Moses, and one for Elias, *not knowing what he said.*" Of course he did not; how should he? If he had been *awake all the time*, he would have been less rash and more practical. So with our friends in the Temperance Movement, who have but just awoke, and who have been asleep for fifty years. Now they are in a hurry, they would have the work done before breakfast to-morrow morning. Let us build three tabernacles; glorify something and somebody. They have had a good time, and they want an outlet, and talk nonsense, "not knowing what they say." In fact they are building tabernacles, not to Christ, or Moses, or Elias, but to themselves.

This may be "gospel," but it looks more like being wise in their generation, than the following of Him who was rich but for our sakes became poor. Possibly those of us who were born before our time, or who have lived too long to fit in with the age, have quite mistaken our calling, and never understood the true meaning of the teaching of Solomon, when he said, "Wisdom is better than gold." In our simplicity it was thought to be so, but since nobody else believed it we have found ourselves quite out of gear with society.

One way of interpreting Solomon's teaching, and which is not only very taking but very profitable, is to say, "I make no charge, you can give me what you like."

When a cabman tells me his fare is "anything I like," I know what that means. One of two things generally happens—either he hopes that I am an ignorant fool, or I prove him to be a designing rogue. Without endorsing the principles of the man who is credited with saying, "Business is business, and religion is religion," I will say that when the "goody-goody" style of teaching, which is so unmanning of men and so unnatural to children, is mixed up with £ s. d., it becomes positively sickening. I confess to a preference for the shop where the goods are marked in plain figures, and where the ultimate result of any transaction can be readily realized.

In a letter which appeared in most of the temperance papers, a few months ago, I was bold enough (and imprudent enough, as some may think) to say that there never was more of the shop in the Temperance Movement than there is to-day.

One or two anonymous letters have come to hand condemning that statement. Had these people had the courage of their convictions, and given me their name and address, I could have dealt with them direct, but as they failed to do that, I will take this opportunity of saying one or two things in justification of that charge.

It must be borne in mind that the temperance teaching of to-day is held up as something so very much more scriptural and in accordance with the spirit of religion than the past. With that I am at issue.

What *is* the history of the past? Did these men who speak so flippantly and so unguardedly of the past know any or many of the men who had to fight, so to speak, with beasts at Ephesus? Well, I *did;* not simply from hearsay, or from what somebody else believed, but from personal intercourse and intimate relationship.

My reference will be confined to the dead, not because there are none living whose eye has not yet become dim, and whose hand has not yet lost its cunning, but because it will refresh my own memory and renew my own soul to have them once more in my vision in the flesh, and will touch the heart and renew the life of other old warriors scattered abroad in the world, as many of them still are.

Surely James Teare will bear comparison for honesty of purpose, purity of zeal, and energy of life, with any man of the present day. And what about John Addleshaw, T. B. Thompson, J. C. Booth, the Rev. R. G. Mason, and Richard Horne? Had these men no understanding of things of which they spoke? And was Simeon Smithard a dumb dog and a blind guide as his melodies touched the heart and won the life of many a wanderer? And what of the Rev. T. I. Messer?

I mention these, not because they were better than others, but because they were men whose lives, from early days in our enterprise, were devoted to the work; and they died as they had lived, full of faith and of the Holy Ghost. And Jabez, too, peace to his memory! I was nearly forgetting him, and I shall forget many, and must of necessity omit the mention of some; but Jabez Inwards was my familiar friend. He crossed my path in early days, and received instruction, conviction, and inspiration, which lived like a burning meteor, and shone like a guiding star. Many are the crowns of his rejoicing, and much is the blessedness of many now living who looked in his face and listened to his words.

The seed was broadcast sown, and not unmixed with either prayers or tears. That seed, like every seed of truth when once sown, is indestructible: it can no more die than can the God of truth. It may be forgotten, as He is forgotten; it may be trampled under foot and despised, as He is often trampled under foot and despised; but with all such things it is but a question of time. The just may have to live by faith, but the right shall triumph. It is an evil day when that which is morally right, and scientifically true, and religiously binding, feeds on excitement and lives by sensation. In such circumstances, degradation becomes a mania, and the publication of one's shame a glory.

Surely the blighting influence of drink is common enough to dispel the necessity for the exhibitions of special examples, and we are now far enough advanced to dispense with "life stories" under special extra charges.

This may be a religious duty, certainly it is one that seems to pay well, and not unlikely to beget the cry in another form and under new circumstances, "Doth Job serve God for naught?"

That circumstances are altered and conditions differ, I know, but the truth is the same at all times and in all places, and we have nothing to-day religiously, scientifically, socially, morally, physically, or commercially, that did not exist forty years ago, and was not proclaimed from temperance platforms and published in temperance papers further back than even that.

Doctors of to-day seldom, if ever, call to mind the labours and teachings of such medical men as John Fothergill, of Darlington; John Higginbottom, of Nottingham; Thomas Beaumont, of Bradford; and Henry Mudge, of Bodmin. These each taught the truths to an unbelieving people, when teetotal doctors walked in an untrodden path and practised what they preached, and suffered, if not in person, very seriously in purse.

The art of medicine is said to be the art of pleasing, and people were pleased to be allowed and to be recommended to take drink, whatever their ailments, more especially if their circumstances would admit of their paying for it. I have more than once, in the presence of these medical men, when their inner life has been revealed, and when sorrow and trial, and even persecution, and not unfrequently neglect, weighed them down and crushed their spirits, been made to feel at what a cost they were true to science and to themselves. Talk of Gospel Temperance! The very men who thus speak are in not a few cases the descendants and connections of some good Christian people of the past, who, to my certain knowledge, withdrew their patronage and closed their accounts with doctors who supplied what they were pleased to call disagreeable physic. Who, I would ask, were the true men in these cases, the honest doctor or the truculent vacillating patient? Or, what is more perhaps to the point, who was the true Christian, the man of fashion and folly, or the man who was true to himself, true to science, and to the God of truth, though it kept him poor, and even threatened his daily bread?

CHAPTER XXXII.

BANDS, HALLS, AND PROCESSIONS.

"THEN drew near unto Him all the publicans and sinners for to hear Him." This teaching conveys a fact and a lesson. The *fact* is, that publicans and sinners found a friend and a sympathiser in Christ; and the *lesson* is, that none are excluded and all may come. The publicans and sinners of that day were in the main a despised and outcast lot, and were not accustomed to be received and treated on the same terms as the rest; hence it was that on public occasions and in great congregations they kept their distance, and at best were only a fringe to the multitude. But when they heard Jesus speak of the blessings He came to bring in the light of a feast, and to that feast every man was invited, and to all it was free, it was news, and not only news but good news, to them. There was music in the voice, and mercy in the means, and the Son of man, who when lifted up would draw all men unto Him, had already touched the springs of life, and the world had become a banqueting house to every child of man.

"They drew near unto Him." The haughty scribe and the proud Pharisee would draw their unsullied robes tighter round them, and the unbelieving Jew and learned Greek would disdain the connection, but the common people heard Him gladly. The righteous and self-sufficient were not called, but the poor, and those who felt their need, had the gospel preached unto them. It is ever so. "Hunger is the best sauce," and helplessness the best soil in which to sow the seed of life.

The mission of Christ and the apostles runs well on all-fours with the mission of the apostles of temperance, and any thoughtful man comparing the history of the one with the other, will see how much of sameness goes through the whole.

The first-fruits of the Temperance Reformation were largely gathered from the ranks of the intemperate. Its special adaptation to their case was readily seen, and soon felt, and the crowds of men rushing to our ranks from that class gave some show of justification to the charge brought against us "that we were a society of drunkards."

This charge, of course, was never true, and every year we live proves it less true than ever, but in early days the proportion of reformed men was much larger than it has been in subsequent years, and that circumstance gave a feature to our movement which shocked the very proper and respectable people of our day, just as the mission of Christ and the apostles shocked the same class in their day. Who does not know how rare a thing it was for the Church to number amongst its members persons who at one time had been notoriously intemperate, prior to the direct efforts made for that purpose by temperance societies? and how common it was then, and is even now, for people reclaimed, if they touched the accursed thing, to be again tenfold more the children of the devil than before?

The records of the Church will show that very many more men fell into drunken habits while members of the

Church than were ever gathered into it by temperance teaching amongst the already intemperate.

Then what comes of the theory about "the grace of God keeping men"? People might as well talk of the grace of God keeping fire from burning, and dirt from soiling, and fever from killing, as talk of drinking communities not being blighted by drink. There are physical and natural laws, with which grace has about as much relationship as an umbrella has with a duck.

The early Methodists, both under Wesley and Hugh Bourne, touched the core of the drink mischief, but they did it by what at the time and to them was an equivalent to teetotalism; and the Salvation Army of to-day are doing it, but only so far as their gospel enforces teetotalism; and it will be done throughout all the Churches in the land when they preach a *full* gospel, and not before.

There is no full gospel where the liquor traffic is tolerated, and the liquor traffic will be tolerated by the State so long as the right hand of fellowship is given to it in the Church. What is the use, and where is the consistency of ministers of the gospel meeting in council and in conference, and asking Government to curtail and suppress the liquor traffic, while the liquor-sellers fill their own pews and build their churches, and they themselves go down on their knees and thank God for the money obtained from such sources?

I am an Alliance man, and a Sunday-closing man, and a limitation man, and every other sort of man which maims and masters the liquor traffic, but I am not satisfied that the Church of God should ask Government to bear a burden grievous to be borne in the abolition of the liquor traffic, while the Church does not touch it with its little finger. Neither am I reconciled to the position of sitting at the feet of men in council meeting who, after adopting reports, and passing resolutions, drink their bottle of wine and tipple their toddy. Surely it is not too much to expect that a bishop should be the husband of one wife, whatever may happen to the rest, and I for one cannot do with men who make such large claims upon others, while they themselves do so little in the same direction. Pray let "Cæsar's wife (at least) be above suspicion."

But to continue a few more specialities of the Temperance Enterprise. Temperance halls, temperance bands, and temperance processions, were at one time quite a rage amongst us. This is not to be wondered at; the wonder is that we have survived it all. In my judgment we should have been happier and more useful had we never had a temperance hall; in many cases we could not afford it, and in others there was much difficulty in knowing what to do with them when got. In some cases it has tended to make us a "sect," a thing to be avoided; in others it has so crippled us with debt, that when the people needed bread, we had nothing for them but a stone. True we were turned out of doors, and had, so to speak, in some cases no home, but that would have passed away with a little patience; indeed it has passed away now. Where there was no building suitable for public gatherings, and a hall could be put up that would meet the wants of the place in general, as well as in special matters, the venture was sometimes justifiable and appreciated; but in very many cases it was not so, and the erection brought trouble and in some cases disgrace.

Temperance bands are a folly and a mistake, especially by societies. There was not one in twenty that did not sooner or later come to grief. The money was wasted and the instruments were perverted. If young men like to establish a band and call it a "temperance" one, well and good, this on their own responsibility may be of service, and be a credit and success. I have known one or two cases where it has been so, but buying instruments and dressing up people at a society's expense is a mistake, and sooner or later brings trouble.

The money spent on halls and bands and processions is something fabulous, and yet there is much to excuse if not to justify it; and it is to be hoped that these are things of the past, but as they have been a feature in the movement, I name them.

The processions in their day had their value, for people at one time would not believe that there were any teetotallers; but when we turned out in thousands and paraded the streets of London and other towns, as we did in early days, and in one case were an hour in passing a given point, that was a long and telling "speech," and had in it an accumulation of facts which took the breath out of many of our gainsayers. The excitement and parade was a thing to be remembered. The flags and banners, the bands and carriages, the footmen and horsemen, were "a new thing under the sun," new to the watching crowds, and not less new to many in the line of procession. Everybody did their best, and put on their best. Russell Square, Bedford Square, Lincoln's Inn Fields, and other open spaces were our gathering grounds, and the joyous shouts and happy recognitions which greeted certain specialities and individualities made the meetings memorable, and the world akin.

All that was needed on the part of the teetotallers was temper and tact and a little patience; the crowd was ever tolerant and appreciative, as most London crowds generally are.

James McCurry was in his glory then, so was James Balfour, so was G. C. Campbell, W. Inwards, and many others.

My friend Harry Smith, the silk handkerchief printer of West Ham, was in the third heavens with joy. He, I remember, in his first procession had a carriage and pair for his bonny little wife and a friend or two and himself, but he would sit on the *box*, that he might see and be seen. There was plenty of room in the body of the carriage, but no, Harry would be on the box, so that when there was a halt and a favourable opportunity, he could have what he called "a lark" with the men about the "pubs."

Harry, on his first arrival, in taking stock of the surroundings, thought he was scarcely up to the mark in the matter of necktie or stock, so he slipped away and made a further investment. Having to finish his toilet in the street, he had not been very successful in the emergency, the stock was put on wrong side up. In one of his harangues to a crowd in front of a gin-shop, one of the men twigged this mishap, and called out—"There is a fellow who does not know how to put his stock on." Harry, who was always equal to the occasion, kept his temper, and simply retorted—"How should I know how to put a stock on? I never had one before." Then turning to the occupants of the carriage, he cried—"Here, wife, put me right, and let these men see what a gentleman *teetotalism* has made of your husband."

Smith, two years before that, was simply a drunken lunatic. He went mad when in liquor, and not unfrequently wrecked his home. One night, when sitting moodily before the fire, he was annoyed by the ticking of a Dutch clock; he sprang from his seat, tore the clock from the wall, and threw it into a mantel glass. I carried for some years a portion of that glass as an evidence of his uncontrolled folly.

When Smith signed, the circumstances were somewhat peculiar. He was a printer at West Ham; the meeting was held in a little chapel at Plaistow near these works. I had been very successful in my visits to Stratford, a little way from Plaistow, and some of the men who worked with Smith had signed with me at Stratford, and they prevailed upon Smith on certain conditions to attend my meeting at Plaistow. The conditions were that "they should lend him a coat to go in, and a shilling for a half-gallon of ale when the meeting was over."

He came, and was caught that night, and was a very marked trophy in the district for years. Subsequently he went to America, and became very famous in the city of New York, and in other American cities, as "the razor-strop man," and made in a comparatively short time a handsome fortune. His investments, however, came to grief in the American war, but I met with him in New York at his usual stall near the Post-Office in the year 1875. He was looking well, and again prospering, having been true all through his eventful life to teetotalism. He gave me a hearty welcome, and never seemed tired of telling of the circumstances under which he had taken the pledge, and gave me a little token of abiding friendship and grateful esteem.

The procession fever was at its height in connection with Father Mathew's work, and it was then that Daniel O'Connell went with the stream. An immense muster was made in Whitechapel and Commercial Road in the east of London, and several carriages and fours made a sensation. On that occasion Mr. O'Connell had one, and I and others were similarly favoured. In that form we were dragged through the streets to the West End. Lord Arundel (who was subsequently Duke of Norfolk) also joined us, so it is quite a mistake to suppose that we never touched the higher circle before these times.

When Mr. O'Connell took the pledge it was essential to his hold on Ireland, and he was wise enough to see it. Cardinal Manning's espousal of the Temperance Cause begot the necessity for the move in the Church of England, and the Church of England begot the necessity for temperance organization in other sects of religion. I do not complain of this, I am not questioning the honesty and sincerity of the parties concerned; but I am bound to say, that while all this shows the progress of the cause, the need for these separate and sectarian operations is begotten, not by true religion, but by the want of it, and indicates rivalry and jealousy in the interest of the individual and sectional "shop" rather than the broad and blessed spirit of a boundless charity towards all, and a patriotism which alone can save a nation.

I think it was President Adams who once said, when asked to take part in a missionary meeting in America, that he would not do that, but he would give a handsome subscription to make the ministers of the country sufficiently Christian to be able to make an interchange of pulpits, and to work in harmony and with brotherly love with one another,

We talk with considerable pride as temperance reformers, of the great Church of England temperance move, of the Catholic guilds, and of the Methodist, Congregationalist, and Baptist temperance sections; but to me there is a sadness in the picture, as there is in many of our national institutions, made necessary because of the infirmities of our race, and the helplessness and lost condition of numbers of our people. Why cannot, and why do not these people work for the national weal on common and ordinary grounds, as others do?

It is simply the old story under new circumstances, of Nicodemus coming by night and upsetting the fixed plan of procedure. They must do it differently, as the original Nicodemus wanted to do. It is always so. Teachers will not be taught, and hence the multiplication of shops and oracles. We have made very little progress in these matters since the Saviour was in the flesh, and James called attention to the offensive practice of giving preference to men because of the clothes they wore, and the rings which decorated their fingers.

It is worth something, however, that a condition of things has been brought about which makes rulers believe, or at least make a show of doing something, and like the late Daniel O'Connell, join the procession. It was policy in him, it is policy in them; but what made the policy a necessity? Public sentiment. And what begot public sentiment? The facts of experience, and the irrefutable and persistent teaching of the previous forty years.

When the late Samuel Bowly presided at the

World's Temperance Convention in the city of London, in the year 1846, he then made an impression on the national mind that resulted in his being singled out as one specially qualified to solve a difficult problem, and guide and direct in questions of dispute. Then it was he became a man of the nation, and retained that position to his death; and the exercise of his rare abilities, and manifestation of Christian charity and loving-kindness, did much to bring about the healthy and more tolerant tone towards the Temperance Question which now exists.

My own part in that Convention was a very humble one, but one circumstance occurred in connection with it which I think worth a record.

"Dicky Turner," who is credited with giving the name "teetotal," had walked all the way from Preston to London to attend that Convention. Thomas Swindlehurst, the first trophy of the Preston Society, who had been crowned king of the reformed men, was also there; and so was also William Howarth ("Slender Billy," as they called him in Preston).

These three men all dined with me in my house in Portland town during that Convention, and made a considerable impression in the neighbourhood, I can assure my readers. They were all reformed men, and each had in him much individuality and marked characteristics. They were thoroughly earnest and most unselfish workers. They have long since gone, not to an unhonoured grave, and so long as temperance has life and history they will in spirit live. Howarth was twenty-four stone weight, and Swindlehurst sixteen or eighteen, so that they had in their day not only value but *weight*. In Lancashire they were in great request to *head* our processions.

Those were days when people judged of men as men judge of pigs, by their weight, and we met the then condition of things by showing "samples," and there can be no doubt that for the time we made a point; at all events, it was hard lines for the *lean* members of our society when they joined the processions.

It is said that on the occasion of a procession through the streets of Wakefield, Mr. Biscombe, who was one of our able advocates in early times, was somewhat conspicuous in it. Now Biscombe was as hungry-looking a dog as could be met in a day's march. He was also badly pitted by small-pox. These circumstances, combined with the fact that while low in flesh he was in colour bad, helped to make him a "target" for the enemy to shoot at. During the procession the parish sexton came running with a large rusty key, represented to be the key of the "bone house," and offering it to Biscombe, begged that he would go and "lock himself up again. What was he doing out, frightening the women and children? Go back," said the sexton, "thou wilt get me into trouble. I had only just gone to get a bit o' dinner. Now thou should not have done so; get in, I tell thee, get in!" That of course was a success; I never heard that my friend Biscombe ever took part in any more processions.

CHAPTER XXXIII.

EXTREMES MEET.

THERE are few positions in life that do not possess some advantages, and it is never well to throw up our hands and give up as lost because of difficulties desperate and troubles overwhelming.

It is astonishing how things do at times right themselves, and nature has within itself wonderful recouping powers. Mixed multitudes will of necessity have in them incongruities, and individual tastes and habits differ as do our faces, and therefore there will be at times strange forms and awkward angles.

To those who move about freely, and see much of men and things, there will often be circumstances into which they are thrown requiring both patience and forbearance, and it cannot be expected that village and obscure life will always have the brightness and promptitude belonging to a more active existence. The thought never suggests itself to such that "circumstances alter cases," and they will frequently sit down with the greatest complaisance and satisfaction where others would be in torture and misery.

I remember on one occasion in Somerset having to lecture in a large village Baptist chapel. The officials in connection with the place were all sunshine, and evidently looking forward to a pleasant evening. The lighting arrangement was so defective I could scarcely see the countenances of the people. There was an abundance of chandeliers distributed about the building, and provision for a sufficient number of candles to illuminate the place, but not a third of these were lighted. Calling one of the officials, I asked if they could not give a little more light. He replied, "Yes; when we have preaching we light up all the candles, but at temperance meetings we only light so many." "Then," I said, "we will call it preaching," and I would not, and did not, proceed until we had preaching light.

There are unseen ways of getting at what is in the heart, and it is evident that these good people (and I am not doubting their goodness) had an impression that teetotalism was a saving of candles, as compared with preaching. I insisted on having preaching light, and for once I suppose it may be presumed I gave them "Gospel Temperance."

I am a thorough believer in the doctrine that "that which is worth doing is worth doing well," and have often been made to feel in my experience how unfairly temperance advocates have been treated, and at what disadvantages they have been put. If some of these starring gentlemen who from time to time favour us with their presence and help, had to give their orations in such rooms, with such lighting, and with such surroundings as have not been uncommon to some of us, their career would be somewhat dimmed of its glory, and their success less pretentious than it was made to appear.

How would an experience like the one described in the following paper harmonize with their notions of proper arrangement? And when I add that the night of the meeting to which I had gone was spent in one room of the shoemaker, in the midst of lapstones, old shoes, rosin and paste, they will perhaps be enabled to see that the widow's mite takes many forms, and the biggest things are often done when there is least pomp and circumstance.

"ALL THAT GLITTERS IS NOT GOLD."

Habit is second nature. What men are accustomed to, not only becomes a necessity, but even when injurious can often be endured without any conscious suffering or inconvenience. It does not follow, however, that because we feel no inconvenience that there is therefore no mischief. Man is an educated animal. It will be seen then how valuable are good habits, and how inconvenient and dangerous are bad ones. Who among us does not know numbers of people whose habits have become a sort of second life, or at least a second coat, and whose artificial wants are more costly, if not more necessary than their daily needs? What a sufferer the snuff-taker is if he happens to misplace his box! and how dreadfully miserable the inveterate smoker, if necessitated to sit in a railway carriage an hour, or even in a lady's drawing-room an evening, without his pipe or cigar! Serve up the best dinner that can be put upon a table and leave out the wine and the beer, and you will be made to feel by the slave of the bottle how shabby you are, and how comparatively worthless all your efforts have been. These uncomfortable feelings, begotten by being deprived of what by habit has become a necessity, are undoubtedly very trying; but then it should not be forgotten that to be compelled to endure that to which our natures have not adapted themselves, is not the less so. While it is wonderful to what nature will adapt itself when by long continuance we become accustomed to it, it is nevertheless true that sudden transition often shocks the system, and suddenly to be deprived of accustomed comfort is an affliction bad to bear. I know something of sudden transitions, and the terrible suffering consequent thereupon; and I am not therefore so little disposed to bear with men whose condition and habit of life makes interference with that condition and habit so annoying, as many may suppose.

In the early days of my public life, I represented a principle everywhere spoken against. The prejudice of the people was so strong, and their bitterness sometimes so great, that it not only resulted in violence and insult from the mob, but in neglect and misrepresentation by those who were considered to be more thoughtful and tolerant. As a consequence, my home accommodation was often of the humblest description. To go to an inn at that time was not only unpleasant, but often unsafe, in addition to which my means were limited.

Persons who kept what was called a spare bed, and who had anything in the way of what was considered social status and respectability to lose, were afraid to have it known amongst their neighbours and friends that they had accommodated such an animal as a teetotal advocate. It was as much as their credit was worth to do so. "The fear of man bringeth a snare." In consequence of this in the early days, we were left much in the hands of the poor. "The poor we have always had with us." The scribes and the Pharisees of old *constantly* did what the scribes and Pharisees of our day do, complained of the *manner*. They did so with the Saviour; anything indeed for an excuse for their own wrong-doing and neglect of doing.

The teachers of the day have always had the presumption and the assumption to exclaim, "Teachest thou us?" Yes! indeed we do. And bad as the world is, it would have been worse had we not done so.

All that glitters, however, is not gold, and the people we hope have learned to take at its proper value all such impertinence and ignorant misrepresentation as I have for a moment stepped on one side to call attention to.

Though the rule was, at the time of which I write, to have hard and humble fare, there were exceptions, and occasionally men who were princes amongst the people did themselves the distinguished honour to open their doors, and devote their mansions to the neglected and maligned temperance advocate. This, though a joy in itself, was often a disqualification for the sterner and tougher work which frequently succeeded it.

Here is a specimen. I was invited to address a meeting in a very aristocratic village, some sixteen miles from Bristol. My host was the squire of the place, and he entertained me with some degree of luxury, and I was attended with no little pomp and circumstance. The next day I was appointed to go to Taunton, some thirty miles west of the village in which I was staying. The junction of the high-road on which the coach travelled by which I meant to reach my destination, was six or eight miles from the village. The morning was fearfully wet, but the squire sent me in great state with a splendid pair of horses and in a handsome close glass carriage, to meet the coach. The humble conveyances we met or passed on the road took to one side with great considerateness. The men working on the road touched their hats either to the carriage or myself, or from a sense of duty which had become a habit, and the women and children did the same, for reasons no doubt equally cogent. Politeness is at all times an agreeable thing, and good manners oil the machinery of life so that it runs much more smoothly. But why confine them to smart carriages and fine coats? "All is not gold that glitters."

Soon after our arrival at the junction of the road was seen the four-in-hand at full speed: signals were made by the squire's coachman to pull up for the fare. This was done in the midst of a terrible downpour of rain. The guard, with promptitude and politeness, opened the door of my carriage, and then, instinctively, turned to the door of the coach, never for a moment supposing that the person who came under so much care and protection could be an outside passenger. Alas! "all that glitters is not gold."

I took a seat on the top of the coach, joining three other gentlemen, just behind the coachman's box. The officials and passengers on the coach were all evidently much concerned for my health and comfort. Offering me their rugs and wrappers, and kindly placing me in the centre of the seat that I might be as little exposed to the wind and wet as possible, we were speedily on our way to the West.

He who held the ribbons, feeling the importance of his position enhanced by the respectable addition made to his highflyer, spoke encouragingly to his team; they, snorting satisfaction at the condition of things, with heads erect and ears alive, made music with their feet; while the guard's bugle discoursed in sweet sounds and dulcet notes airs familiar to every country swain. These things combined made travelling in bygone times less irksome and much more joyous than the inexperienced can conceive. On and on we went, with so much vigour and life, that despite the elements, the heart's blood kept warm and the mind's imagining active. Wayside doors flew open, and bright eyes looked up, and welcome smiles greeted us. Turnpike gates stood back, and old Joey, with his well-kept stud, in front of the old hostelry, had a cheery word of welcome for his new charge, which had done their work so well. Then replacing them by the next on duty, with a friendly slap on the back of the off-wheeler, he exclaimed, "Go it, my beauties." A word of encouragement from the "whip," and the well-known intimation, "all right," from the guard, and once more we are on the wing.

During the short interval at the wayside inn, I was somewhat amused, if not confused, by the, what seemed to me, painful efforts of some of my fellow-travellers to add to my comforts and get me "something." All the while I could not but feel that it was the carriage they were paying attention to, and that they had yet to learn "All that glitters is not gold."

I did not, however, refuse to take all I could take, asking no questions, and keeping my own counsel. Storm succeeded storm, and I began to wish for a home and a fireside. I had a friend who I knew would make me welcome when I got to Taunton, and as we both richly enjoyed a joke, we would get the laugh at the expense of the gentlemen who had paid me, even at their own inconvenience, such very marked attention, and that enjoyment would be all the greater from the fact that such men, as a rule, at that time would not touch knowingly a teetotal advocate with a pair of tongs.

At this moment, and when within some few miles of

Taunton, was seen an object in the distance standing right in the middle of the road. When we drew nearer it proved to be a man, who was in a great state of excitement, for with uplifted hands and loud noises he was signalling the coach to stop. Just at that moment it rained as if the bottom had tumbled out of the heavens, and all was coming down at once, and neither horses nor men were in the humour to stand still. A little way from the man in the centre of the road, was a donkey and cart. Talk of Patience on a monument! Job himself might have learnt a lesson from this docile and enduring creature. While everything else seemed troubled and restive, there it stood unconcerned.

The man in the road, as soon as the coach had stopped, and he could sufficiently calm himself down to find words to give utterance to what he wanted, said, " Is Mr. Whittaker there?"

Everybody looked at everybody else, but no response. He then went into particulars, explaining that if Mr. Whittaker was there he was not to go on to Taunton, for the teetotal meeting that night was to be held at North Curry, and North Curry was only three miles from there, and it was seven from Taunton, and as it began at seven o'clock, there would not be time to go there and back, in addition to which there was no conveyance; then, pointing to the chariot near him, he said, " I have brought this for him, and he *must* go with *us*."

Men may talk of courage and bravery, but I have an impression that it is much easier to face a cannon, and take the city to the sound of martial music and amidst the din of war, than boldly to admit your name in such circumstances as those in which I was that day placed. This was, I admit, a terrible trial, and I was strongly tempted to deny my name. There was, however, but one alternative. I must either pronounce myself, or disappoint the meeting: the former would mortify myself, the latter be an injustice to the public, and a wrong to this poor man. I determined upon the former.

Oh for a Hogarth or a Cruikshank to have depicted the countenances of that company at that moment! The guard did not handle my luggage so tenderly as when I arrived, neither was he so considerate of my person. The bag was not carried by *him* to the *other* conveyance, neither was I politely *helped* into it. The passengers who had paid me so much attention looked down their noses, and the coachman stuck his tongue in his cheek, while I could have sunk in my shoes.

There was no " All right," this time, from the guard, but, "Go ahead, Bill," instead, and the moment Bill did so, a great horse-laugh burst from the lot, as they left me with my new friends.

I confess to being somewhat annoyed by this son of Crispin, for that was what he was, that he had not managed this business in a more quiet and less demonstrative way. But when I came to learn, as I subsequently did, that though only a poor bachelor shoemaker, living, working, and sleeping in one room, he had that day, with the best of motives, and to save me expense and trouble, walked to Taunton and back, a distance of fourteen miles, to prevent disappointment and add to my convenience: after which he had begged the use of this humble conveyance and *walked* with it three miles more to the point where we met, that *I* might ride and to some extent be protected from the weather, I felt that while it was true that "all that glittered was not gold," it was not the less true that here and there in our journey through life was to be found *a diamond in the mud.*

CHAPTER XXXIV.

FAITH AND PHYSIC.

THAT numbers of men abstain from intoxicating liquors who are but little if at all influenced by Bible teaching needs no proof. They have no faith in the drink, and wishing to make the best of this life they take care of the present. Numbers more abstain who *have* faith in the drink, but believing themselves called upon to abstain from things lawful and useful in themselves that they may be useful to others, they practise what to them is a considerable self-denial.

In either of these motives there is sufficient reason and abundant vitality to keep alive the practice of teetotalism. There is, however, yet another class, and not by any means a small one. These not only believe the drink to be dangerous, but worthless, and they have the clearest and most abiding conviction that both Church and State are called upon to take hold with no gloved hand of this delusion to man and enemy to God: of that number I am one. That men are influenced by different reasons and act from different motives is no new thing, and our platform is broad enough for all. It is therefore a needless and meddlesome interference with individual liberty to ask for reasons and question motives. It is enough that the action in itself is right. We have from the first been more or less subject to amendments and improvements, but they none of them change our nature, and never will. We differ in our form of thought, as we do in our form of face, and as we agree to differ in the one why should we not do so in the other? As temperance teachers we have nothing to do with *motives*; if it were so, there would be plenty to trouble us in connection with the working of the different societies: those concerned have thought it wise in this way to put forth their strength, and so long as the chief end (the deliverance of the land from the drink thraldom) is secured, we may tolerate even where we cannot approve.

That we form and manage our societies just as we form our social connections, and manage our personal operations in life, is not to be wondered at, however we may at times have occasion to regret it. These things cannot be cured, they must therefore be endured. Personally I have endured a good deal in this direction, and do so still. This setting up of a fresh business, which after all is not a fresh business, this opening of another shop, and this too sometimes where there are more now than can honestly live, may give prominence to persons which could not be obtained without it, but it is *not* an advance of principles, and often exists at the cost and humiliation of honester, abler, and better men. "All men have not faith," was the utterance of one in times past, as he looked at those who seemed as if they belonged to the elect; and we are not now, and never have been, free from those who may be justly called weak in the faith.

Every one who abstains does not do so because drink is bad, yet it *is* bad whether they believe it or not. And until there is something like a national conviction that the liquor itself is a danger and a mischief, there is but little hope of national sobriety and oneness of life amongst temperance reformers. The exceptions made in all the early pledges, in what were supposed to be the interests of religion and the requirements of health, left loopholes by which vast numbers have slipped away from us, and by which floods of destruction have gone through our ranks; and it is only because there have been here and there bulwarks of resistance set up by men who dared to be true, that preachers and physicians were disturbed in their *fancied* security, and the Church and the sick chamber have at length begun to see that both true science and true religion are not only not helped but very seriously hindered by their intimate and needless relationship with this mother of mischief, the liquor traffic. The dogma of the priest and the authority of the physician is now little if any more than is that of any other man, and the people will not accept on the *ipse dixit* of either priest or physician that which common sense and everyday experience refutes.

The temperance pledge of what is known as the old Temperance Society, after declaring the adherent's willingness to abstain from ardent spirits, made *exceptions* in the interest of medicine and religion; and when the teetotal pledge was adopted the same form was continued, with this difference, that we included *all* intoxicating liquors. That was undoubtedly a big stride, and was quite as much as could be taken at the time, but in taking it we patted on the back a *great delusion* in physic, and gave licence to a dangerous and irreconcilable practice in connection with religion.

There might never have been written in the interests

of religion the exhortation, "Have no fellowship with unfruitful works of darkness," for the Church has held on to this rag of rottenness in its ordinances, and even yet taboos those who never could and never will be a party in such practices. Some dozen or fifteen years ago, at an official meeting of the Church of which I was a member, a question was raised by a member as to the propriety of some who were then present absenting themselves from the Lord's Table. The president of the meeting was new to us, and this was his first appearance amongst us. Fortunately he was a man of wisdom and judgment, or consequences might have been serious. He in reply to the question said, "he hoped none would be guilty of such conduct." I at once responded by saying, "Yes, I am." I knew the attack was made on myself, so I made short work of it. He very kindly replied, "Perhaps it is not convenient, Brother Whittaker." "No," said I, "that is not the reason; it is no means of grace to me administered in such a form, it is an *offence*, and troubles me, and I am better and happier away." All that I wanted was peace; I had never troubled the Church, and did not wish the Church to trouble me on the subject, for I was satisfied in due time the thing would right itself. The minister was shocked; he had never met with anything so *extreme*, but desired the discussion might be suppressed, and as he lived next door but one to myself, he would call some day and hoped to be able to remove my scruples.

Shortly he called, according to promise, and the following conversation took place:—

"Well now," said he, "as to that matter raised at the local preachers' meeting the other day, let me put it to you thus: Did it never strike you that as it is the almost universal practice of the Church to observe the ordinance in this way, and that good men for ages have done as we now do, that you might be wrong?" Looking him in the face, I said, "Mr. Wilson, did it never strike you that 'they all forsook Him and fled'?" Rising from his seat and taking me by the hand, he said, "Good-morning, brother, I think we had better let it rest." "I think so, too," said I, and it has rested ever since so far as I am concerned, but it has *broken* those relations with the Church which had been intimate, and I think useful, for more than thirty years.

Is not this a big evil and a great wrong? The person who raised the question in the meeting ought to have been the last to do it. His own sister was the widow of a man who had been reformed by the Teetotal Society, and who for a few years did a great amount of good work in the Church, travelling the country and filling many of our principal pulpits. He was often exhausted by his excessive labours, and foolish and ignorant Christian people put wine into his gruel and *medicinally* treated him with drink, thus kindling the old fire within him, making the last state of that man worse than the first; and so he died.

Will the Church never awake to this folly, and will the members of our households continue blind to the death, as to the madness of giving countenance to such a domestic foe?

A lady highly connected, sensitive in nature, refined in taste, and cultivated in mind, some time ago was placed in one of those excellent institutions, in which persons overcome by the passion for drink seek help and deliverance. She felt, after many months' residence, recovered, and longed to return to her family and home. She had a religious concern to take the sacrament. She did so, and within three weeks' time was back again more helpless if possible than ever.

I saw her before she went home, and I saw her after she returned to the institution. It was at the Table of the Lord where the fire of hell was kindled in that lady's life, and I left her with a bleeding and an aching heart.

Is there no guilt in the Church and in the family in that case? I know there is, and I for one am prepared to stand alone, and be without fellowship and friends rather than taint my soul and becloud my life by going with the multitude to do evil.

Here is another recent acquaintance, a lady who in early life was a teetotaller. She married as such. She was well connected and in every way desirable. Her husband was not a teetotaller, but both were religiously inclined, and were members of the Church and active in the Sabbath-school. The doctors got hold of her a few years after she was married, and though the semblance of past respectability was kept up for years, the mischief was working, and ultimately the havoc made was manifest to all around. The home is a very hospitable one, and the desire to do and get good never leaves it, and that no doubt tones down much that would be very objectionable in its absence. Yet there is death in the pot, and all who know what pitch in the bosom means, know that such people live as the moth lives in the presence of the lighted candle—they *may* survive, but they *often* do *not;* and the question comes, shall we remove the flame or *kill* the fluttering life?

"Why destroy him with thy meat for whom Christ

died?" surely has some force in cases like these; and it should never be forgotten that "no man liveth to himself." Home hospitality and genial friends are very agreeable accompaniments to life; but if we may buy gold too dear, may not our social joys be purchased at such a price as to beget the inquiry, "Is thy servant a dog, that he should do this great wickedness, and sin against God?"

There is no true benevolence apart from self-sacrifice, and if that be absent, so likewise is true religion. "He who was rich, for our sake became poor." There is the kernel of all that followed; and we are only Christian so far as we are Christlike, and no more. Custom and company and fashion do not ignore *facts*, and cannot make wrong right be they never so agreeable and respectable and common.

Do these people know that the sight, the smell, and the presence of the liquor is to some persons an irresistible temptation? What then must be the effect when it touches the lip and fires the blood! Don't talk to me about what people ought to do for themselves, by way of excusing the performance of what is clearly a duty on our part towards them. If what we ought to do and what they ought to do were put into a bag together and shaken up, which, I wonder, would come out first? Of course everybody *ought* to do right, but if the right-doing of some people is made difficult by the thoughtlessness and self-gratification of others, what then?

Truly we live in a land of shams, shops, and shoddy; and if these were confined to our trade and teaching they might in the main be laughed at, but when they touch our religion and taint our morals, the sooner some one with a whip of small cords clears us out the better.

The learned nonsense men have talked in justification of custom, and from which custom they have sought to enforce a law and sanctify a wrong, has been very confusing to many, and misleading to others. Learning is not necessarily sense or wisdom. A knowledge of letters is not a knowledge of life. Dead languages do not make living men. They may feed skeletons, but they neither warm the blood nor nerve the flesh. They are at best but a valley of dry bones, and so far from such being the guide and inspirers of our life, they rather need that we should breathe upon them than that they should rattle their old bones in our ranks.

What is it to me that the original Greek, or Latin, or Hebrew, meant this, that, or the other? and what do I care what the authorities and the learned say was the practice and belief one thousand years ago, in the presence of revealed facts and the evidence of my own senses to-day?

When living in the suburbs of London forty years ago, in the garden at the rear of my house was an apple-tree; it seldom bore fruit, but when it did bear fruit it was always an *apple*, never a pear, a plum, or a cherry. Now there was no necessity for me to dig down deep to find the roots of that tree in *order* to know what kind of tree it was. I knew it by its *fruit* and I know what drink is by the logic of facts, and the every-day evidence of my senses. What need have I to see whether the roots can be traced to Noah's vineyard, the marriage of Cana, or the Pope's big toe? It is *not* the roots about which I am concerned, it is the *fruit*, that settles my business, and the fruit is *bad*. "Do this in remembrance of Me," no more means that I should take intoxicating liquors, even if the Saviour Himself did (of which there is no proof), any more than that if I wanted to go to London to-morrow morning I should go round the town to hire a donkey, because when Jesus entered Jerusalem He rode on an ass.

I have a more excellent way in both cases, and I should not need to go far from home to find an ass if I had not sense to see and wisdom to use what was best adapted to the altered circumstances. "Except in religious ordinances," is a foolish and needless exception.

When the late Rev. F. Beardsall abolished the exceptions from his pledge, he was only a little before the times, and the various temperance societies are gradually but certainly coming round to sounder views and safer teaching. This was Mr. Beardsall's pledge,—" I promise to abstain from and discountenance the use of all intoxicating liquors." The whole is there. That is my theory, that is my practice, and in my judgment it is the wisest and best.

When John Higginbottom, F.R.S., the eminent surgeon of Nottingham, announced to a crowded meeting in Exeter Hall, London, the uselessnesss of drink as a medicine, and challenged and defied contradiction, he confirmed me in my resolve not only not to take the drink at a religious ordinance, but he also settled the physic question.

Holding up the pledge and reading it, he stopped at the *exception* for medical purposes. Why that exception should be put there he could not see—"except for medical purposes." "There is not," said he, "a single disease that ever intoxicating liquor cured, but there are scores that it has caused, and hundreds that it has aggravated; and could I have all the strong drink there is in existence in the compass of a nutshell, I would set my foot upon it and crush it in the earth, by doing which I should do service to my God and to my country!"

I am far from blaming either doctors or ministers in every case. They are after all very much what the people make them, and there are no doubt numbers of cases where people fall back *unjustly*, for an excuse for what they do, to these influences. Still the readiness and flippancy with which drink is commended and approved by such is most dangerous. The stuff is not only in everybody's cupboard, but was at one time in almost everybody's mouth, and there is no quackery palmed upon the public more delusive in its tendencies or more dangerous and useless than is this.

We are taught to believe that the practice of medicine is a science. Science means certainty, but who does not know that medical practice is anything but that? and its history, when understood, is but little calculated to beget that confidence which it is desirable to cultivate in those in whose hands our life and health are often trusted.

Medical men either know or they do not know the nature and property of intoxicating liquors; if they know, then where is their fidelity, where their honesty in tolerating and frequently commending this thing? If they do not know, of what value is their diploma, and by what law of rhyme or reason must an inquest be held over my dead body in case I die without a certificate from such? I know it is said the "art of medicine is the art of pleasing," and it would certainly seem like it, for those of us who have had much experience in this matter know that if we want drink treatment we can have it, while those of us who want teetotal treatment can have that also. Science is very accommodating, and evidently often very *un*scientific.

Many years ago, in the eastern counties, I got a letter of introduction from a clergyman with whom I had been visiting, to a banker in a neighbouring town. It was hoped by this introduction I might be able to hold a temperance meeting there under somewhat favourable circumstances. I called at the banker's private house; he was out for a walk, but I was asked to take a seat as his return was momentarily expected. Presently in he came. In the presence of his wife I explained the object of my visit. During the interview the lady interrupted by saying, "I beg, Mr. Whittaker, you will not attempt to persuade my husband to become a teetotaller: he is very delicate, he has to live by rule; he has been out now for a walk, he has to do it every day to get up circulation, he suffers very much from a languid circulation, his heart sometimes almost ceases to beat, and sometimes in the dead of the night the household is alarmed by what appears to be the suspension of all pulsation. We have consulted eminent"—they are always *eminent*—"medical men, both in town and country, and they are agreed that a little brandy is the best thing to give him under these circumstances, so you see he could not join you." "Well, madam," I replied, "I regret to hear so poor an account of your husband, but my object is not at this time to get him to join us; it was thought if he would be good enough to take the chair it would help to secure me a hearing, and in other ways forward the cause." "Oh dear, no! the excitement would be too much." "Then," said I, "may I beg the favour of your presence at the meeting, for it is important that some person of influence in the town sides with us." "That could never be," said she, "for I am quite an invalid." "That is most unfortunate," said I. "It is most unfortunate," she responded; "I am a martyr to palpitation; it is dreadful; I am sometimes taken so bad with these violent beatings. Did you," she inquired, "ever suffer from palpitation?" "No," said I; "never." "Then you have much to be thankful for." "Indeed, I have, madam; I am quite aware of that." "Well sir," she went on to say, "not unfrequently the household is disturbed throughout the entire night in trying to allay these terrible and alarming symptoms—nothing does it but a little brandy. We have consulted eminent medical men in town and country, and they are agreed it is the best thing we can do." I could only express my sorrow at so much suffering, and intimate as politely as I could, that to my mind it was a marvellous thing that her husband took brandy because his heart would not go, and she took it because hers went too fast. But then in both cases they had been advised by *eminent* medical men. Indeed, if they had not been eminent, they would have been laughed at or sent to school again.

The danger and unwisdom of this drink medicine is in the fact that there is usually more difficulty in getting people to leave off taking it than there is in getting them to begin, and the folly and futility is seen when we consider how common it is to take this physic in company, and in the social circle, and on days of festivity. How true is the story in this case, of the man who was well, would be better, took physic and died. I am not without experience and practical knowledge in matters of which I now speak. My family and social relations, as well as my public ones, have taught me lessons; in marriages, births and deaths, my experience has been equal to most men, and were I to particularise, the facts would astound many.

We marry, and are born, and live and die, and get through all the duties and belongings of life at our house without the drink, and we go through the world so far as our personal wants are concerned as if drink had no existence. We believe when that necessity arises our work will be done, and the sooner we are off the better. Should it be a delusion, well what of that? We raise monuments to men who die for their country, and sometimes very questionably so. Surely there is as much credit and honour in dying for the truth.

I recently had a very trying illness. It was not considered dangerous, but it was irritating and tedious. My doctor was not a teetotaller, but he knew I was. Now I have but little respect for that teetotalism of which nobody knows anything. He never troubled himself to talk to me about drink. He watched me carefully and treated me well. I was anxious to get better, for I had broken down in the midst of useful and happy work, and when the doctor was asked the probable time it would take, he thought "Three months." Well, it was all over in a month, and there has been no relapse, which he thought likely, and he admitted his astonishment.

Thirty years ago the most serious and dangerous illness of my life laid me low at Whitehaven. I was unfortunately badly housed and badly nursed, and I could not be removed. Two medical men, both of whom believed in drink attended me there. They were respectable and very considerate, and did very well for me.

A Quaker lady, seeing my helpless condition, wrote to my wife, who crossed the country in trying circumstances (it took her two days to do it), to nurse me, and the change was manifest directly. "One good nurse is worth a dozen bad doctors," and nobody knows the value of a good nurse better than doctors themselves.

My wife soon had me well enough to venture on my way home. The doctor called to see me before I left, and during our interview he said, "Well, you have had a narrow escape, and it will be some time before you recover your strength and vigour." "How long, doctor?" "Three months at least; and now the disease is gone and you are convalescent, it will speed on your recovery if for a time you take a little *stout* daily. I say this in all candour and honesty," said he, "but you can please yourself." Turning to him and smiling, I said, "The worst is over, is it not?" "Yes," said he. "And over," said I, "without the drink?" "Yes, certainly." "And over sooner than you expected?" "Yes, I admit that." "Does not the greater include the less, doctor, and having conquered the big foe am I to fall before the lesser one?" "Well, you will not get your strength so soon without it," said he. What happened? I was in perfect health in two weeks from that time, and I was to be three months with the help of stout, and I have never had another attack since. The disease from which I suffered was erysipelas in the face and head. It was a fearful attack.

I could fill a volume large as this book will be, with cases of this kind. One more. A son of mine at nineteen years of age came home from his apprenticeship with a very bad attack of typhus fever; he had previously to that been away in a very delicate state, he had grown rapidly and was threatened with symptoms of consumption. He went to Matlock for a month, and received much benefit; his return to business was urged, and he went, but it was not long after that when he came home in the condition named.

It was a very trying case, and his constitution being weak the most serious consequences were anticipated. The illness was of long continuance, and as he was the son of the family, who had been more than any other the companion of his mother in my all but constant absence from home, the affection was strong on the part of his mother, while the suspense was living death.

The neighbours were very kind, and walked about our home with tender tread, and every morning looked to see if any signs of life were still manifest in the house. One of them, the minister's wife living near to us, and a teetotaller, met me near the door one day when things were very dark, and said, "May I send you a bottle of wine for your son? I thought perhaps you would not like to get it yourself." I mention this to show what was working in the minds of the people. This was kindness in the extreme, Christian kindness.

This son was all the world to his mother, and I sometimes wonder how it was that I did not give way, but we were all one in this matter, we had no faith in the physic, and we could only watch and wait, as the weary tossed mariner waits for the morning, the morning which of all others was big with consequences to me and my house. On that morning three doctors were to meet and consult together about my son. They met, and after seeing him sent for me into the drawing-room. The senior one said, "We have sent for you, Mr. Whittaker, to ask if there would be any objection to our trying a little wine for your son."

He was at the time unconscious, and as they said, in very critical and almost hopeless circumstances. This was a fearful trial and a terrible responsibility. The hope and joy of the family dying, and the refusal of that which was thought might save his life rested with me.

Turning to these three men, "Gentlemen," I said, "this is cruel. Some of you have been attending my son for weeks and months, you were sent for to save his life, that life has been in your hands; you have never before consulted me as to what should be done, you have prescribed and directed, and we have carried out your instructions to the letter, and now he is dying you lay the onus on me, it is cruel! Will you promise me my lad shall live if he has the wine?" No, they could not do that. "Do you mean to tell me that you have nothing in your surgeries that will produce the same effect as you *suppose* this wine would produce? If so, why send me to a publican for physic?"

One of them was touched and said, "Well, as your feelings are so very strong in the matter, I think I can send you a mixture that will do quite as well." Then said I, "In the name of mercy and fair-play *do it*," and the lad lives and is Chairman of the Scarborough School Board to-day, while the doctors one and all are *dead*. Had he died the town would have cursed me, and the Church with clasped hands and devout aspirations would have pleaded with God that this sin be not laid to my charge. Is not all this a solemn mockery and a miserable infatuation, and is it not high time that every man who knows and feels the truth as applied to this practice, be faithful at all costs? Who does not see that had my son taken the wine and lived, the *wine* would have got the credit of that life, and to that extent weakened the household faith in teetotalism, while the drinking world would have laughed at our helpless necessities and encouraged itself in the idiotic delusion that drink is the panacea for the ills to which flesh is heir. I blame no man for doing what he feels to be right in these circumstances, but I do ask that our principles have fair-play, and that the prejudices of custom and habit do not ignore facts nor belie science.

The temperance public cannot do a better deed than sustain the London Temperance Hospital in its noble and successful efforts to refute the dogmatic lie which teaches that drink is a necessity in surgical operations and medical practice, and the Church will show a truer wisdom in cleansing itself from the smell of liquors than it is doing in asking Government to bear a burden grievous to be borne in the suppression of the liquor traffic, a burden which the Church has itself as yet not touched with its little finger.

CHAPTER XXXV.

REFLECTIONS AND PROSPECTS.

THE temperance advocate by his calling has special opportunities to study character, and get a true knowledge of life. This was especially so in early days. We mixed much in domestic circles, and with families of varied circumstances and characteristics. We not only saw what was its outward development, but we learned much of the inner workings. There was a oneness and a sympathy, which made our intercourse most refreshing, and it was under these circumstances that attachments were formed which only ended with life. The joy and gladness in each other's company was a thing to live, and our periodical renewals were not only red-letter days but festivals in the best sense. Jubilees came not by years, but by months and weeks, and in that way our labour was rest, and our pain sweet. By these means our minds were filled with real life, and it was because of this that we were able to speak that which we knew, and testify that which we had seen.

Then, again, the platform of a temperance meeting was one of the best schools for training any one ambitious of public life this country offered, and the bench and the bar, the pulpit and the press, owe much to it. Some of the first men extant in all these departments are indebted to the experience gained in our meetings, and there has been a wonderful influence exerted from our platform in the minds of all ranks and conditions of men. The ear has been educated to listen, and the mind to reason, and the heart to feel; and there has been no machinery in operation in this land during the last fifty years which has been more useful and wholesome in its teaching, than has been the platform on which the temperance advocate has stood. It has been the wellspring of sober-mindedness in matters of trade, and the platform of arbitrament in cases of war and disputes. There home life has found its best friend, and provident habits and personal thrift their constant and most persevering advocates. The nation owes an unpaid debt of gratitude for its services, while religion itself has had its sheet anchor in our midst. That we have had our inconsistencies and defects it would be folly to deny; to say we had not, would be to declare we were not human. All societies have in them a mass of humanity, where *we* are that is, and there much that is common to all must happen to us, and yet we have our specialities, and have often been credited with a power not possessed by others.

I have more than once in my experience been asked by a fellow-member in the Church to speak to some brother who was known to have a weak side on the drink business, and see if I could not induce him to become a teetotaller: thus at once admitting that the Church was unable to do what it was supposed teetotalism might do. And yet how very slow many of these people have been to see any necessity for themselves to be placed in such a position as to be able to preach a full gospel to every child of man.

The gospel that does not meet every case cannot be

a complete one, and yet such men as I here refer to admit the inefficiency of the one in which they themselves have been satisfied to rest. Every man's eyes are not in his head, some have got them in their stomachs, some in their shops, some in their pockets, and some in society, and everything is seen by them through these mediums. They admit what is true, they see what is right, but they lack the moral power and need the true manhood essential to complete the case.

Instead of when they awake springing from their beds and taking the plunge needful for the invigorating bath, they lie with their eyes wide open and reason themselves into further indulgence; thus are opportunities lost and the means by which manly life is secured slip through their hands.

These can only be moved by that power which enables the eagle to stir up her nest, and flutter over her young, and bear them on her wings, and it is that knowledge which has again and again inspired temperance advocates with thoughts that breathe and words that burn, and which quickened into active life many an indulgent Christian, and put in motion the Church which was dead while it lived.

In making books it is said there is no end, and certainly in this compilation my difficulty is to know when to stop. Bulky books are an abhorrence, and dry details a bore, so I must (notwithstanding temptations to the contrary) make a finish whether I have done or not.

That there would be many imperfections, I knew when I began; but that I should be compelled to have so many omissions is a trouble, but I am helpless.

R. D. Alexander, of Ipswich; S. Jarrold, of Norwich;

Joseph Tucker, of the Bury, Bedford; Potto Brown, of Huntingdonshire; the four Misses Proctor, formerly of Selby; the home of the Saunders family, of Market Lavington, Wilts; the quiet resting-place nestling under the Roseberry Topping, and known as Langbury, the home and estate of John Richardson;—all have in them a history worth telling, and from them came, and in them were lives worth living. These, like many others, such as the homes of the Ridleys of Hexham, the Hutchinsons and Morrells of Selby, the Palmers of Reading, and good Joseph Spence of York, scattered all over the country, have in their day been centres in which have been treasured the life-longings of noble deeds, and out of which have gone weakness made strong, and darkness made light.

The sturdy yeoman of Langbury stood like a rock when the tempest was high. The Proctors of Selby cheered the mind and warmed the heart of many a battered warrior and weary traveller. Joseph Tucker, the country squire and Christian gentleman, did deeds as sheriff of his county and lord of his manor that live in lasting esteem in the minds of men who know what true manhood is; while the festivals and galas held annually at Houghton, and instituted by Potto Brown, gave joy and gladness by the week together to vast numbers assembling in that centre of Huntingdon, and that home of profuse and generous hospitality.

These memories are amongst the sunny sides of my life, and these localities the green pastures of my resting-places. I have felt for many years how I should like to tell them how much they were loved and appreciated, and yet now I try to do it in *every* case they are beyond my reach! With them and many more, such as with *her* also who for nearly forty years was my partner in life, the opportunity is gone, and there is only left to me the melancholy pleasure of living in the past. Yes, there is a joy in melancholy. It is worth something to know and feel that there have been times when brightness and blessing filled the heart, and when no sorrow was big enough to beget a cloud, and no disappointment bad enough to paralyse a purpose.

These memories, while they touch my heart and check my breath, help me to write this book, and to cherish the hope that these records will keep alive the spirit which has done so much in the past.

The temperance warfare has a history, and one that should be known; this is my contribution towards it. The work is not yet done, very far from it, there will be wars and rumours of wars, and many who now live will have to fight. Where there is national iniquity there is national guilt.

The liquor traffic in this land, like slavery in America, has perverted and seared the national conscience and tainted the national life. Indeed it has become our life. That being so, separation means death. It was so in America, it will be so here. The price will be great. It was great there, it will be great here; but as in one case so in the other, it will have to be paid.

We may count the cost as soon as we like, but pay we must either in money or kind, or both. Let there be no mistake about it; it is not going to be done by a breath or mere waving of the hand. The nation will fight for its life.

The question now is not so much what *is* the nation's life, but what is *believed* to be its life. It is the *belief* we have to deal with. My conviction is that the nation believes a lie. It believes in drink. It has not yet believed in teetotalism. When it does, the Church and the State will make short work of the drink business. We have had "Moses and the prophets," and have not believed. It may be that we should not believe did one rise from the dead. What then? Are we to fight? It looks like it. That is to say, there must to some extent be *force*, and the weakest will go to the wall. Who then will put forth the hand, and in what direction shall the hand be put?

We have had enough of Easter holidays, and sham fights, and guerrilla warfare. It is waste of powder, and a cowardly way of killing a foe. Why not once again listen to a wholesome and much-needed exhortation? "If the Lord be God, serve Him; if Baal, serve him." With decision and determination the business is settled, and we may ground our arms and live in peace. That force is no remedy may have its true side, but it has a side on which it is not true. Ask the man whose troublesome tooth had to be brought into unpleasant contact with the horrid forceps whether that be so or not? Proving that, even in cases where an article may have been both useful and ornamental, a condition of things may arise when even at the cost of *force* and pain it is wisdom to get rid of it. What then if drink ever was all that some men now think it to be? have not conditions arisen which would make it the highest wisdom at all pain and costs to root it out? If then we keep up a standing army of hundreds of thousands, that we may if needs be cope with a foreign foe; and spend annually many millions of hard-gotten gain to cover this forethought, surely it is not utopian to provide for the extirpation of an *internal* enemy, which has been pronounced by the youngest son and brightest and best specimen of the royal household of these realms, "England's greatest foe!"

Then let him that has no sword sell his coat and buy one. There is that which is more than meat, and there are moments in a man's life when to falter is to fail. Out upon the chicken-hearted policy which is the language of the cowardly spies who, frightened by the giants, would sell even the promised land for a mess of pottage.

No! God has ever had His Calebs and His Joshuas, and He has them now.

The land is ours, it is a goodly land: let us go up and possess it.

TEMPERANCE LITERATURE.

OUR NATIONAL VICE. The Claims of Temperance on the Christian Church. By R. B. GRINDROD, M.D., LL.D. Edited by his Son. Crown 8vo, cloth, price 5s.

ILLUSTRIOUS ABSTAINERS. By FREDERICK SHERLOCK. Author of "Heroes in the Strife," etc. Fifth Thousand. Crown 8vo, 3s. 6d.

"Advocates of the cause of total abstinence will be highly interested and as highly edified by the perusal of a bright little volume entitled 'Illustrious Abstainers.' It is refreshing to find enumerated such personages as, President Hayes, Sir Henry Thompson, Dr. Richardson, Sir Henry Havelock, Elihu Burritt, and John Howard. It is an excellent book."—*Illustrated London News*.

SUNLIGHT AND SHADOW; or, Gleanings from my Life Work. Comprising Reminiscences of 37 years' experience on the Platform and among the People, at Home and Abroad. By JOHN B. GOUGH.

Cheap Edition. With Portrait and Illustrations, 8vo, cloth, 3s. 6d.; Without Portrait and Illustrations, cloth, 2s. 6d.

"This brilliant and entertaining work is full of stirring incidents, telling anecdotes and instructive reminiscences of men and things, both in Great Britain and America. A more charming book we do not know."—*Freeman*.

TEMPERANCE STORIES.

THE WESTONS OF RIVERDALE; or, The Trials and Triumphs of Temperance Principles. By E. C. A. ALLEN. New Edition, handsomely bound, crown 8vo, 2s.

"An excellent temperance story, admirably calculated to further the cause of total abstinence."—*Watchman*.

THE SISTERS OF GLENCOE; or, Letitia's Choice. A Temperance Story. By EVA WYNNE. Sixteenth Thousand. Cloth Elegant, 5s.

"Its life pictures are skilfully drawn, and the most wholesome lessons are enforced with fidelity and power."—*Temperance Record*.

LONDON: HODDER AND STOUGHTON, 27, PATERNOSTER ROW.

JUST IN TIME; or, Howard Clarion's Rescue. By Mrs. G. S. REANEY, Author of "Our Daughters," etc. Crown 8vo. Handsomely bound. 5s.

DAISY SNOWFLAKE'S SECRET. A Story of English Home Life. By the same Author.
Cheaper Edition, Crown 8vo, cloth, price 3s. 6d.

"Winning in style, pure and earnest in tone, and of commanding interest."—*Daily Review.*

"Daisy's character is a charming one."—*British Quarterly Review.*

"In 'Daisy Snowflake's Secret' we have temperance of the most advanced character, the most wholesome lessons being woven with artistic skill into a web of interesting narrative that will be certain to find multitudes of admiring readers."—*Temperance Record.*

BIOGRAPHICAL WORKS.

D. L. MOODY; his Earlier Life and Work. By Rev. W. H. DANIELS, M.A., Chicago. With Steel Portrait and Illustrations. Third Edition. Crown 8vo, 3s. 6d.

"Mr. Daniels knew all about Mr. Moody's early life and all about his work at Chicago. The biographical part of his work is excellently done; it is as interesting as a romance. Our readers will find it very interesting and very stimulating."—*Congregationalist.*

GEORGE F. PENTECOST, D.D. A Biographical Sketch, with Bible Readings and Experiences with Enquirers. 3s. 6d.

"Mr. Pentecost is the ablest evangelist who has ever crossed my path."—*D. L. Moody.*

"An interesting record of earnest evangelistic work. Mr. Pentecost's career has been a varied one, and many curious incidents are placed on record."—*Rock.*

ELIZABETH PRENTISS, The Author of "Stepping Heavenward": Her Life and Letters. By the Rev. G. L. PRENTISS, D.D. Second Edition. With Portrait and Illustrations. 7s. 6d.

"It is the inner history of a woman of genius. The book is charming reading to those who love to study human nature under varied aspects. It is good to be brought into contact with such a lovely soul, and to trace the path she trod."—*Academy.*

CHRISTMAS EVANS, The Preacher of Wild Wales, His Country, his Times, and his Contemporaries. By PAXTON HOOD. Second Edition. Crown 8vo, 7s. 6d.

"A wonderfully interesting narrative."—*British Quarterly Review.*

LONDON: HODDER AND STOUGHTON, 27, PATERNOSTER ROW.

JOHN HOWARD, THE PHILANTHROPIST, and his Friends. By JOHN STOUGHTON, D.D., Author of "History of Religion in England," etc. Crown 8vo, 7s. 6d.

WILLIAM PENN: the Founder of Pennsylvania. By JOHN STOUGHTON, D.D. With Steel Portrait. 7s. 6d.

"An excellent life of William Penn. Few men are better qualified than Dr. Stoughton for the task. He is a skilled writer in full sympathy with his subject. He has visited Pennsylvania, and learnt much on the spot which no reading in this country could impart."—*Athenæum*.

GEORGE FOX and the EARLY QUAKERS. By A. C. BICKLEY. Crown 8vo, 7s. 6d.

CHRISTIAN WOMANHOOD. By MARY PRYOR HACK. Uniform with "Consecrated Women" and "Self Surrender." Elegantly bound. 5s.

"We know no more suitable present for a young lady than this charming book, with its sketches of Mary Fletcher, Elizabeth, last Duchess of Gordon, Ann Backhouse, Frances Ridley Havergal, and others. It will be a very fountain of inspiration and encouragement to other good women."—*Sheffield Independent*.

CONSECRATED WOMEN. By MARY PRYOR HACK. Fourth Thousand. 5s. Handsomely bound.

"The memorials are all deeply interesting, bright, and vivid."—*Freeman*.

"Some of these brief biographies are deeply interesting."—*Record*.

"The stories of such philanthropic women are profoundly touching."—*Spectator*.

SELF-SURRENDER. By MARY PRYOR HACK. A Second Series of "Consecrated Women." Second Thousand. 5s. cloth elegant.

CONTENTS: *Anne Askew—Isabel Brown—Helen Herschel—Anne Maurice—Elizabeth Long—Mary Jane Graham—Lydia Read—Harriet Jukes—Susannah Gibson—Agnes Jones.*

"A most delightful book, written by a woman, about women, and for women—though it may be read by men with equal pleasure and profit. Each of the eleven chapters contains in brief the life, history, and work of some sister who was made perfect either through service or suffering."—*Christian*.

LONDON: HODDER AND STOUGHTON, 27, PATERNOSTER ROW.

THE LIFE OF THOMAS COOPER. Written by himself. With Portrait. Thirteenth Thousand. 3s. 6d.

"A most interesting volume."—*Leisure Hour*.

"The book is full of recollections of literary and political celebrities with whom the author came in contact at different times."—*Graphic*.

SPENT IN THE SERVICE. A Memoir of the Very Rev. Achilles Daunt, D.D., Dean of Cork. With Selections from his Letters, Diaries, and Sermons. By Rev. F. R. WYNNE, M.A., Dublin. With Portrait, 5s.

"We feel grateful to Mr. Wynne for giving us so lifelike a sketch of a very beautiful character."—*Literary Churchman*.

ROWLAND HILL: His Life, Anecdotes, and Pulpit Sayings. By V. J. CHARLESWORTH. With Introduction by C. H. Spurgeon. Tenth Thousand. With Portrait, 3s. 6d.

"Our friend Mr. Charlesworth has written a life of Rowland Hill, which in our judgment surpasses its predecessors in giving a full-length portrait of the good man."—Rev. C. H. SPURGEON.

BROWNLOW NORTH: The Story of His Life and Work. By the Rev. K. MOODY-STUART, M.A. 3s. 6d.

"The ability and faithfulness with which Mr. Moody-Stuart has discharged a task which largely demanded both tact and discrimination, has been generally acknowledged."—*Record*.

CHARLES G. FINNEY. An Autobiography. With Fine Portrait. Crown 8vo, cloth, 5s.

"The history of this man appears almost as unique in modern times as was that of the great Apostle of the Gentiles in the early days of the Church. We cannot, within the ordinary limits of our space, give our readers a fair idea of the intense and thrilling interest of this volume."—*Christian*.

MODERN HEROES OF THE MISSION FIELD. By the Right Rev. W. PAKENHAM WALSH, D.D., Bishop of Ossory, Ferns, and Leighlin. Second Thousand. Crown 8vo, 5s.

The lives sketched in this volume all belong to the present century, and include:— Henry Martyn, William Carey, Adoniram Judson, Robert Morison, Samuel Marsden, John Williams, William Johnson, John Hunt, Allen Gardiner, Alexander Duff, David Livingstone, and Bishop Patteson.

HEROES OF THE MISSION FIELD. By the same Author. Second Edition. Crown 8vo, 5s.

"Brilliant sketches."—*Literary Churchman*.

"We can heartily recommend his book to our readers."—*Spectator*.

LONDON: HODDER AND STOUGHTON, 27, PATERNOSTER ROW.

www.ingramcontent.com/pod-product-compliance
Lightning Source LLC
Chambersburg PA
CBHW080345190426
43201CB00045B/2153